50 _Hikes_

In Utah

Day Hikes from the Red Rocks Deserts to the Uinta and Wasatch Mountains

CHRISTINE BALAZ

THE COUNTRYMAN PRESS · WOODSTOCK, VT.

THE COUNTRYMAN PRESS
Woodstock, Vermont

AN INVITATION TO THE READER

Over time trails can be rerouted and signs and
landmarks altered. If you find that changes have
occurred on the routes described in this book,
please let us know so that corrections may be
made in future editions. The author and publisher
also welcome other comments and suggestions.
Address all correspondence to:

Editor, 50 Hikes Series
The Countryman Press
P.O. Box 748
Woodstock, VT 05091

Explorer's Guide 50 Hikes in Utah
97-1-58157-182-0

Maps by Erin Greb Cartography,
    © The Countryman Press
Book design by Glenn Suokko
Text composition by PerfecType, Nashville, TN
Interior photographs by the author unless
    otherwise specified

Published by The Countryman Press,
P.O. Box 748, Woodstock, VT 05091
Distributed by W. W. Norton & Company, Inc.,
500 Fifth Avenue, New York, NY 10110
Printed in the United States of America

10 9 8 7 6 5 4 3 2 1

50 Hikes in Utah at a Glance

HIKE	DISTANCE (in miles)
1. Limber Pine Trail	1.4
2. Naomi Peak	6.4
3. Tony Grove Nature Trail	1.3
4. White Pine Lake	7.4
5. Maughan Hollow	2.9
6. Wind Caves	3.4
7. Riverside Nature Trail	2.7
8. Green Canyon Trail	7.8
9. Beirdneau Trail to Wind Caves Way	4.1
10. Waterfall Canyon	2.4
11. Wheeler Creek Trail	3.9
12. Ogden Overlook from Snowbasin	5.4
13. Skull Crack Canyon	4.7
14. White Rock Bay	7.3
15. Frary Peak	6.8
16. Little Mountain Summit to Mountain Dell Overlook	4.2
17. Rattlesnake Gulch to Pipeline Trail	3.2
18. Mount Aire	3.4
19. Dog Lake from Upper Big Water	5.2
20. Willow Heights to Willow Lake	2
21. Silver Lake Loop	0.9
22. Brighton to Dog Lake and Lake Mary	2.4
23. Red Pine Lake	6.6
24. Snowbird to Hidden Peak	3.2
25. Albion Basin to Catherine Pass	3

RISE IN FEET	VIEWS	GOOD FOR KIDS	WATERFALLS	NOTES
200	★	★		Views of 500-year-old limber pines, as well as Bear Lake
1,950	★			Panoramic views of Bear River Range and Mt Naomi Wilderness
150	★	★		Interpretive nature trail around Tony Grove Lake
1,200	★			Lengthy and pleasant hike around Mt Magog to White Pine Lake
800	★			Short and steep journey into less traveled reaches of Logan Canyon
1,100	★	?		Gorgeous hike up Logan Canyon's steep slopes
250	★	★		Interpretive and shady riverside trail
1,100		?		Tree-covered, canyon-bottom hike
1,800	★			Short, steep hike to ridge separating Green and Logan Canyons
1,200	★	?	★	Popular hike in Ogden-area Wasatch
700	★	★		Broad, creek-side trail with views Snowbasin
1,000	★	?		Tree-lined hike to yawning overlook onto Ogden
650	★	★		Short stroll overlooking the popular Causey Reservoir
755	★			Wide-open views of northern Antelope Island
2,100	★			Antelope Island's tallest peak
900	★	★		Generous views and solitude given its nearness to Salt Lake City
850	★	?		Popular Salt Lake City-area hike
2,000	★			Ascends to peak on ridge between Millcreek and Parleys Canyons
1,400	★	★		Pleasant, rolling trail
750	★	?		Gorgeous views across Big Cottonwood Canyon
150	★	★		Kid-perfect, lakeside interpretive trail
800	★	?		Tour of Brighton Resort in Summer
1,900	★			Views of the u-shaped Little Cottonwood Canyon and alpine Wasatch
2,900	★			Free tram ride down!
950	★	?		Route to ridge separating Little and Big Cottonwood Canyons

50 Hikes in Utah at a Glance

HIKE	DISTANCE (in miles)
26. Tibble Fork Loop	4.2
27. Silver Lake Flat to Silver Lake	4.6
28. Pine Hollow	3.6
29. Stewart Falls from Sundance	3.5
30. Lakes Country Loop	7.5
31. Wall Lake and Notch Mountain Trail	5.7
32. Notch Mountain Trail: Bald Mountain Pass to Lilly Lakes Trailhead	9.8
33. Bald Mountain	2.8
34. Amethyst Basin	10.9
35. Fisher Towers	4.3
36. Delicate Arch from Wolfe Ranch	3.1
37. Dead Horse Point Rim Trail	8.4
38. Cohab Canyon	3.4
39. Cassidy Arch	3.3
40. Golden Throne	3.9
41. Chimney Rock Loop	3.5
42. Calf Creek Falls	6.6
43. Escalante River to Natural Bridge	3.7
44. Queens Garden/ Navajo Loop/ Rim Trail	3
45. Losee Canyon Trail	6
46. Arches Trail	0.75
47. Watchman Trail	3.1
48. Emerald Pools	2.2
49. Angels Landing	5.5
50. Canyon Overlook Trail	1

RISE IN FEET	VIEWS	GOOD FOR KIDS	WATERFALLS	NOTES
1,100	★			Tree-lined trail speckled with mountain meadows and clearings
1,500	★			Open, alpine landscape
1,250	★	?		Tree-covered route with a trail's end view of Mt Timpanogos
650	★	★	★	Gorgeous waterfalls on the slopes of Mt Timpanogos
1,100	★	?		Flat, fast trail
1,000	★	?		Popular tour of many Uinta lakes
1,000	★			Long, mellow trail with more solitude than most
1,200	★			Feels like the top of the world!
2,000	★			Diverse landscape on the Uintas' northern slopes
750	★	?		Remarkably unique features in a classic desert landscape
550	★	★		Perhaps the most popular hike in all of Utah
150	★	?		Incredible rim-side views of the Colorado River and its canyons
900	★	?		Hidden canyon near Fruita
550	★	★		Colorful geology and a massive natural arch
700	★	?		Stunning Wild West landscape
900	★			Perhaps this book's most scenice desert hike
400	★	?	★	Popular, interpretive trail
150	★	?		Many easy river crossings
850	★	?		Up-close views of Bryce Amphitheater's colorful formations
600		★		A small, picturesque canyon reminiscent of Bryce, but without crowds
200	★	★		Easy add-on to Losee Canyon, or a stand-alone hike with great vistas
450	★	★	★	Excellent views of lower Zion Canyon from peninsula
300		★	★	Easy hiking to lower pools; more strenuous to upper pools
1,600	★	★ (to lookout)		Spectacular exposure; avoid in bad weather
170	★	★		Short and interesting hike in Pine Creek Canyon

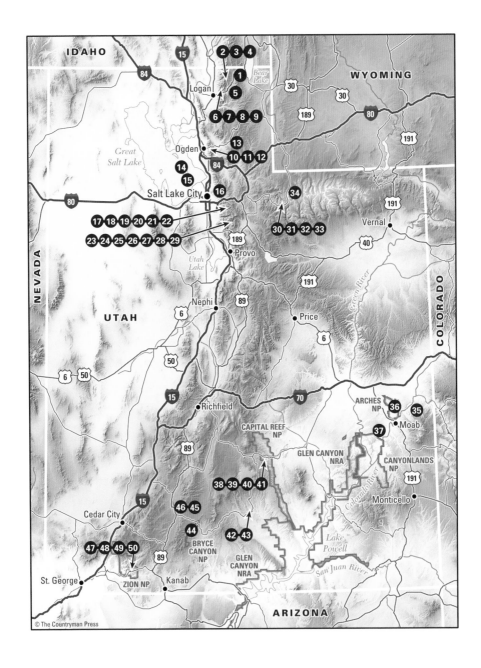

Contents

Introduction 13

1. Limber Pine Trail 21
2. Naomi Peak 25
3. Tony Grove Nature Trail 30
4. White Pine Lake 34
5. Maughan Hollow 38
6. Wind Caves 42
7. Riverside Nature Trail 47
8. Green Canyon Trail .52
9. Beirdneau Trail to Wind Caves Way 57
10. Waterfall Canyon 62
11. Wheeler Creek Trail .67
12. Ogden Overlook from Snowbasin 71
13. Skull Crack Canyon .76
14. White Rock Bay 79
15. Frary Peak 84
16. Little Mountain Summit to Mountain Dell
    Overlook 88
17. Rattlesnake Gulch to Pipeline Trail 92
18. Mount Aire 97
19. Dog Lake from Upper Big Water 102
20. Willow Heights to Willow Lake 106
21. Silver Lake Loop 110
22. Brighton to Dog Lake and Lake Mary 114
23. Red Pine Lake 118
24. Snowbird to Hidden Peak 123
25. Albion Basin to Catherine Pass 128
26. Tibble Fork Loop 132
27. Silver Lake Flat to Silver Lake 136
28. Pine Hollow 141
29. Stewart Falls from Sundance 145
30. Lakes Country Loop .149
31. Wall Lake and Notch Mountain Trail 154
32. Notch Mountain Trail: Bald Mountain Pass
    to Lily Lakes Trailhead 159
33. Bald Mountain 163

34. Amethyst Basin 167

35. Fisher Towers 172

36. Delicate Arch from Wolfe Ranch 177

37. Dead Horse Point Rim Trail 182

38. Cohab Canyon 187

39. Cassidy Arch 191

40. Golden Throne 195

41. Chimney Rock Loop 199

42. Calf Creek Falls 203

43. Escalante River to Natural Bridge 207

44. Queens Garden/Navajo Loop/Rim Trail 211

45. Losee Canyon Trail 216

46. Arches Trail 221

47. Watchman Trail 224

48. Emerald Pools 228

49. Angels Landing 232

50. Canyon Overlook Trail 237

Introduction

ABOUT THIS BOOK

This book contains a broad variety of day hikes spanning from the Bear River Range of northern Utah to the Salt Lake City–area canyons and Zion National Park. The hikes in this book range from 1 to 13 miles in length, and contain as little as 100 feet of elevation gain–or as much as 3,000 feet. The routes tour through high-alpine terrain, canyon forests, low-elevation deserts, and everything in between. Seeing it unfit to combine multiday backpacking journeys with 3-mile outings, I intentionally kept all of the hikes within a one-day distance.

Additionally, I often clumped multiple hikes together with the idea that people traveling somewhere to hike–particularly to some of Utah's most beautiful areas–would likely want to explore the destination more than just one hike would allow. So if you're planning a trip to the Logan area, for example, you'll find yourself with a good selection of hikes, all within 45 driving minutes of each other.

Though geographical variety is important, this book does not include variety for variety's sake alone. That is, if a region of Utah is truly too bland, flat, remote, or otherwise less-than-ideal for hiking, I did not force it into the book. After all, narrowing Utah's hikes down to a selection of just 50 is already a challenging task. I saw no need to dilute these hikes with lower-quality or logistically unfeasible alternatives simply in the name of spreading out dots on a map.

MOUNTAINS, CANYONS, DESERTS, AND BASINS: UTAH'S GEOLOGY

With the exception of perhaps California, Utah arguably has the most diverse geography of any state in the United States. Within its boundaries stand burnt-orange sandstone arches, towering alpine peaks, and vast desert salt flats. Standing as low as 2,180 feet at Beaver Dam Wash, and as high as 13,528 feet at Kings Peak in the Uinta Mountains, this state contains more than 2 vertical miles of relief. And with an area of nearly 85,000 square miles, its spans 5 degrees of latitude and 5 degrees of longitude.

Utah's northern half is largely dominated by major mountain ranges and broad valleys standing between them. The Wasatch Mountains, possibly Utah's most famous range, run from southern Idaho past Logan and Salt Lake City to just south of Provo. This mountain range is considered to be the westernmost portion of the Rocky Mountains, which stretch eastward all the way to Denver. West of the Wasatchs stands the Great Basin, with its enormous salt flats, scattered mountain ranges, and–of course– the Great Salt Lake.

The Uinta Mountains, Utah's tallest range, occupy the northeastern corner of the state. A rarity in North America, this enormous range actually runs from the east to the west (rather than from the north to the south). In fact, the Uintas are the tallest range in the contiguous U.S. that have this alignment, with peaks ranging from 11,000 to 13,528 feet in elevation.

In this northern half of Utah, trails typically tour mountainous terrain—covered with evergreen forests and aspen groves, open meadows, and above-timberline scree. Yet there are exceptions. The trails of Antelope Island explore an utterly different environment—that of a stark and otherworldly desert.

The southern portion of Utah is largely dominated by the geologically famous Grand Staircase. Containing roughly 9,000 vertical feet of relief, this enormous geological feature runs from Cedar Breaks National Monument in the north to the Grand Canyon in the south. From Cedar Breaks, it descends in colorful strata past Bryce Canyon; the Pink and Grey Cliffs; Kolob and Zion Canyons; and the White, Vermillion, and Chocolate Cliffs.

Trails in this southern portion of the state vary enormously. Like those of northern Utah, they can be of lofty, thin-aired elevations. However, they can just as likely tour sun-baked, low-elevation slickrock.

No matter where you find yourself in this state, prepare yourself for a pleasant experience by dressing properly and carrying plenty of food and water. Generally speaking, this is high, dry, and big country—whether you're in the desert or on a mountain.

TIPS FOR HIKING AND WELL-BEING

Clothing

In a state that regularly sees a temperature range in excess of 120 degrees Fahrenheit, there is obviously no single suggestion that will cover this subject. However, it is safe to say that synthetic materials and wool are universally the best choice. In hot and cold, dry and wet weather, these wick sweat and insulate no matter what. Furthermore, loose, shade-giving clothing breathes well and provides protection from the sun.

Especially on longer or steeper hikes, you would be wise to carry a spare pair of socks in your pack. To avoid blisters while hiking, I wear wool or synthetic socks and typically change into a dry pair halfway into the hike—after letting my feet air out for a few minutes.

Finally, even on the hottest of days, it never hurts to throw a jacket, hat, and pair of gloves into your pack—especially when hiking in the mountains. Nearly all of the trails in this book climb in their first half, and then descend in their second. This means that during the first half of the trip, hikers work up a sweat. But upon reaching higher elevations, they turn downhill and reduce their exertion significantly. This lessened effort, combined with accumulated sweat and cooler, high-altitude temperatures, can render a jacket quite handy.

Sunblock

Utah is a land of high elevations, few clouds, and relatively low latitude. The sun, therefore, has little trouble getting to—and burning—people's skin there. Regardless of the season, it's always wise to apply at least one coat of the stuff before you begin. And if you sweat a lot, you probably should reapply during the trip. Even in winter, when the sun hangs lower in the sky, sunblock is indispensable—especially for those hiking over snow or pale earth. These light-hued surfaces reflect the sun's rays back off the ground, intensifying their effects.

Altitude

Though Utah has no 14,000-foot peaks like its neighbor, Colorado, a huge number of its mountains can rightly be considered high or even very high in elevation—particularly among folks accustomed to living at or around sea level. And though it's extremely unlikely anyone will come down with a case of altitude sickness on any of this book's routes,

Carved sandstone steps leading toward the Canyon Overlook in Zion National Park   DAVID SJÖQUIST

it is almost guaranteed that everyone hiking them will be affected in much more subtle ways. When not minded, these subtle effects can be just as dangerous as the acute.

Firstly, people are more susceptible to sunburns at higher altitude. The atmosphere at altitude is thinner; the sun's rays hitting the skin are therefore much stronger. Secondly, regardless of temperature or cloud cover, humans become dehydrated much more quickly at altitude. When hiking up high, bring more water or sports drink than you usually would. Thirdly, the reduced amount of oxygen at elevation inhibits performance, causing hikers to slow from their normal pace. If hiking much higher than you're accustomed to, do yourself a favor and allow plenty of time.

Water and Electrolytes

Given Utah's very dry and sunny climate, it should not surprise you that hydration is of critical importance for hikers in the Beehive State. Combining the area's climate with its generally high altitudes, this topic becomes even more vital. When loading your pack, water and electrolyte beverages should be of top priority. Though sports drinks are not crucial for all journeys, they do help the body hydrate vastly better than water alone—and should therefore accompany hikers on hot or strenuous routes.

Food

Food is a matter of personal preference for all hikers. However, those heading out for long journeys should consider bringing a sizeable snack with balanced macronutrients. Low blood sugar can turn a pleasant stroll into an arduous journey. Worse yet, it can alter behavior and impair judgment.

Minimizing Impact

Utah has more than 2.8 million residents—generally active ones, at that. As such, many

Late spring snow in Bryce Amphitheater

Introduction

Cryptobiotic Soil

of the area's trails see a huge amount of traffic. Because of the undeniable human presence in Utah's mountains, it is absolutely critical that hikers do all they can to minimize their personal impact. As a user of Utah's trails, you should never litter and never take shortcuts. When you encounter a puddle or muddy section of trail, do not step outside of a trail to avoid it; this will only widen the area and worsen the situation.

Avoid disturbing plant life whenever possible. Utah has a harsh climate with very little precipitation and violent temperature swings. Though plants do grow here, they struggle to do so; look around you, and see if you don't agree.

Cryptobiotic Soil

Cryptobiotic soil is a very strange beast indeed. Growing in locations that most plants cannot, this symbiotic combination of cyanobacteria, algae, fungus, lichens, and mosses forms a living ground cover that prevents erosion. Slow growing in nature, clumps of this soil take decades to mature. Fragile, these specimens can be killed with a single footprint. When cryptobiotic soil is killed, the ground has no cover and becomes extremely vulnerable to wind erosion. Avoid stepping on cryptobiotic soil by staying on the trail. If you get off trail for some reason, you can avoid this by walking in washes and on top of stones.

Mammals

Lions and tigers and bears, oh my! While Utah has no tigers, it indeed has bears and mountain lions—as well as moose, badgers, and numerous other species. Though wild animals generally like to keep to themselves, they are inherently unpredictable. As a result, Utah history contains a long list of animal attacks. Educate yourself about how to avoid animal attacks—and how best to survive

The peculiar sandstone shapes of Red Canyon

DAVID SJÖQUIST

them. When hiking, make enough noise so as not to surprise any animals that may be nearby. And remember, bear spray makes an excellent companion.

Snakes

According to Utah State University, Utah is home to 31 species of snakes. Though most of the species here are utterly nonthreatening, 7 of these species are venomous. All belonging to the viper family, these species are the following: speckled rattlesnake, Mojave rattlesnake, western rattlesnake, midget-faded rattlesnake, Hopi rattlesnake, Great Basin rattlesnake, and sidewinder. Though it might be challenging for any nonbiologist to identify these species, it should be fairly easy for anyone to avoid them by simply looking out for, and leaving alone, any snake they encounter.

Like other animals, snakes prefer to keep to themselves. Snake sightings, therefore, are surprisingly rare. Yet they still occur—and often when you least expect them to. As much as possible, watch where you're stepping, and listen for warning rattles. Keep an eye on your pets, and try to prevent them from approaching snakes.

Insects and Arachnids

Given its harsh winters and dry climate, Utah has a fairly benign population of creepy-crawlies. Most all species, like flies and mosquitos, will only be annoying at worst. Nevertheless, this state has its fair share of threatening species. When you're out and about, you'll want to watch out for ticks, spiders, and scorpions.

Unfortunately for the human race, Utah is home to both the Rocky Mountain wood and American dog tick species. Quite common, particularly in grassy and wooded areas during spring and early summer, these ticks can be very dangerous to human and pet health.

Though less than 0.25-inch long (when not engorged), these ticks carry a disgusting host of dangerous diseases, including Rocky Mountain spotted fever, tularemia, and Colorado tick fever. If bitten by a tick, contact a physician. Be sure to remove the tick in its entirety (including the head), and circle the bite with a pen for future monitoring.

According to Utah State University, nearly all of Utah's venomous spiders are of no medical significance to humans. The major exception to this rule is the black widow spider. These are recognizable as an oily black and sleek spider with a bright red hourglass spot on the abdomen. These spiders spend most of the time on their webs, and typically only bite when disturbed. As with many other poisonous critters, the bites of these spiders are usually only lethal among very young children or the ill and elderly.

Scorpion stings typically present like bee stings in human adults, but pose a lethal threat to the very young or sickly and elderly. Scorpions tend to live under rocks and in crevasses. Be careful when disturbing stones, and avoid sticking your hands into dark places. If you're curious about this topic and would like to read further, visit Utah State University's Web site, www.usu.edu.

Poisonous Plants

You'll be safe from most of Utah's poisonous plants if you don't eat them. However, there are a few common plants that you should watch out for—particularly in wet areas. These are the common and well-known species of poison ivy and poison oak.

Poison ivy can be recognized as a small shrub or vine with leaves growing in distinctive groups of three. Though there are many varieties of poison ivy, each with its individual characteristics, there is one good rule of thumb regarding all of them: "Leaves of three? Let it be."

A boy playing in the chilly pool beneath Calf Creek Falls, Grand Staircase-Escalante National Monument

DAVID SJÖQUIST

Poison oak grows as a dense shrub or as a vine. Its leaves typically grow in clusters of three—but can also grow in groupings of five, seven, or even nine. Though the leaves appear quite a lot different than those of poison ivy, the same "leaves of three" rule applies.

Both plants produce oil that is present on all parts—from the leaves to the stems and even the roots. This oil, when left on the skin, causes an itchy, allergic reaction. The severity of the reaction depends on the affected individual, and varies tremendously from case to case. In the worst instances, this can becomes extreme and even life threatening.

If any part of you touches these, your best defense is to wash with soap and water as soon as possible; water alone will not remove the oil. If you believe that you or someone else has been exposed to a poisonous plant, call the Poison Control Center (1-800-222-1222).

Cell Phones

Cell phones, in large part, cannot be depended upon in Utah's backcountry. Naturally, cell phone coverage depends on the provider. But there are many, many large expanses in Utah that have absolutely no service. As of the writing of this book, there was virtually no coverage in the Bear River Range, Uinta Mountains, and many parts of the Wasatch Mountains. There was very little to no service in the Grand Staircase-Escalante National Monument or Great Basin. This list is by no means comprehensive; a good guideline is that you should never expect service in mountainous terrain—particularly in canyons. Even though you might only be 5 miles from a city, mountainous topography could easily prevent your phone from picking up a signal.

1

Limber Pine Trail

Type: Forest; broad, groomed dirt; loop

Season: Spring–Fall

Total Distance: 1.4 miles round-trip

Time: 0.5–1 hour

Rating: Easy

Elevation Gain: 200 feet

Location: Logan Canyon, east of Logan

Maps: USGS GARDEN CITY US TOPO

Contact: Uinta-Wasatch-Cache National Forest: Logan Ranger District, 1500 E. US 89, Logan UT 84321; 435-755-3620; www.fs.usda.gov/uwcnf

Trailhead GPS Coordinates: Limber Pine Parking Area: N41 55.498 W111 28.322

Comments: A short and interpretive hike, this serves as a great educational addition to other Logan Canyon hikes–or as a stand-alone route.

OVERVIEW

Though short in distance, Limber Pine Trail offers a decent variety of plant life, terrain, and views. This diversity, as well as the numerous interpretive signs along the way, renders the trail a worthy addition to other Logan Canyon explorations, or as an outing in and of itself. Hikers not only learn about the local wildlife along the way, but they also see the namesake limber pine–or rather a cluster of limber pines–aged to be 560 years old.

THE TRAIL

The Limber Pine hike originates at a clearly signed trailhead immediately off US 89 and just east of Beaver Mountain. From the parking lot, a short connector trail heads south and joins the loop trail in just a few hundred feet. This chapter's route arbitrarily heads to the right and takes the loop in a counterclockwise direction; however, on this pleasant trail, the route of travel does not matter. Along the way, roughly a dozen interpretive signs explain various plant and animal phenomena of Logan Canyon.

The initial section of this trail takes hikers through a forest of tall fir, pine, and aspen trees surrounded by a blanket of shrubby undergrowth. Already within the first few minutes of walking, a handful of informative placards appear. Among the first of the interpretive signs is one that explains snow as the reason for a dramatic Z-shaped kink in the trunks of one of these mature trees.

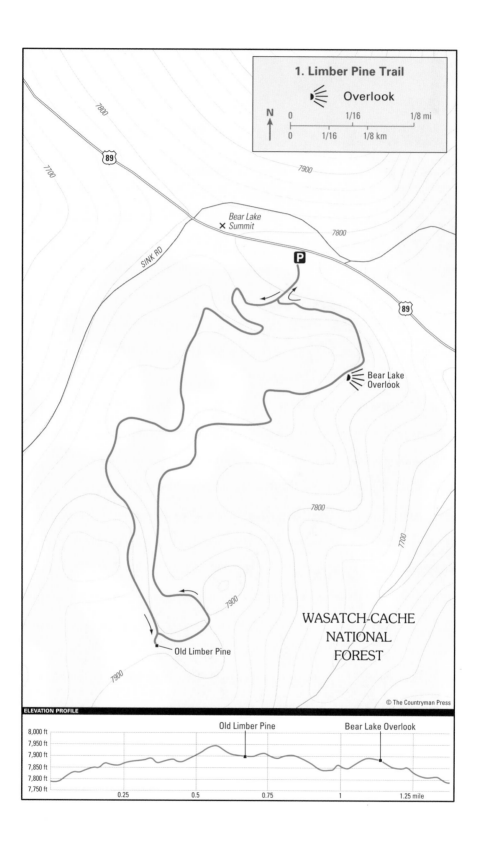

1. Limber Pine Trail

Overlook

N

| 0 | 1/16 | 1/8 mi |
| 0 | 1/16 | 1/8 km |

7800

7700

89

7900

Bear Lake
✕ Summit

7800

SINK RD

P

89

Bear Lake
Overlook

7800

7700

7900

WASATCH-CACHE
NATIONAL
FOREST

Old Limber Pine

7900

© The Countryman Press

ELEVATION PROFILE

| | Old Limber Pine | Bear Lake Overlook |

8,000 ft
7,950 ft
7,900 ft
7,850 ft
7,800 ft
7,750 ft

0.25   0.5   0.75   1   1.25 mile

The broad, groomed Limber Pine Trail

CHRISTINE BALAZ

After about 0.3 mile of walking, the trail pops up and out of the forest and enters a section of sagebrush and grass. Here the trail roughly traces the crest of a very rounded ridge. You will stay in this environment roughly 0.2 mile as the trail rolls up and over rounded hilltops and offers views of the surrounding mountains in all directions.

As quickly as it left the forest, the route enters it once again at roughly 0.5 mile into the route. Shortly afterward, the forest begins to thin and small, blocky boulders of cream-colored dolomite dot the trailside. Similar to limestone, this rock is often mistaken for its more common cousin.

At 0.7 mile from the trailhead, you come upon a cluster of benches alongside a wooden fence. In front of the fence stands the trail's namesake limber pine. Actually a cluster of trees (rather than a single organism), this limber pine group has been determined to be 560 years of age. Though it would not appear remarkable to the casual observer, this trees indeed have peculiar shapes, with knotted bases and pronged trunks.

Scientists theorize that the responsible party for this intimate formation of trees is actually a bird—the Clark's nutcracker. This species eats the nutrient-rich seeds of limber pines, and stores extra seeds underground for later consumption. Naturally, the birds sometimes forget some of these cached seeds. Left buried, some of the seeds naturally germinate later.

After passing the limber pine, the path descends gradually through shady forest for 0.3 mile's worth of looping meanders. At 1.0 mile into the hike, the trail enters yet another clearing marked by grass and sagebrush. After passing eastwardly through the clearing, the trail reaches an overlook of Bear Lake. This natural body of water, which straddles the border of Utah and Idaho, is the second-largest freshwater lake in Utah—behind Utah Lake, west of Provo.

After passing this viewpoint, the trail bends first to the north, and then to the west. From this loop, a fair number of faint shortcut trails head north and back to the parking lot. Resist the temptation to bushwhack on these false paths, as the real connector trail awaits less than 0.2 mile from the Bear Lake overlook.

FEES, RESTRICTIONS, AND PERMITS
Dogs and bikes OK; National Forest restrictions apply

560-year-old limber pines   CHRISTINE BALAZ

2

Naomi Peak

Type: Mountain; dirt with some rocky sections; out-and-back

Season: Spring–Fall

Total Distance: 6.4 miles round-trip

Time: 2–4 hours

Rating: Moderate/Strenuous

Elevation Gain: 1,950 feet

Location: Tony Grove, Logan Canyon, east of Logan

Maps: USGS NAOMI PEAK US TOPO

Contact: Uinta-Wasatch-Cache National Forest: Logan Ranger District, 1500 E. US 89, Logan UT 84321; 435-755-3620; www.fs.usda.gov/uwcnf

Trailhead GPS Coordinates: Tony Grove Lake Parking Area: N41 53.684 W111 38.522

Comments: This hike offers relatively little effort to reach one of the higher peaks—and the panoramic views afforded by it—in the upper reaches of the Bear River Range, a branch of the Wasatch Mountains.

OVERVIEW

The hike to Naomi Peak is a very pleasant ramble through subalpine and alpine terrain to the rocky summit of this tall mountain—the tallest in the Bear River Range, which spans the border of Utah and Idaho. Though Naomi has a rather lofty elevation of 9,979 feet, the hike to it requires a surprisingly moderate amount of climbing to reach, distributed very evenly throughout the trail's 3.2-mile length. From the summit, hikers enjoy 360-degree views of the Bear River Range as well as portions of the Mount Naomi Wilderness.

THE TRAIL

Located in the upper reaches of Logan Canyon, the trail to Naomi Peak departs from the end of Tony Grove Road. Even before the hike begins, the road itself provides a generous helping of scenery as it winds up the drainage of the namesake Tony Grove Lake. During spring, the hillsides sport a rich covering of lush grasses and wildflowers; in autumn, the vast fields of aspen, maple, and scrub oak paint the hillside with their orange, red, and pink foliage. Wildlife—such as porcupine, deer, and moose—are commonly spotted along this steep road. Drive carefully to avoid a collision.

The road terminates in a large parking area, and the trail departs from the far end of this lot. Marked by a map-bearing kiosk and trail signs, the trailhead is hard to miss. Follow signs for Naomi Peak and White Pine Lake; these trails begin as one.

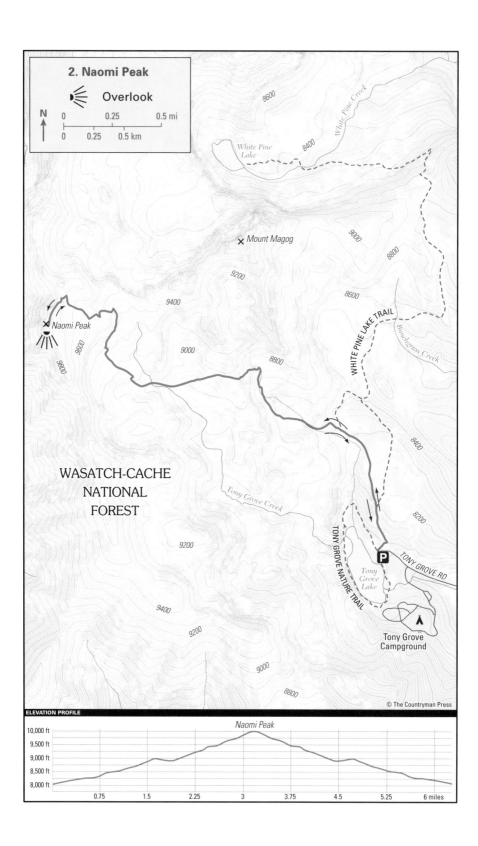

2. Naomi Peak

Overlook

N

| 0 | 0.25 | 0.5 mi |

| 0 | 0.25 | 0.5 km |

White Pine Creek

8600

8400

White Pine Lake

9000

8800

× Mount Magog

8600

9200

9400

WHITE PINE LAKE TRAIL

Bunchgrass Creek

× Naomi Peak

9800

9600

9000

8800

8400

8200

WASATCH-CACHE
NATIONAL
FOREST

Tony Grove Creek

TONY GROVE NATURE TRAIL

P

TONY GROVE RD

9200

Tony Grove Lake

9400

9200

9000

Tony Grove
Campground

8800

© The Countryman Press

ELEVATION PROFILE

Naomi Peak

| 10,000 ft |
| 9,500 ft |
| 9,000 ft |
| 8,500 ft |
| 8,000 ft |

0.75   1.5   2.25   3   3.75   4.5   5.25   6 miles

From the trailhead, the route climbs gently through an open expanse of sagebrush, grass, and small boulders. After less than 0.1 mile, you reach a (broken) backcountry register; 0.2 mile later, the trails split at a signed junction. The route to Naomi Peak takes the left of the two forks. Though the sign indicates a distance of 3.3 miles to the summit, only 3.0 miles actually remain.

After this junction, the trail continues climbing through the same boulder-dotted, open landscape. Stands of mixed aspen and evergreen trees line the trail on either side. The trail assumes a steeper pitch and, 0.6 mile into the hike, it passes by a notable outcropping of terraced quartzite. Less than 0.2 mile later, the trail passes by an unmarked post and a faint junction; stay left here. If you

View northeast from Naomi Peak onto Mt Naomi Wilderness CHRISTINE BALAZ

Large gully on the slopes of Naomi Peak

were to take this path, you would eventually connect with the White Pine Lake Trail.

Beyond this junction, the trail continues its relatively steep ascent. After 1.0 mile of total walking, hikers enter the first of several tiered basins with flat meadow floors. At 0.2 mile later, the trail reaches a higher tier of the same basin. Still climbing, it passes directly beneath short cliff bands and enters into a shallow gully, which it follows along until eventually reaching a ridge.

The path continues to climb from meadow to higher meadow, threading through gullys en route from one to the next. After 2.0 miles, the trail passes by a massive wash. Gouged deeply into the steep mountainside, this wash contains large boulders moved into place by violent spring runoff waters.

At 2.3 miles into the route, you enter the bottom section of the route's largest cirque, crowned with cliffs and rocky peaks. Naomi Peak, the nearest to the trail, is actually rather difficult to discern from this perspective—despite being the tallest point in the Bear River Range. After entering the cirque, the trail curves to the north and then to the east. At 2.5 miles, hikers can peer down into the top of the deep wash of which they had seen the bottom 0.5 mile earlier.

After this wash, the trail leaves the cirque by passing around its eastern shoulder. It then veers rather sharply to the north and then west. After a short section of switchbacks, the path straightens out on its final approach to the summit ridge. Once at the ridge, you encounter a sign demarking a border, west of which stretches the Mount Naomi Wilderness. This boundary, which runs parallel to the ridge, separates this nearly 45,000-acre wilderness area from the Cache National Forest.

Beyond this sign, the summit stands just 0.2 mile to the west. Shortly before the true peak of the mountain, the trail deteriorates into multiple faint paths. Above the treeline at this point, you should have no trouble route-finding.

Each of the numerous paths to the summit requires a short, but very casual, scramble to the rocky summit of Naomi Peak. In all directions from the top, the tall peaks of the Bear River Range stretch high into the sky. To the west, the city of Logan can be seen; because of this, fairly spotty cellular reception is actually available on the mountain's summit.

To return to the parking area, hikers must simply retrace their steps. Because of the generally gentle grade of the trail, the return trip should be easy and quick. If extra time allows, you can consider adding a trek to White Pine Lake (Chapter 4 in this book) or a stroll around Tony Grove Lake (Chapter 3).

FEES, RESTRICTIONS, AND PERMITS
A $5 day-use fee is required of all parked vehicles; dogs OK; National Forest restrictions apply (though the trail encounters the Mount Naomi Wilderness, it never crosses into it)

3

Tony Grove Nature Trail

Type: Mountain; dirt and gravel; loop

Season: Spring–Fall

Total Distance: 1.3 miles

Time: 0.5–1 hour

Rating: Easy

Elevation Gain: 150 feet

Location: Tony Grove, Logan Canyon, east of Logan

Maps: USGS NAOMI PEAK US TOPO

Contact: Uinta-Wasatch-Cache National Forest: Logan Ranger District, 1500 E. US 89, Logan UT 84321; 435-755-3620; www.fs.usda.gov/uwcnf

Trailhead GPS Coordinates: Tony Grove Lake Parking Area: N41 53.684 W111 38.522

Comments: A short, yet interesting, tour around Tony Grove Lake, the Tony Grove Nature Trail is a worthy stand-alone hike or educational addition to the other Tony Grove–area routes.

OVERVIEW

The Tony Grove Nature Trail begins at the end of the Tony Grove Road and follows the shores of Tony Grove Lake. Along the way, it passes roughly a dozen interpretive signs that depict the local animal and plant life, as well as the history and geology of the basin. With shady beaches located near its southern end, this loop trail is an excellent destination for picnickers.

THE TRAIL

The Tony Grove Nature Trail is a loop that departs from the upper, western end of the Tony Grove Road. Arbitrarily, this route description takes the loop in a counterclockwise direction, thereby leaving the parking lot at its northwestern edge. The trailhead, with a small kiosk and signs, is easy to recognize. Three hikes originate at this point; stay left to follow the Tony Grove Nature Trail.

From the lot, the path heads northward and gently uphill through open fields of sagebrush and grass. In early summer, these expanses are filled with colorful wildflowers such as lupine, bluebells, elephant's head, and scarlet gilia. Almost immediately after leaving the parking lot, the trail passes the first of the route's many interpretive signs explaining the area's natural phenomena.

Quite quickly, the trail enters a rather moist environment by way of a long boardwalk. Here the path, surrounded by thick shrubs, curves to the west before it enters into a stand of tall fir and pine trees. Shortly afterward, you remerge into an open field

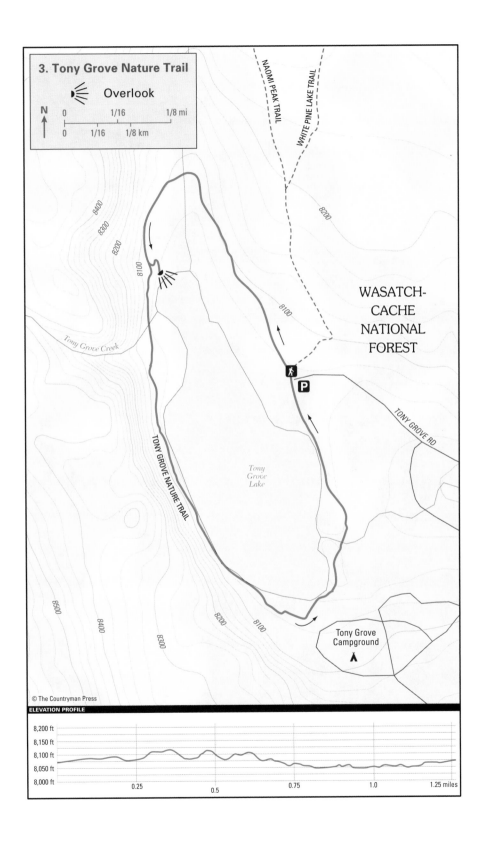

3. Tony Grove Nature Trail

Overlook

N

| 0 | 1/16 | 1/8 mi |
| 0 | 1/16 | 1/8 km |

NAOMI PEAK TRAIL

WHITE PINE LAKE TRAIL

8400
8300
8200
8100

8200

8100

Tony Grove Creek

WASATCH-
CACHE
NATIONAL
FOREST

P

TONY GROVE NATURE TRAIL

TONY GROVE RD

Tony
Grove
Lake

8500
8400
8300
8200
8100

Tony Grove
Campground

© The Countryman Press

ELEVATION PROFILE

8,200 ft					
8,150 ft					
8,100 ft					
8,050 ft					
8,000 ft					

0.25   0.5   0.75   1.0   1.25 miles

Boardwalk leading into shrubs on the northeastern corner of Tony Grove Lake   CHRISTINE BALAZ

before again crossing into yet another stand of trees by way of another boardwalk, which curves leftward to face south.

Emerging from the trees, hikers come face-to-face with broken quartzite cliffs. These rock faces line the long length of Tony Grove Lake's western shore, depositing scattered boulders onto the hillsides below. As the trail straightens out, it enters a long section with open views across the lake encircled by conifer-covered mountains.

At 0.4 mile into the hike, a short spur trail dips down and toward the lakeshore. Here an interpretive sign spells out the importance of the thick sedges and rushes lining the shore. Hikers here also begin to see dolomite rocks scattered about. Roughly 430 million years old, these rocks were once a sea bottom; today they are filled with fossilized small sea creatures such as trilobites, sea lilies, and corals.

Beyond this spur, the trail continues its due-south trajectory, passing through a cluster of rather large boulders and then directly by another short quartzite cliff; quartzite is metamorphosed sandstone. This particular sample was once the beach that lined the ancient sea from which the local dolomite came. A remarkably hard rock, quartzite has an approximate hardness of 7 on the Mohs Scale—on which talc is a 1 and diamond is a 10.

Though hard, these quartzite cliffs are nevertheless extremely broken. Strangely enough, this fracturing was caused by fungi, algae, and plants. Lichens, a symbiotic partnership of algae and fungus, root themselves on the rocks. These growths produce acid, which breaks down the rock. This degraded rock, combined with deceased and decaying lichens, creates soil in which ferns and even trees grow. The roots of these growing plants further crack the rock, breaking it into blocks. With bigger cracks and even more soil present, the cliffs become home to more and bigger plants, furthering their destruction.

Passing the cliff band, the trail reaches a few flat-boulder outcrops on the lake's edge; these make for excellent viewing platforms. If those are occupied, walk a bit farther along and enjoy the sights while sitting on a bench.

Roughly 1.0 mile into the hike, the trail passes the southern edge of the lake and bends to the east to follow its shoreline. Here it enters a forest of evergreen trees with an open, sandy floor. Leading right up to the waters of the lake, this sandy shore makes for an excellent shaded picnic spot.

On its final stretch, the trail curves northward and nears the dam responsible for Tony Grove Lake. The path itself heads to the east of, and below, the dam. After passing it, the trail ends in the northwest corner of the Tony Grove parking lot. Though this chapter's hike ends here, two more are possible from the very same trailhead: one to Naomi Peak (Chapter 2 of this book) and another to White Pine Lake (Chapter 4).

FEES, RESTRICTIONS, AND PERMITS
A $5 day-use fee is required of all parked vehicles; dogs must be leashed; National Forest restrictions apply

4

White Pine Lake

Type: Mountain; dirt; out-and-back; side trips possible

Season: Spring–Fall; best in fall foliage season

Total Distance: 7.4 miles round-trip

Time: 3–4 hours

Rating: Moderate/Strenuous

Elevation Gain: 1,200 feet (800 feet en route to lake; 400 feet on the return trip)

Location: Tony Grove, Logan Canyon, east of Logan

Maps: USGS NAOMI PEAK US TOPO

Contact: Uinta-Wasatch-Cache National Forest: Logan Ranger District, 1500 E. US 89, Logan UT 84321; 435-755-3620; www.fs.usda.gov/uwcnf

Trailhead GPS Coordinates: Tony Grove Lake Parking Area: N41 53.684 W111 38.522

Comments: A somewhat long hike in the Bear River Range, this hike first ascends, then descends to reach White Pine Lake; remember to save some energy, food, and water for the return trek and the climb it requires.

OVERVIEW

The hike to White Pine Lake begins at the upper, westernmost point of Tony Grove Road in Logan Canyon. The trail heads north from there, ascending for its initial 2.4 miles before descending rather steeply to its endpoint at White Pine Lake. This petite lake stands at the bottom of a cirque formed by Mount Magog and Mount Gog, two of the taller peaks in the Bear River Range.

THE TRAIL

The Tony Grove area of Logan Canyon is a large, high-elevation region that contains the tallest peaks of the Bear River Range. Filled with rocky summits, open meadows, and mountain lakes, this area contains numerous trails that explore its reaches. The White Pine Lake Trail is but one of these, and shares its origin with two other trails departing from the end of Tony Grove Road.

Cleary signed, the trailhead is easy to recognize. From the northwestern corner of the parking lot, the White Pine Lake Trail heads uphill and northeast through open fields. During the first part of the journey, hikers are surrounded by wildflowers, grass, and sagebrush, as well as quartzite boulders of varying sizes. The trail climbs gradually through this subalpine landscape for 0.2 mile before reaching a signed junction. Here the Naomi Peak and White Pine Lake trails divide; this chapter's route takes the right-hand fork.

After passing this junction, the trail continues climbing a short distance before reaching a flat meadow and leveling off. This flat

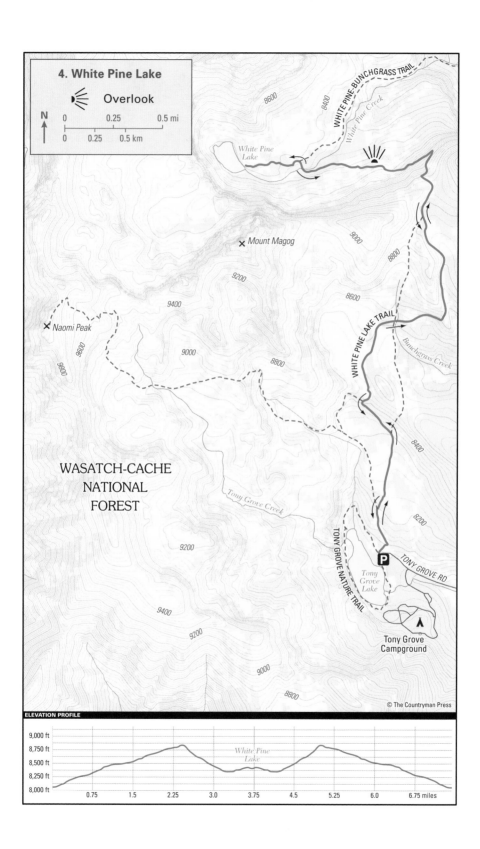

4. White Pine Lake

Overlook

N

| 0 | 0.25 | 0.5 mi |
| 0 | 0.25 | 0.5 km |

8600

8400

WHITE PINE-BUNCHGRASS TRAIL

White Pine Creek

White Pine Lake

× Mount Magog

9000

8800

8600

9200

9400

× Naomi Peak

9600

9800

9000

8800

WHITE PINE LAKE TRAIL

Bunchgrass Creek

8400

WASATCH-CACHE
NATIONAL
FOREST

Tony Grove Creek

8200

9200

TONY GROVE NATURE TRAIL

P

TONY GROVE RD

Tony Grove Lake

9400

9200

Tony Grove Campground

9000

8800

© The Countryman Press

ELEVATION PROFILE

9,000 ft								
8,750 ft				White Pine				
8,500 ft				Lake				
8,250 ft								
8,000 ft	0.75	1.5	2.25	3.0	3.75	4.5	5.25	6.0	6.75 miles

White Pine Lake

space, largely devoid of trees, offers relatively far-reaching views of the greater landscape—including that of the pointy Mount Magog to the northwest, elevation 9,750 feet.

The path more or less makes a beeline through this meadow, then reaches a hillside at its northern edge. Here it enters a forest of mixed aspen and evergreen trees and ascends the hillside in a series of switchbacks. In the middle of this ascent, the trail passes a junction with a faint side trail; if taken, this faded cut-across reaches the Naomi Peak Trail (Chapter 2 of this book) after roughly 0.5 mile. Stay straight here.

Once past this brief section of climbing, you reemerge into yet another open, flat meadow. Even larger than the last, this plateau offers yet better views of Mount Magog to the northwest. Here, the path heads to the northeast as it crosses this open space, eventually entering into a stand of tall aspen roughly 1.5 miles into the hike.

About 0.2 mile later, the trail curves distinctly to the north and enters the bottom of a broad gully. It stays at the bottom of a natural channel and follows it on its due-north trajectory for roughly 0.3 mile. To the left, the gully is clear of trees and filled with grass; on its eastern side, it sports a healthy forest of evergreen and aspen trees.

After reaching the top of this gully, the trail bends slightly to the east as it passes beneath a section of broken rocks and enters a thick grove of aspen. Here the trees, regardless of size, have twisted and gnarled shapes. Caused by snow and wind, these grotesque shapes are interesting and hard to miss.

At 2.4 miles into the route, the trail reaches a ridge and then begins descending at a rapid rate. Here you enter a thick forest of tall evergreen trees and descend via a series of rather steep switchbacks. Less than 0.2 mile later, the trail reaches the final of these hairpin turns and continues losing elevation in a straight, westward course.

As you drop in elevation and the hillside loses steepness, the forest, too, sheds some of its thickness. The path passes through occasional fields of grass offering views of Mount Gog to the north. You cross a small creek 3.1 miles into the route, and a larger one by way of a bridge 0.2 mile later. Just beyond the bridge, the trail reaches a meadow and a signed junction within it. From here, the White Pine–Bunchgrass Trail leads away to the east; this chapter's route, however, heads left.

At 0.3 mile after this fork, the trail arrives at White Pine Lake. This small, natural lake is surrounded by a crown of mountains—the tallest peaks of which are Mount Magog to its south and Mount Gog to the north. Mount Magog, elevation 9,750 feet, is the taller of the two; Mount Gog is only slightly shorter, with a top height of 9,714 feet.

From here, hikers return to the trailhead by turning around and following the same trail back. In the first 1.3 miles of the return trip, 400 feet of elevation must be gained; it is a good idea to save some energy and rations for this return trek.

Mixed forest and fields surrounding White Pine Lake Trail   CHRISTINE BALAZ

FEES, RESTRICTIONS, AND PERMITS

A $5 day-use fee is required of all parked vehicles; dogs OK; National Forest restrictions apply

5

Maughan Hollow

Type: Mountain; dirt; out-and-back; side trips possible

Season: Any; best in fall foliage season; may be hot in summer

Total Distance: 2.9 miles round-trip

Time: 1–2 hours

Rating: Moderate

Elevation Gain: 800 feet

Location: Right Hand Fork, Logan Canyon, east of Logan

Maps: USGS TEMPLE PEAK US TOPO

Contact: Uinta-Wasatch-Cache National Forest: Logan Ranger District, 1500 E. US 89, Logan UT 84321; 435-755-3620; www.fs.usda.gov/uwcnf

Trailhead GPS Coordinates: The Grotto: N41 46.495 W111 36.588

Comments: A steep and relatively untrafficked hike in lower Logan Canyon, Maughan Hollow offers hikers solitude and the chance to explore.

OVERVIEW

Maughan Hollow is but one of many trails located at the end of the Right Hand Fork Road in Logan Canyon. This particular route, like its neighbors, heads into this portion of lower Logan Canyon by way of a narrow gulch that eventually reaches higher, more open landscape. The trail peters out in an open hilltop field; from here, it is possible to continue the journey by off-trail exploration, or connect to the other area trails. Having a map in hand is advised for those planning to link up with other trails or embark on a significant exploration of the area.

THE TRAIL

The Maughan Hollow Trail departs from the end of a road mapped as Old Ephraim's Grave Trail–but commonly called Right Hand Fork. This road departs south from US 89, just 8.9 miles east of Logan Canyon's mouth. The trailhead is located at the end of this road's left-hand fork.

From the large parking area, the well-worn trail departs to the east. Just 0.1 mile from the trailhead, you come upon a fork in the trail. This chapter's hike up Maughan Hollow takes the left branch; the Right Hand Fork Great Western Trail takes the other. Almost immediately after this intersection, the Maughan Hollow Trail bends to the left and enters its namesake gulch. Here you embark on a steady, rather steep ascent.

Composed of orange soil, this singletrack trail sticks to the the left-hand side of this V-shaped gully. As it climbs, the path stays parallel to, but just above, the hollow bottom and the shrubbery it contains. At this point of the trail, the hillsides on either side of Maughan Hollow are steep and covered only with grasses and sagebrush.

Shortly into the trail's initial ascent, it enters a stand of scrub maple trees. This shade cover lasts but a moment, as the path quickly reemerges into the open. Roughly 0.4 mile from the trailhead, the steepness eases off

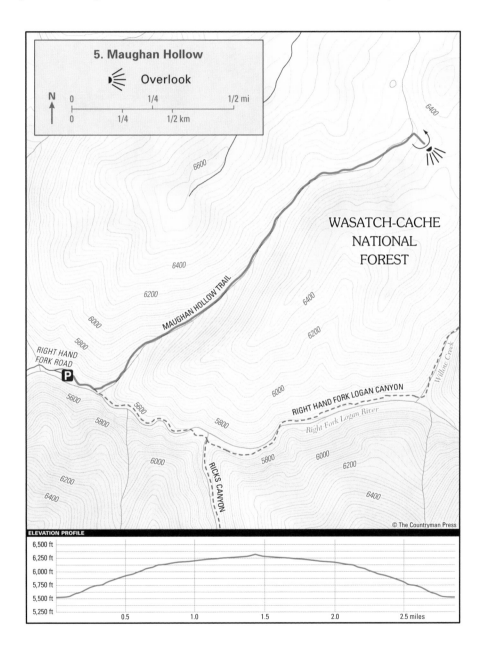

The initial ascent up Maughan Hollow

significantly, but not entirely. Here the trail changes from a roughly 18 percent grade to one of approximately 11 percent, which it maintains for the next 0.5 mile.

At 0.75 mile into the hike, the trail passes beneath the branches of a large cottonwood tree. Hot and tired hikers should consider taking a break here, as there won't be a better opportunity for shade on the remainder of the hike.

Just 0.1 mile later, the views of the surrounding mountains open up significantly. And 0.9 mile from the trailhead, you must pass through a barbed wire fence by way of a gate. Beyond this, the trail levels off significantly, and the slopes on either side of it grow noticeably less steep. Here the bottom of Maughan Hollow is generally moist, and the trail stays left and well above it. On the left-hand side of this depression, expanses of sagebrush are only interrupted by an occasional juniper tree. To the right, groves of aspen trees blanket the gently rolling landscape.

As the trail continues to climb, the hollow's depth and steepness continues to lessen. Due to the presence of grazing cattle, the trail begins encountering many side trails. However, at this point in the route, the real trail is easy to recognize as the one that runs parallel to the bottom of Maughan Hollow.

Roughly 1.3 miles into the hike, the trail levels off as it reaches the top of the hollow, and the hollow disappears into the surrounding landscape. At this point in a flat field, the trail itself is nearly impossible to distinguish from the game and cattle trails crisscrossing this high, open space. By 1.4 miles, the hollow has utterly disappeared, and the single trail has become unrecognizable among countless dozens of animal paths.

Here, you have the choice to attempt a loop route, meeting up with either the Little Cottonwood Creek Trail to the west or the Willow Creek Trail to the east. However, the overwhelming presence of animal paths and the utter lack of clarity at this point renders you rather helpless without a detailed map and excellent sense of direction. Rather than attempt a loop route, many hikers may instead choose to enjoy the open views afforded by this grassy mountaintop by wandering to a pleasant picnic spot.

To return to the car, hikers may simply turn around and follow Maughan Hollow to its base. On the way down, views of the Bear River peaks to the south are generous between the walls of this drainage.

FEES, RESTRICTIONS, AND PERMITS
No fees; dogs OK; National Forest restrictions apply

View down into Maughan Hollow from top plateau　　　CHRISTINE BALAZ

6

Wind Caves

Type: Mountain; dirt; out-and-back; side trip possible

Season: Any; outstanding in fall foliage season

Total Distance: 3.4 miles round-trip

Time: 1.5–2 hours

Rating: Moderate

Elevation Gain: 1,100 feet

Location: Logan Canyon, east of Logan

Maps: USGS MOUNT ELMER US TOPO

Contact: Uinta-Wasatch-Cache National Forest: Logan Ranger District, 1500 E. US 89, Logan UT 84321; 435-755-3620; www.fs.usda.gov/uwcnf

Trailhead GPS Coordinates: Wind Caves Trailhead: N41 45.743 W111 42.228

Comments: A popular and scenic hike, this leads to a distinctive set of limestone caves and arches in lower Logan Canyon.

OVERVIEW

The Wind Caves Trail is a pleasant, single-track path with steady climbing on the north side of Logan Canyon. The trail winds through low- and mid-level vegetation to reach this formation more than 1,000 feet above the canyon floor. As such, it offers fantastic views of Logan Canyon. Sometimes called the Witch's Castle, the Wind Caves is a distinctive set of caves and arches carved into an otherwise unbroken band of limestone.

THE TRAIL

Many times, popular Wasatch trails near cities leave something to be wanted. However, this is not the case in Logan Canyon—where many of the most beautiful trails are actually located rather low in the canyon and therefore near town. The Wind Caves Trail, just 5 miles east of Logan, is both one of the most accessible and scenic in the canyon.

The Wind Caves Trailhead can be recognized as a rather large pullout on the north side of the road. Adorned with a multipanel kiosk, this parking area is hard to miss. Only one trail departs from this trailhead, rendering the route-finding quite simple. You should take a moment to look at the overview maps and information on the kiosk before departing.

From the parking area, the trail to the Wind Caves leads west and down the canyon. The trail begins climbing immediately at a steady yet comfortable grade. During its initial 0.6 mile, though the trail stays

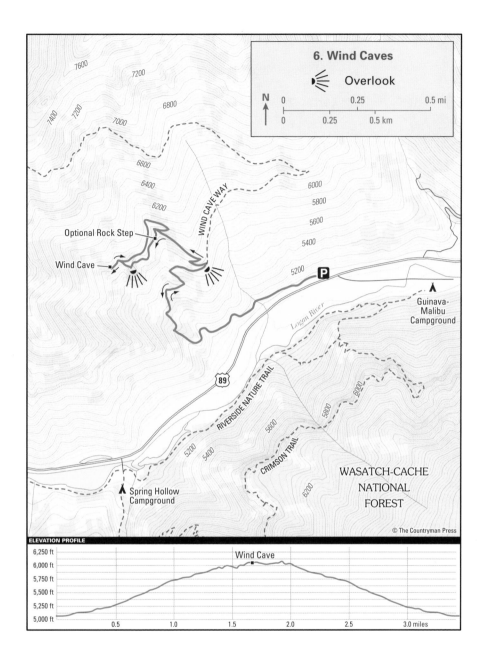

more or less parallel to the road, it climbs more than 300 feet above it. As it gains elevation, the path passes through mixed sections of shrubs and grass, providing hikers with excellent views of the Bear River Range across and down Logan Canyon.

After this initial westward stretch, the trail bends to the northwest and enters a gully. It

View up the Wind Caves Trail toward limestone outcrops

Wind Caves

follows this small drainage and climbs more or less directly uphill—at a noticeably steeper grade—for 0.2 mile. While in this gully section, the trail enjoys a rather dense covering of shrub maple and the occasional juniper. During the autumn months, these maple trees absolutely glow with orange, red, and pink foliage—contributing to Logan Canyon's nickname, "Little Vermont." It is also in this section that the trail offers its first glimpses of the Wind Caves.

At 0.8 mile into the hike, the trail breaks out of the gully and heads to the right. Climbing at a more mellow grade once again, it wraps around a bulging hillside. Having left the gully, the trail enters a landscape of grassy, open expanses. Facing east for the first time, you now enjoy a completely different set of views.

At 1.1 miles into the hike, the trail comes to a junction with a faint path. Unmarked but for a bare post, this easy-to-miss trail is ac-

tually the Wind Caves Way Trail. To stay on this chapter's route (the Wind Caves Trail), make a sharp, left-hand turn and follow the well-worn trail. Hikers that go right here (and therefore take Wind Caves Way Trail) do not go to the Wind Caves; rather, they climb to the ridgeline and meet up with the Bierdneau Trail of Green Canyon (Chapter 9 of this book) after 3.5 miles.

After passing this junction, the trail makes two switchbacks and then heads west and uphill toward the caves. At 1.4 miles into the hike, a post marks yet another junction. Though the post clearly held a sign at some time in the past, it no longer does. From here, two trails lead to the caves. Many young people take the left fork, which heads across a limestone terrace and then up a short, scrambly ledge. Though the majority of this left-hand trail is suitable for anyone, the initial rock step renders it impassible for less agile folks and dogs.

Wind Caves

The best trail takes a sharp right at this post, leading to the east—and seemingly in the wrong direction for a few hundred yards. Shortly afterward, though, this trail switches back to the west and makes its way over to the cave after just 0.4 mile, approaching it from above.

No matter which route you take to the caves, the final section of the journey is filled with crisscrossing paths. Despite the large number of scattered trails, the caves should nevertheless be easy to locate at this point. Once at the caves, hikers are able to look down onto Logan Canyon through a pair of conjoined arches. In good weather, this area provides a pleasant spot for picnicking.

From the caves, hikers must return to the trailhead via the same route, unless extending their hike with a trip up the Wind Caves Way Trail. Because hikers face out and away from the mountainside, the views on the way down are generally even better than on the way up.

FEES, RESTRICTIONS, AND PERMITS
No fees; dogs OK; National Forest restrictions apply

7

Riverside Nature Trail

Type: Canyon; broad dirt; out-and-back; side trips and extensions possible

Season: Any; best in fall foliage season

Total Distance: 2.7 miles round-trip

Time: 1–2 hours

Rating: Easy

Elevation Gain: 250 feet

Location: Logan Canyon, east of Logan

Maps: USGS MOUNT ELMER US TOPO

Contact: Uinta-Wasatch-Cache National Forest: Logan Ranger District, 1500 E. US 89, Logan UT 84321; 435-755-3620; www.fs.usda.gov/uwcnf

Trailhead GPS Coordinates: Spring Hollow Campground: N41 45.191 W111 43.011

Comments: This trail is short, pleasant, and surprisingly beautiful.

OVERVIEW

The Riverside Nature Trail follows the southern shore of the Logan River from the Spring Hollow Campground to the Guinavah-Malibu Campground. Adorned with informative signs along the way, this accessible, mellow, and very pleasant trail offers unexpectedly beautiful views of nearby wetlands and more distant mountainsides. Those hoping to extend the route may easily do so, either by adding a trip on the River Trail (to the west and downstream of the Spring Hollow Campground) or by tacking the more strenuous Crimson Trail onto the journey.

THE TRAIL

This chapter's tour of the Riverside Nature Trail begins at the Spring Hollow Campground in the lower reaches of Logan Canyon. Located just above the third dam, this campground is a popular access point for fishermen and hikers alike. As such, a parking lot for day-use recreationalists stands at the entryway to the campground. Here, information on the area is posted on a large kiosk, including an overview map of the campground showing the locations of the trailheads within it.

The Riverside Nature Trail departs from Site 12, on the western side of this campground. Hikers must walk roughly 50 yards through the campground to reach Site 12. A sign describing the route marks the actual trailhead there.

After leaving the campground, the trail immediately passes over a small stream by way

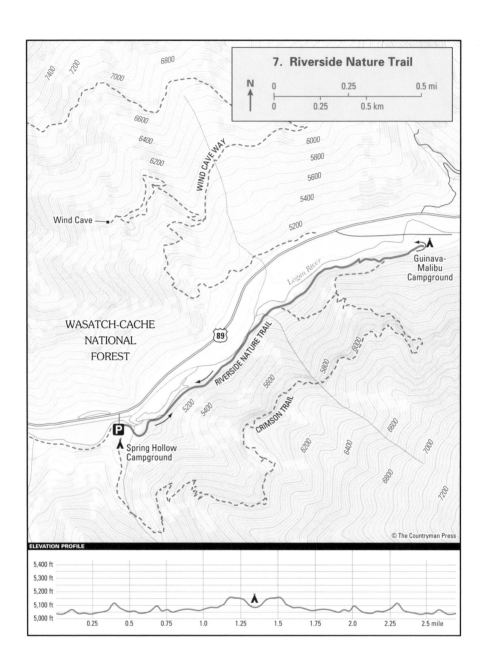

7. Riverside Nature Trail

N

| 0 | 0.25 | 0.5 mi |

| 0 | 0.25 | 0.5 km |

7400 7200

6800

7000

6600

6400

6200

WIND CAVE WAY

6000

5800

5600

5400

5200

Wind Cave

Logan River

Guinava-
Malibu
Campground

WASATCH-CACHE
NATIONAL
FOREST

89

RIVERSIDE NATURE TRAIL

5200

5400

5600

5800

6000

CRIMSON TRAIL

6200

6400

6600

6800

7000

7200

P

Spring Hollow
Campground

© The Countryman Press

ELEVATION PROFILE

| 5,400 ft |
| 5,300 ft |
| 5,200 ft |
| 5,100 ft |
| 5,000 ft |
| 0.25 | 0.5 | 0.75 | 1.0 | 1.25 | 1.5 | 1.75 | 2.0 | 2.25 | 2.5 mile |

View west onto Logan River from Riverside Nature Trail CHRISTINE BALAZ

of a footbridge. Shortly afterward, you pass by the first of about a dozen interpretive signs. Along the way, these point out various components of the environment and describe their importance within the ecosystem. Without these signs, many interesting aspects of this wetland habitat would go unnoticed by the vast majority of hikers.

Though hikers on the Riverside Nature Trail find themselves generally surrounded by lush, canyon-bottom plant life, the trail nevertheless offers many more views than one would expect. At times, the path comes quite near the incredibly clear waters of the Logan River. In these places, you emerge from the trees and enjoy views of the canyon's opposite side, with its mountain walls, cliffs, and peaks. Often, too, the trail climbs sufficiently high above the river to provide similarly open vistas.

Continuing east, the trail passes numerous signs pointing out components of the marshes and wetlands along the river, as well as the various vegetation zones of the canyon. At 0.6 mile from the trailhead, a clearing allows for cross-canyon views of the Wind Caves (Chapter 6 of this book). Located roughly 1,000 feet above the river, this series of caves and natural arches have been eroded into the long limestone cliff bands stretching much of the length of Logan Canyon.

Riverside Nature Trail heading out of Spring Hollow Campground

At 1.0 mile into the hike, the trail passes a warning sign just before the dirt path becomes a boardwalk. Just beyond this it passes beneath a band of limestone cliffs roughly 30 feet tall. Here the boardwalk keeps hikers out of a swampy area by the adjacent line of cliffs they would otherwise be forced to walk through.

The trail climbs up and away from these cliffs to reach a signed junction with the Crimson Trail. If you were to take this trail, you climb roughly 1,000 feet through a series of tight switchbacks, then descend to reach the Spring Hollow Campground 3.0 miles from this junction.

Hikers that wish to continue on the Riverside Nature Trail have but 0.1 mile remaining to reach the Guinavah-Malibu Campground where water spigots offer potable water during peak (summer) season. From this upper campground, the quickest route back to the Spring Hollow Campground is to retrace the Riverside Nature Trail—unless, of course, there is a shuttle car waiting at this campground.

FEES, RESTRICTIONS, AND PERMITS

A $5 day-use fee is required of all parked vehicles; dogs OK, must be leashed in the parking lot and campground; National Forest restrictions apply

Green Canyon Trail

Type: Mountain; dirt; out-and-back; side trips and extensions possible

Season: Any

Total Distance: 7.8 miles round-trip

Time: 2.5–4 hours

Rating: Easy/Moderate

Elevation Gain: 1,100 feet

Location: Green Canyon, east of Logan

Maps: USGS SMITHFIELD US TOPO and USGS MOUNT ELMER US TOPO

Contact: Uinta-Wasatch-Cache National Forest: Logan Ranger District, 1500 E. US 89, Logan UT 84321; 435-755-3620; www.fs.usda.gov/uwcnf

Trailhead GPS Coordinates: Green Canyon Trailhead: N41 46.132 W111 46.187

Comments: Offering a lot of distance at an extremely gentle grade, this trail is therefore very popular among mountain bikers; stay alert to avoid being startled or run over.

OVERVIEW

This long and pleasant trail stretches along the tree-covered bottom of Green Canyon for nearly 4.0 miles. This narrow canyon, which sits east of Logan and north of the more popular Logan Canyon, climbs slowly into the Bear River Range and toward the Mount Naomi Wilderness. Though surrounded by trees most of the time, the shady Green Canyon Trail nevertheless passes through occasional open sections, allowing hikers to stay cool whilst enjoying intermittent views of the charming canyon.

THE TRAIL

The Green Canyon Trail beings in a large parking area located 0.6 mile into the canyon, along Green Canyon Drive/1900 North Street. Though it is possible to start this hike at the mouth of the canyon, most people do not, as the upper canyon offers a much better trail and more pleasant atmosphere.

The trailhead is impossible to miss, as it contains a pit toilet and kiosk in a parking area with room for dozens of cars. Posted on the kiosk is a topographical map of the area. This map shows this route and Beirdneau Trail (Chapter 9 of this book), as well as designated wilderness and national forest lands.

From the trailhead, the path heads due east and across a grassy field. For the remainder of its journey, this trail stays quite near and parallel to Green Canyon Drive—even crossing it multiple times. Though the idea of these crossings might, at first, seem to detract from the experience, these road

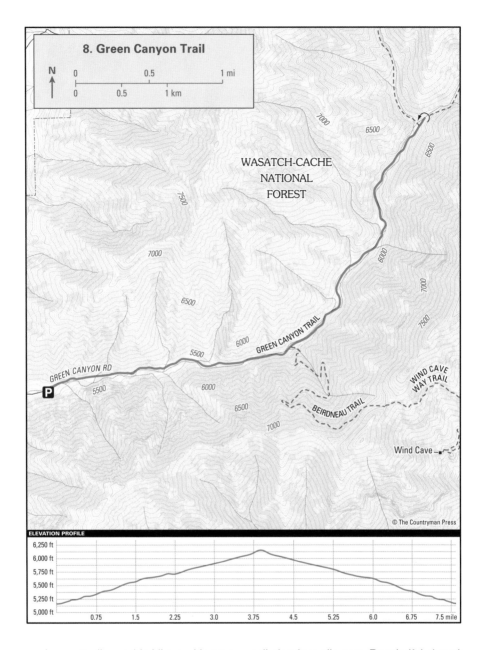

8. Green Canyon Trail

N

| 0 | | 0.5 | | 1 mi |
| 0 | 0.5 | | 1 km | |

WASATCH-CACHE
NATIONAL
FOREST

7000
6500
6500
7500
7000
6500
6000
5500
6000
GREEN CANYON TRAIL
6000
7500
GREEN CANYON RD
5500
6000
6500
7000
WIND CAVE WAY TRAIL
BEIRDNEAU TRAIL
Wind Cave

© The Countryman Press

ELEVATION PROFILE

6,250 ft	
6,000 ft	
5,750 ft	
5,500 ft	
5,250 ft	
5,000 ft	

0.75 1.5 2.25 3.0 3.75 4.5 5.25 6.0 6.75 7.5 mile

crossings actually provide hikers with more instances of open views—making the hike a little more scenic than it might otherwise be. Additionally, this rather rough dirt road sees little traffic and therefore creates little noise pollution for trail users. Be mindful, though, when crossing the road, so as to avoid injury.

After passing through this grassy field, the trail heads into a section of juniper trees and scrub maple. Soon after, it enters a

The rolling Green Canyon Trail

picnic area with yet another kiosk and pit toilet. Here the history of the greater Logan area is illustrated on a sign. You can read about fossils, the Shoshone people, Spanish explorers, trappers, the founding of Logan, the quarrying of limestone in Green Canyon, and the construction of the LDS Temple from this limestone among other interesting facts. This quiet little canyon has seen a lot, from ancient musk ox and mammoth species to famous mountain men like Jim Bridger.

Just 0.3 mile into the canyon, the trail crosses the road for its first time and passes by a blocky limestone cliff with a significant cave. Crossing the road again immediately, the trail heads into a thick stand of scrub maple and other low-lying trees and brush.

As it continues up the canyon, the trail more or less maintains the same relaxed tra-jectory. It climbs gently, and occasionally rolls as it goes. Though it remains mostly in the forest, the Green Canyon Trail occasionally comes into more open areas, either by entering into grassy fields or by crossing Green Canyon Drive.

At 1.8 miles from the trailhead, the Beirdneau Trail (Chapter 9 of this book) departs to the south from a small roadside trailhead. Shortly after this, the Green Canyon Trail bends to the left to follow the canyon bottom, which arcs subtly to the northeast. Beyond this point, the canyon walls grow noticeably less steep, giving way to a wider canyon.

At 3.2 miles from the trailhead, the ecosystem changes subtly, and tall evergreen trees slowly start replacing deciduous shrubs as the dominant group. Shortly

Cave low in Green Canyon

after this, the trail curves back to the right. About 0.3 mile later, the trail passes through an open, grassy section.

At 3.9 mile from the trailhead, the path joins the road, and this chapter's route ends in a parking lot. Though the road ends here, a trail continues climbing into the upper reaches of Green Canyon from this point. Though less popular (likely due to its steeper grade and its longer distance from Logan), this section of trail leads into the Mount Naomi Wilderness after 1.7 miles.

To reach their car from this point, hikers must turn around and follow the Green Canyon Trail back to the parking area. Given its pleasant downhill grade of roughly 5 percent, the 3.9-mile return trip can be completed rather quickly. Those with extra energy should consider adding the more strenuous 4.0-mile Beirdneau Trail hike (Chapter 9) to their trip.

FEES, RESTRICTIONS, AND PERMITS
No fees; dogs and bikes OK; National Forest restrictions apply; those extending the journey into the Mount Naomi Wilderness (1.7 miles beyond this route's end) must not bring wheeled vehicles of any kind

9

Beirdneau Trail to Wind Caves Way

Type: Mountain; dirt; out-and-back; extensions possible

Season: Spring–Fall

Total Distance: 4.1 miles round-trip

Time: 2–3 hours

Rating: Moderate

Elevation Gain: 1,800 feet

Location: Green Canyon, east of Logan

Maps: USGS MOUNT ELMER US TOPO

Contact: Uinta-Wasatch-Cache National Forest: Logan Ranger District, 1500 E. US 89, Logan UT 84321; 435-755-3620; www.fs.usda.gov/uwcnf

Trailhead GPS Coordinates: Beirdneau Trailhead: N41 46.387 W111 44.215

Comments: This trail offers a generous amount of shade, rendering it rather pleasant to hike on days when other trails would be too hot.

OVERVIEW

A relatively short–yet steep–hike, the Beirdneau Trail ascends the steep south wall of Green Canyon to its ridge. There it offers views down into Logan Canyon to the south, and joins the Wind Caves Way Trail, which heads down into this canyon. As the entirety of the Beirdneau Trail lies on a north-facing slope, it enjoys ample shade provided by thick evergreen forests for much of its length.

THE TRAIL

The trailhead for this hike is located along Green Canyon Drive, approximately halfway up the Green Canyon Trail (Chapter 8 of this book). From this small, crude parking area, the trail heads south and immediately begins climbing the steep, north-facing wall of Green Canyon by way of a broad gully. Adorned with a light forest of low-growing scrub maple trees, this portion of the hike is especially beautiful during the autumn months.

This initial gully section doesn't last long, however. After just 0.1 mile, the trail bends to the right and cuts westwardly across the hillside. As it does this, the trail emerges from the fold of the gully and reveals views down Green Canyon and into the Cache Valley.

This southwestward trajectory continues just 0.1 mile before the trail hooks sharply back to the left. Facing southeast at this point, you gain ever-better views of upper Green Canyon. To the northeast, the broad summit of Mount Elmer, elevation 9,655 feet, can be seen framed by the canyon walls.

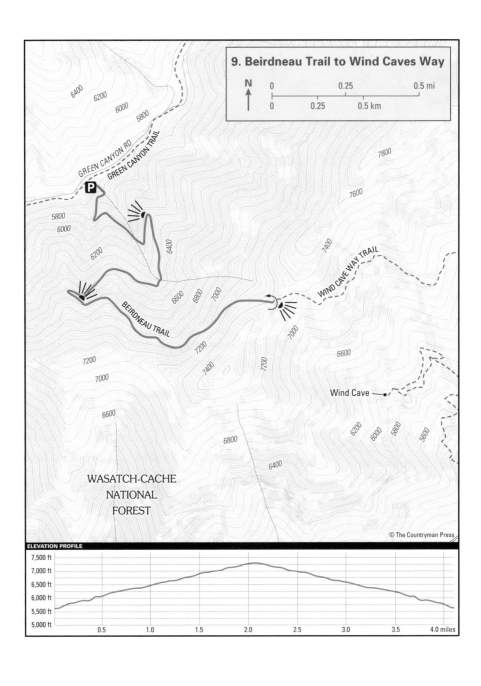

9. Beirdneau Trail to Wind Caves Way

**WASATCH-CACHE
NATIONAL
FOREST**

Wind Cave

© The Countryman Press

ELEVATION PROFILE

However, as you enter onto east-facing slopes, you also enter into thick evergreen forest once again—trading views for pleasant shade.

After arcing yet farther to the east, the trail makes a distinct hairpin turn to the right, roughly 0.5 mile into the hike, and heads southwest again. As the trail emerges onto a west-facing slope of the mountainside, the forest lightens once again, providing yet better views toward the west and down into Green Canyon.

At 0.8 mile into the hike, the trail switches back to the right yet again and heads more or less due west for 0.4 mile. As it does this, it traverses in and out of canyon-wall folds, and therefore through alternating patches of dense forest and open vistas.

At 1.2 miles into the hike, the trail passes through its final switchback, and heads to the east once again. Here, the grade lessens up noticeably. Though you will find yourself mostly surrounded by forest from here to the top, the canopy nevertheless opens up distinctively 0.1 mile after the hairpin turn, offering a final elevated view of Green Canyon's upper reaches to the east.

The last stretch of trail sports the cover of a beautiful evergreen forest. Tall and well-spaced, these conifers let just enough light through their branches to allow for a thin carpeting of low-laying undergrowth. On either side of the trail, Douglas fir tree trunks have characteristic J-shaped curves at their bases. When these trees were saplings, the steep earth around them shifted. Though the tree roots remained in place, the shifting earth caused the trees to slant downhill. Yet as the trees continued growing, their tops grew upright and toward the sun. Though the trees' trunks today are almost entirely straight, the lower curves remain.

As you continue uphill, the top of the trail remains hidden by trees until very near the

Beirdneau Trailhead   CHRISTINE BALAZ

end. The ridgeline can only be discerned through the dense canopy as you come very close to it. The actual top of this trail—and the ridge itself—is marked by a small clearing in which a collection of logs has been arranged for lounging purposes. You can enjoy a snack and drink in the clearing, and then walk through this area to the east to an overlook. Here, beyond the crest of the ridge, the Beirdneau Trail becomes Wind Caves Way and drops down into Logan Canyon, which lays parallel to and south of Green Canyon. Hikers continuing down into Logan Canyon

Looking down into Logan Canyon from the top of Beirdneau Trail

eventually meet up with the Wind Caves Trail (Chapter 6 of this book).

Unless you have parked a shuttle car at the Wind Caves Trailhead in Logan Canyon, you will return to your car by turning around and retracing your steps down into Green Canyon. Once back at the Beirdneau Trailhead, you may add an extension by walking along the Green Canyon Trail (Chapter 8)—either by following it up the canyon for up to 2.1 miles or down the canyon for 1.8 miles.

FEES, RESTRICTIONS, AND PERMITS
No fees; dogs OK; most of this hike falls within the Mount Naomi Wilderness, where wheeled vehicles of any kind are not allowed, and wilderness restrictions apply

10

Waterfall Canyon

Type: Mountain; dirt; out-and-back

Season: Fall–Spring; ice possible in winter

Total Distance: 2.4 miles round-trip

Time: 1–2 hours

Rating: Moderate

Elevation Gain: 1,200 feet

Location: Ogden-area Wasatch Mountains

Maps: USGS OGDEN US TOPO

Contact: Weber Pathways, 2661 Washington Blvd., Ogden, UT 84401; 801-393-2304; www.weberpathways .org

Trailhead GPS Coordinates: East end of 29th Street, Ogden: N41 12.679 W111 55.912

Comments: Relatively short and extremely accessible, this hike climbs considerably to an impressive waterfall just outside Ogden.

OVERVIEW

Part of the incredible and extensive Weber Pathways trail system, Waterfall Canyon is one of the most popular hikes in the Ogden area. Departing from the eastern edge of town, this trail climbs quickly along the city-side foothills before plunging into the namesake fold in the Wasatch Mountains. Once in Waterfall Canyon, the trail climbs steeply as it follows alongside a stream, then terminates at the base of a 200-foot waterfall cascading down a face of vertical quartzite. During springtime, the waterfall surges most impressively down this lofty drop.

THE TRAIL

The Waterfall Canyon Trail begins in a large, obvious parking lot at the "top" (east end) of 29th Street in Ogden—where the city ends and the Wasatch Mountains dramatically begin. The path departs from underneath a large and obvious kiosk at the southern end of this parking lot. However, once past the kiosk, the route loses its obviousness temporarily in a junction of trails. The most direct path to Waterfall Canyon (and the route followed by this chapter) is taken by heading directly east and uphill (rather than south). Hikers feeling at all uncertain about the route should take a moment to study the overview map permanently posted in the parking lot kiosk.

After its initial eastward climb, the trail bends gradually to the south, and encounters another trail after about 0.2 mile. Here signs correctly indicate that you should take

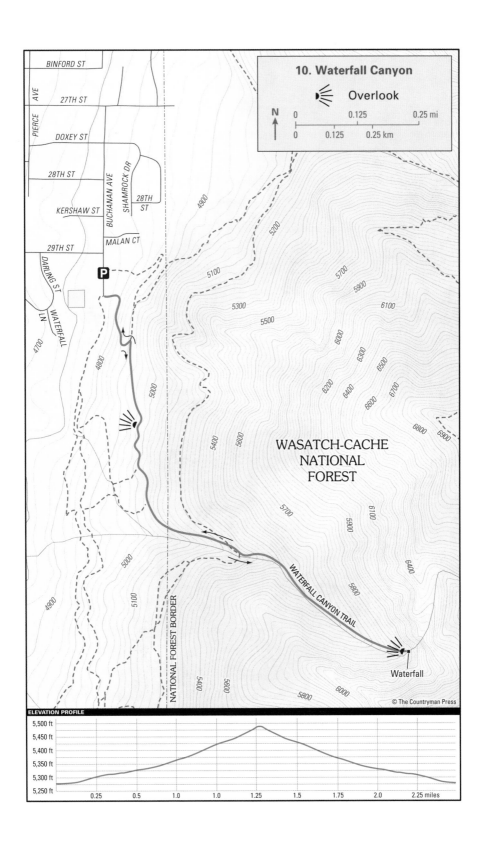

10. Waterfall Canyon

⟋⟍ **Overlook**

N

| 0 | | 0.125 | | 0.25 mi |

| 0 | 0.125 | 0.25 km |

BINFORD ST

27TH ST

PIERCE AVE

DOXEY ST

28TH ST

BUCHANAN AVE

SHAMROCK DR

28TH ST

KERSHAW ST

MALAN CT

29TH ST

DARLING ST

WATERFALL LN

P

4700

4900

4800

5000

5100

5200

5300

5500

5400

5600

5700

5900

6100

6000

6200

6300

6500

6400

6600

6700

6800

6900

WASATCH-CACHE
NATIONAL
FOREST

5700

5900

6100

6400

5000

5100

4900

5000

WATERFALL CANYON TRAIL

5900

Waterfall

5400

5600

5800

6000

NATIONAL FOREST BORDER

© The Countryman Press

ELEVATION PROFILE

5,500 ft									
5,450 ft									
5,400 ft									
5,350 ft									
5,300 ft									
5,250 ft									
	0.25	0.5	1.0	1.0	1.25	1.5	1.75	2.0	2.25 miles

Waterfall Canyon's namesake destination

a right to head south and toward Waterfall Canyon.

From here, the broad and well-maintained trail climbs gradually higher and higher onto the Ogden foothills as it heads south. Increasingly broad views of Ogden, the Wasatch Mountains, and eventually the Great Salt Lake and its mountainous Antelope Island can be had through the low-lying scrub oak and sagebrush characteristic of Utah's mountains. Don't expect much shade on this route, particularly in the afternoon; these sparsely vegetated, west- and south-facing slopes offer very direct exposure to the sun's warmth.

After about 0.6 mile of total walking, the trail reaches the mouth of Waterfall Canyon and crosses a stream by way of a small footbridge. Here it veers distinctly to the east and steepens in grade as it climbs higher into the canyon, paralleling the stream that flows beneath the namesake falls. At this point, the trail again splits into multiple paths. However, the exact route to the falls is unimportant here—all paths lead uphill and to the same point, and all after a very similar length of walking. Because of the popularity of the route, you'll notice that as many as three or four parallel trails sometimes exist within the same area.

After just 0.6 mile of steep and rocky climbing, you'll find yourself at the obvious end of this hike—where the trail terminates in a craggy and tight cirque of orange quartzite. From a notch high on the north side of the canyon, a perennial stream falls roughly 200 feet onto a bed of jagged quartzite slabs. Here you can cool off in the mist of the falls, or even dip your head under the stream. To the west, views of Ogden and the mountains of Antelope Island can be stolen through the walls of the narrow canyon.

View northwest onto Ogden

From here, the only feasible route out is to reverse your path and follow the exact same route back down Waterfall Canyon. Once you've descended the 0.6 mile of steep Waterfall Canyon to reach the footbridge at the mouth of the canyon, you may extend your journey slightly by turning south (instead of heading north) at the mouth of the canyon. Doing so will take you approximately 0.6 mile farther south yet, and lead you to the mouth of Strong Canyon, up which no trails go. To return to the parking lot from here, head west and downhill for a few hundred yards, and then follow either of the two parallel trails heading due north back to the 29th Street parking lot.

FEES, RESTRICTIONS, AND PERMITS

Dogs permitted on-leash, clean up and pack out all solid dog waste; much of the land surrounding the trail is private property, stay on the path at all times

Out of Sight, Out of Mind

A word of warning: Though in the last few decades, Ogden has matured and gentrified in leaps and bounds, it still has a higher crime rate than many other parts of Utah. When parking anywhere in Ogden, be sure to conceal all valuables. Better yet, leave all valuables at home or carry them with you.

11

Wheeler Creek Trail

Type: Mountain canyon; dirt; out-and-back; side trips and extensions possible

Season: Spring–Fall

Total Distance: 3.9 miles round-trip

Time: 1.5–2 hours

Rating: Easy/Moderate

Elevation Gain: 700 feet

Location: Ogden Canyon

Maps: USGS HUNTSVILLE US TOPO and USGS SNOW BASIN US TOPO

Contact: Cache National Forest: Ogden Ranger District, 507 25th Street, Suite 103, Ogden, UT 84401; 801-625-5112; www.fs.usda.gov/uwcnf: or Weber Pathways, 2661 Washington Blvd., Ogden, UT 84401; 801-393-2304; www.weberpathways.org

Trailhead GPS Coordinates: Wheeler Creek Trailhead (across from Pineview Dam): N41 15.210 W111 50.673

Comments: A moderate and shady canyon-bottom hike, Wheeler Creek is pleasant in summer and a great option for those short on time.

OVERVIEW

The Wheeler Creek Trail is a broad and flat dirt path that follows the decommissioned Art Nord Road up Wheeler Creek Canyon. The trail is cooled by a parallel, namesake creek and in the afternoon—when the sun settles in the western half of the sky—nearly the entire route is shaded by trees. Along its ascent and at its terminus, this trail encounters numerous other paths of the Weber Pathways trail network. As this trail is shared by hikers, mountain bikers, horses, and even cross-country skiers, it is a good idea to stay alert and listen for oncoming traffic.

THE TRAIL

The route begins at fairly sizeable parking lot in Ogden Canyon just across the road from, and slightly west of, the Pineview Dam. Only one trail departs from this lot, making the route-finding quite simple at this point. From the parking area, the broad, dirt path climbs steadily and gradually through deciduous trees and past limestone cliff bands. As the route progresses, the trail maintains a near distance to Wheeler Creek, providing hikers with a pleasantly cool temperature and relaxing "nature" sounds of running water.

As the Wheeler Creek Trail climbs higher, deciduous trees blend with evergreen species, and thick, leafy shrubs yield to grass and talus. At 1.1 miles into the hike, a large, pyramidal mountain comes into view. Here the trail forks, sending one branch around either side of it; to remain on this chapter's

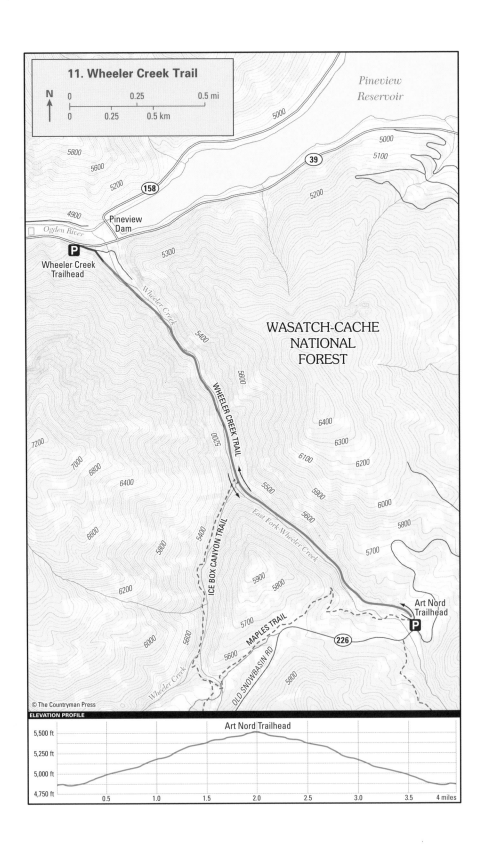

11. Wheeler Creek Trail

N

| 0 | 0.25 | 0.5 mi |

| 0 | 0.25 | 0.5 km |

Pineview Reservoir

5000

39

5000

5100

5800

5600

5200

158

5200

4900

Ogden River

Pineview Dam

P
Wheeler Creek Trailhead

5300

Wheeler Creek

5400

5600

WASATCH-CACHE NATIONAL FOREST

WHEELER CREEK TRAIL

5200

6400

6300

6200

7200

7000

6800

6400

6100

5900

6000

5800

5700

5500

5600

East Fork Wheeler Creek

6600

ICE BOX CANYON TRAIL

5400

5800

5900

5800

Art Nord Trailhead
P

6200

5700

MAPLES TRAIL

226

6000

5600

5600

OLD SNOWBASIN RD

5800

Wheeler Creek

© The Countryman Press

ELEVATION PROFILE

Art Nord Trailhead

5,500 ft								
5,250 ft								
5,000 ft								
4,750 ft	0.5	1.0	1.5	2.0	2.5	3.0	3.5	4 miles

route, stay straight (and to the left side of the mountain). However, you may take a right and cross the creek; doing this leads into Icebox Canyon and around the right side of the mountain. Both routes connect with the Maples Trail at their terminus; together these three trails (Wheeler Creek, Icebox Canyon, and Maples) form a triangular path around the mountain.

After the junction with the Icebox Canyon Trail, the Wheeler Creek Trail enters into a zone of tall, widely spaced aspen trees. Shortly afterward, Wheeler Creek Canyon opens up and the steep hillsides on either side of the trail give way to broad, grassy slopes ornamented with occasional trees. Here the views open up significantly as well, revealing plentiful scenery of the surrounding mountains as well as the lofty peaks of Snowbasin Resort towering high above the landscape to the west. Mount Ogden, at 9,570 feet, is the tallest of these summits.

Shortly after the canyon opens up, the Wheeler Creek Trail ends at the Maples Trail. There a large structure of logs stands with placards depicting different aspects of the ecosystem. Here you can learn about various species and their role in the local environment, as well as the Forest Service's management of this riparian area since 1936.

Our route ends in the Art Nord Trailhead parking lot (along UT 266). To return to your vehicle, turn around and retrace your steps to the parking lot. Alternatively, you can extend your journey by taking a sharp right-hand turn onto the Maples Trail. Follow it westward and uphill; this meets up with Icebox Canyon Trail at the Wheeler Campground after 3.2 miles; here you can take another right-hand turn to join the Icebox

View of Snowbasin from top of Wheeler Creek Trail   CHRISTINE BALAZ

Canyon Trail and follow it downhill for about 1.5 miles. This will dump you back on the Wheeler Creek Trail at the junction described earlier in this chapter (just 1.1 miles above the Wheeler Creek Trailhead).

FEES, RESTRICTIONS, AND PERMITS
No motorized vehicles allowed; horses and mountain bikes OK year-round

Extend the Journey
Just above the trailhead, a wooden sign foretells the mileage to certain points along this trail network. From here, it is just 1.8 miles to this route's turnaround point; however, if you wish to take a long run or mountain bike ride, you can easily extend the journey by way of the numerous looping side trails, You'd be clever to carry a map with you in order to navigate the numerous trail junctions this would entail. If you're fairly confident in your navigational skills, you may simply visit Weber Pathway's website and sketch a map of your own to carry in your pocket.

Local Legend, Art Nord
Arthur George Nord was born in 1892 and died in 1957. During his lifetime, Nord was a local legend among conservationists. Working for the U.S. Forest Service from 1915 to 1956, Nord had a tremendous impact on the restoration and management policies directly affecting the Ogden-area Wasatch Mountains. Nord was a powerful leader able to marry public use policies and watershed restoration efforts. It is largely because of his early conservationist efforts that humans today continue to enjoy the Ogden-area environment without destroying or severely disrupting local habitat.

12

Ogden Overlook from Snowbasin

Type: Mountain; dirt; out-and-back; side trips possible

Season: Spring–Fall

Total Distance: 5.4 miles round-trip

Time: 2–4 hours

Rating: Moderate

Elevation Gain: 1,000 feet

Location: Snowbasin Resort, Ogden Valley

Maps: USGS SNOW BASIN US TOPO and USGS OGDEN US TOPO

Contact: Snowbasin Resort, 3925 E. Snowbasin Road, Huntsville, UT 84317; 1-888-437-5488; www.snowbasin.com: or Cache National Forest: Ogden Ranger District, 507 25th Street, Suite 103, Ogden, UT 84401; 801-625-5112; www.fs.usda.gov/uwcnf

Trailhead GPS Coordinates: Parking Lot #2: N41 13.111 W111 51.759

Comments: A moderately high-elevation route, this extremely pleasant trail winds gradually through the aspen trees and fields of Snowbasin's slopes to reach an impressive viewpoint overlooking the city of Ogden to the west.

OVERVIEW

The Ogden Overlook Trail follows along a dirt road (closed to motor traffic) before reaching a decommissioned campground, transforming into singletrack, and ascending the slopes of Snowbasin Resort. The path climbs extremely gently and steadily as it winds its way up the mountainside in large, looping switchbacks. Along the route, you'll pass through patches of aspen and evergreen trees, as well as open grassy areas affording views of Snowbasin and the more distant Ogden Valley and Wasatch Mountains. At the trail's terminus, a bench allows for relaxation while taking in the views of the Ogden metro area below. Many longer side trips are possible from this route; pack extra water and food if you plan to extend your journey.

THE TRAIL

Locating the Ogden Overlook Trailhead is reasonably straightforward, given the clear signing of Snowbasin's parking lots. At the northwesternmost portion of Parking Lot #2 a gate and signboard mark Maples Road, which serves as the beginning of this trail. Closed to traffic, this pedestrian-only dirt road heads due north and slightly downhill through forest and open fields. After about 0.5 mile, the road begins climbing gradually. Just afterward, you'll notice the Maples/Wheeler Creek singletrack trail on your right; stay straight to keep on this hike's route.

As you climb, you'll notice several singletrack shortcuts between the meanders of the

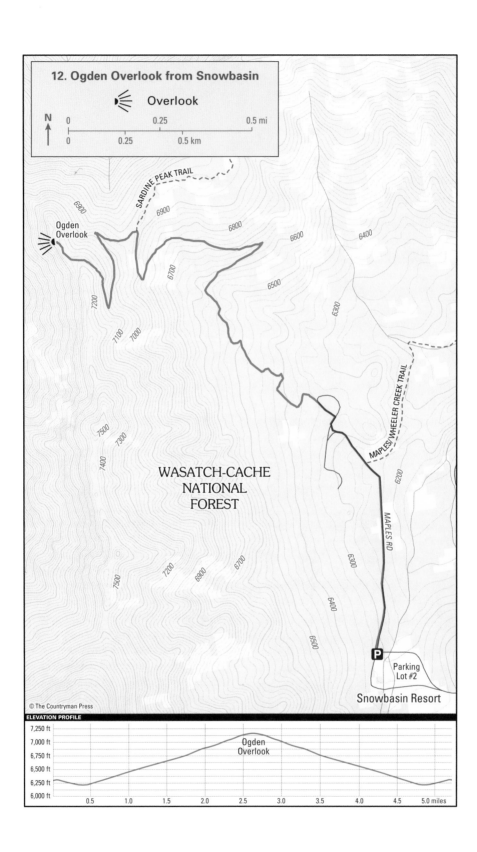

12. Ogden Overlook from Snowbasin

Overlook

N

| 0 | 0.25 | 0.5 mi |

| 0 | 0.25 | 0.5 km |

SARDINE PEAK TRAIL

6900

6900

6800

6600

6400

Ogden
Overlook

6700

6500

7200

6300

7100   7000

MAPLES/ WHEELER CREEK TRAIL

7500

7300

6200

7400

WASATCH-CACHE
NATIONAL
FOREST

MAPLES RD

7500

7200   6800   6700

6300

6400

6500

P

Parking
Lot #2

Snowbasin Resort

© The Countryman Press

ELEVATION PROFILE

7,250 ft					Ogden					
7,000 ft					Overlook					
6,750 ft										
6,500 ft										
6,250 ft										
6,000 ft	0.5	1.0	1.5	2.0	2.5	3.0	3.5	4.0	4.5	5.0 miles

Trail lazily ascending toward Ogden Overlook

CHRISTINE BALAZ

gravel road; take whichever you please, as all routes end up at the same place. After 0.8 mile of total hiking you come upon a decommissioned campground, which sends the road funneling naturally into a singletrack path. Here a wooden sign for Ogden Overlook and the Sardine Peak Trail stands next to another trail map. Take a second to look at the map and orient yourself.

Once on the singletrack, you can expect steady—yet very gradual—climbing on a nice, buffed-out path. This dug-out, serpentine route winds gently up through aspen stands, open fields, and evergreen. Because of its extremely pleasant grade and smooth nature, this trail is a big hit among mountain bikers. Be sure to keep your eyes and ears tuned for incoming bikes; though trail etiquette would have bikers yield to hikers, there are no guarantees that you won't have to do some yielding yourself.

As you climb, you'll catch glimpses of Snowbasin Resort in the foreground and the Ogden Valley and surrounding mountains in the distance. At 1.9 miles into the route you'll pass under a set of power lines; just 0.1 mile later, you'll encounter a ridgeline junction with the Sardine Peak Trail. To the right you'll see Sardine Peak, a small hump in the foreground. Here a small, wooden sign directs you to the left and toward the Ogden Overlook.

From this junction, the environment changes slightly as the trail ascends at roughly the same grade and enters forests of tall evergreen trees. After 0.7 mile of trail is the highpoint of this route: the Ogden Overlook. From here, the mountains fall steeply away toward the west, exposing generous views of the city of Ogden—the eastern edge of which lies only 3 beeline miles away.

If you turn around and retrace your steps exactly, you'll arrive at your vehicle in about

Bench at Ogden Overlook

CHRISTINE BALAZ

2.7 miles. However, if you wish to extend your journey, simply head back 0.7 mile to the junction with the Sardine Peak Trail. Take a left rather than heading straight, and you'll lengthen your trip by 3.4 miles of very similar terrain and pleasant pathways.

FEES, RESTRICTIONS, AND PERMITS

No motorized vehicles allowed on the path, but bicycles OK; use the trail only when dry

Extra Loop: Sardine Peak Trail

If you're considering adding an extra side loop to your hike, take time to study (or take a picture of) the maps at the trailhead (or beginning of the singletrack) if you didn't bring a map of your own. Adding a large loop with the Sardine Peak Trail is easily done, but requires correct navigation of a few trail junctions. The total loop (with a side journey to the Ogden Overlook) is 8.7 miles. In addition to the extra distance, the loop adds some climbing as well as views down onto the Pineview Reservoir in the Ogden Valley.

Much larger side loops, which link sections of trail called Art Nord, Middle Fork, Wheeler, and Green Pond are possible; however, these are significantly lengthier than the Sardine Peak Trail loop and therefore are almost exclusively done by mountain bikers. If you're interested in exploring these, however, visit the Weber Pathways' Web site (www.weberpathways.org) for more information.

13

Skull Crack Canyon

Type: Mountain; dirt; out-and-back

Season: Spring–Fall; hot in summer

Total Distance: 4.7 miles round-trip

Time: 2–3 hours

Rating: Moderate

Elevation Gain: 650 feet (400 feet on the way out; 250 feet on return trip)

Location: Causey Reservoir, Ogden Valley

Maps: USGS CAUSEY DAM US TOPO

Contact: Cache National Forest: Ogden Ranger District, 507 25th Street, Suite 103, Ogden, UT 84401; 801-625-5112; www.fs.usda.gov/uwcnf

Trailhead GPS Coordinates: Causey Reservoir: N41 17.377 W111 34.960

Comments: A moderate hike, this tours the rolling hillsides above the Causey Reservoir.

OVERVIEW

This route traverses the southern shores of the Causey Reservoir, roughly 25 miles east of Ogden and 10 miles east of Ogden Valley's hamlets of Eden and Huntsville. Though the reservoir is extremely popular among canoeists and kayakers in the summer, the trail itself offers a surprising amount of solitude. Even on the most crowded of lake days, there's a good chance you'll have the entire trail to yourself. A relatively short hike, this route climbs for the first half of its outward journey, then descends to reach the waters of the reservoir at its end; turning around, you'll climb back up to the trail's high point before coasting back down to the parking area.

THE TRAIL

The name Skull Crack Canyon sounds rather foreboding. However, this trail is neither dangerous nor extreme. In fact, the name of this path comes from a local story of two men hunting with mules in the canyon in the 19th century. According to legend, one of the animals got out of control. A hunter struck the mule on the head with his gun barrel, cracking its skull. So even though the history of this trail's name is rather brutal, you can at least hike knowing that you will not be in danger of head-cracking on this route.

The Skull Crack Canyon Trail begins south of the Causey Dam, at the northern end of a large and obvious parking lot there. The trailhead shares its location with a gate and an unofficial boat ramp. Here the obvious dirt singletrack path begins, rather flat and paral-

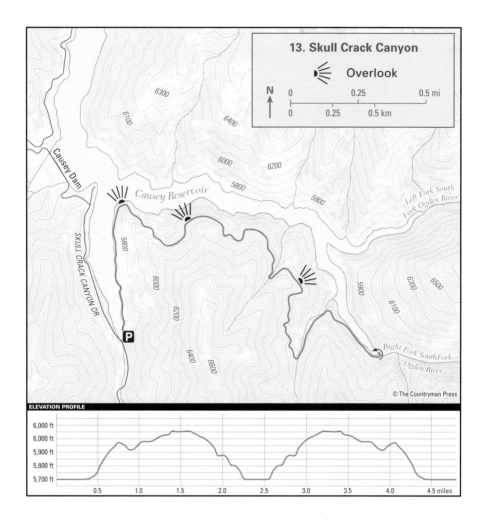

ELEVATION PROFILE

6,000 ft
6,000 ft
5,900 ft
5,800 ft
5,700 ft

0.5 1.0 1.5 2.0 2.5 3.0 3.5 4.0 4.5 miles

lel to the shoreline at first. After approximately 0.3 mile of hiking, the route becomes significantly steeper, climbing quickly above the deep waters of the reservoir below. During springtime, these waters carry sediment stirred up by the swift spring runoff, and are reddish brown. However, by summer—when the current has calmed down—the reservoir becomes a deep greenish blue.

As the trail ascends higher and higher, it enters into zones of scrub oak and airy patches of pine forest. At 0.5 mile into the route, a side trail forks off to the left, accessing an overlook. Here you might spot young people cliff jumping—not a recommended activity as spring waters can (and do) relocate perilous debris each year. The opaque waters of the reservoir can easily conceal deadly logs and other subsurface hazards.

The trail continues to climb about 1.0 mile after the turnoff, affording good views of the reservoir and cliff bands of limestone plunging into it. The higher the trail ascends, the thicker the scrub oak becomes. Though fine for hikers—especially those wearing pants—this shrub species makes mountain biking a little difficult. The presence of rounded quartzite boulders in the trail also further complicates this particular section of trail for mountain bikers.

After 1.5 total miles of hiking, the trail turns noticeably to the right and winds downhill and away from the reservoir. Descending through a side canyon, the trail leaves the scrub oak zone and leads into a slightly marshy area and through a grove of aspen trees. At 0.8 miles from where the trail began descending, it reaches the shoreline of the reservoir at its easternmost point. From here, the only route back is via the trail on which you came . . . unless a friendly boater is willing to give you a ride.

FEES, RESTRICTIONS, AND PERMITS

The Causey Reservoir is considered a day-use area only, so no camping is allowed; no restrictions for pets; boaters must wear a personal floatation device, and boat speed must be kept wakeless

Causey Reservoir

The Causey Reservoir was built over the course of five years in the 1960s. Occupying 142 acres along the South Fork of the Ogden River, this reservoir stands at an elevation of 5,700 feet. No alpine lake by any means, the reservoir has a slightly higher altitude that nevertheless provides some relief from the summer heat of Utah's valleys. Here people fish for brown, rainbow, and cutthroat trout from nonmotorized boats. If you wish to enjoy the reservoir, be aware that there are no boat-launching facilities or campgrounds.

Causey Reservoir from Skull Crack Canyon Trail

CHRISTINE BALAZ

50 Hikes in Utah

14

White Rock Bay

Type: Desert; dirt; lollipop-shaped

Season: Fall–Spring

Total Distance: 7.3 miles round-trip

Time: 3–4 hours

Rating: Moderate

Elevation Gain: 755 feet

Location: White Rock Bay, Antelope Island State Park

Maps: USGS ANTELOPE ISLAND NORTH US TOPO

Contact: Antelope Island State Park, 4528 West 1700 South, Syracuse, UT 84075; 801-773-2941; www.stateparks .utah.gov/antelope-island

Trailhead GPS Coordinates: White Rock Bay: N41 01.500 W112 14.400

Comments: This trail offers no shade along its entire course; think twice before embarking on this journey in the summer.

OVERVIEW

A reasonably flat trail exposing many vistas of the eerily beautiful Great Salt Lake and its environs, White Rock Bay Trail allows hikers to cover a fairly long distance with relatively little effort. Beginning at Antelope Island's White Rock Bay, this trail gently climbs to higher ground before splitting into a loop. Taken clockwise, this hike offers views of the Ogden-area Wasatch Mountains, the mountains of Antelope Island, and the Oquirrh Range—as well as the southwestern portion of the Great Salt Lake, Stansbury Bay, and a mountain range of the same name behind it.

THE TRAIL

White Rock Bay Trailhead is located near the western shores of Antelope Island, toward its northern end. As this island is a state park, you must pay a day-use fee on the western edge of Syracuse before crossing over the causeway and onto the island. When talking with the tollbooth ranger, be sure to ask for a trail map. Though rudimentary, these park-issued maps do a lot to help navigate the island's usually unsigned network of trails.

The White Rock Bay Trail itself departs from a well-signed day parking area at the southern end of a campground bearing the same name. To join the trail, head south out of this parking lot and cross through an opening in a chain-link fence. At this point, you'll have to choose from two trails; the White Rock Bay Trail departs to the left and cuts an arching path up the hillside in front of

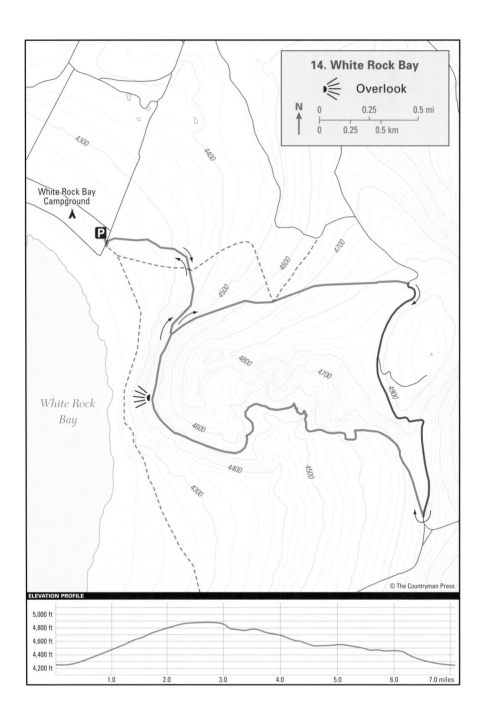

14. White Rock Bay

Overlook

N

| 0 | 0.25 | 0.5 mi |
| 0 | 0.25 | 0.5 km |

4300

4400

White Rock Bay
Campground

P

4500

4600

4700

4800

4700

4900

White Rock
Bay

4600

4400

4500

4300

© The Countryman Press

ELEVATION PROFILE

| 5,000 ft |
| 4,800 ft |
| 4,600 ft |
| 4,400 ft |
| 4,200 ft |

1.0 2.0 3.0 4.0 5.0 6.0 7.0 miles

you—first heading east, then south, and eventually west again.

After 1.0 mile of climbing, this broad and sandy trail reaches the loop portion of this lollipop-shaped journey. Arbitrarily, this chapter's route takes the clockwise version of this loop, requiring you to take a left at this junction.

Though you'll have only climbed about 200 vertical feet to reach this point, you'll notice that the views at this elevation are already markedly better than at lake level. In the foreground, you'll see gnarled, black quartzite boulders; farther afield stands the White Rock Bay itself, as well as the Stansbury Mountains on the horizon.

Once on the loop portion of the hike, the trail continues to climb at a very similar rate as before. As you walk eastward and up-

ward, the peaks of the Ogden-area Wasatch Mountains come into view beyond the grassy hillsides in the foreground. On Antelope Island it is quite easy to imagine what the Salt Lake Valley would have looked like 170 years ago, before the July 1847 arrival of the Mormons in Utah.

After 1.3 miles of due-east travel and steady climbing, the trail approaches and merges with a dirt road, which comes into the trail from the east. To stay on the trail, continue straight and follow the intuitive path as the route takes a rounded U-turn to the southwest. (To get off the route, you would have to make a sharp left-hand turn onto the dirt road.)

The trail then skirts a sizeable knoll to its east, bending around this feature to do so. At 0.5 mile from the last junction, the path en-

Ogden-area Wasatch from White Rock Bay Trail CHRISTINE BALAZ

Antelope Island's slopes as viewed from White Rock Bay Trail   CHRISTINE BALAZ

counters another split; stay right to remain on this route. (If you take a left, you'll reach a cluster of operational buildings near the top of this hill after about 0.4 mile of climbing on the spur called the Beacon Knob Trail.)

At 0.5 mile after the junction, the trail curves back toward the north as it wraps around the base of the hill, and then takes a looping switchback downhill before continuing to the south. Here, the Wasatch Mountains towering over Bountiful and Salt Lake City are perfectly reflected on the mirrorlike surface of the Salt Lake's Farmington Bay.

At 3.8 miles into the hike, the trail reaches a junction at which you must take a very sharp right-hand turn to head north and return to your vehicle. If you were to stay straight here and continue heading south, you could extend your journey another 7.5 miles by taking the Split Rock Loop Trail or

another 4 miles by taking the Elephant Head Trail. In either case, you would be wise to carry a map with you.

As the trail works its way northwest and back toward your car, it meanders and rolls along the hillsides of the island's interior. At times, the views consist entirely of arid, grassy slopes; at other times, views of the Great Salt Lake can be seen beyond them. After about 5.5 total miles, the trail makes its way west enough to reveal White Rock Bay once again, whose reason for the name should be obvious at this point.

The trail bends gradually to the north and, after about 6.3 total miles, it reaches the end of the loop. From at this point, take a left to return to the parking area the same way you came. From here your car should be visible, just 1.0 mile downhill and to the north.

50 Hikes in Utah

FEES, RESTRICTIONS, AND PERMITS

Dogs OK on leash, mountain bikes permitted; $9 day-use fee required to enter the state park; national parks passes not accepted

Farmington Bay Waterfowl Management Area

Farmington Bay occupies the far southeastern corner of the Great Salt Lake. The marshy wetlands surrounding this bay contain a variety of habitats, including open saltwater expanses, freshwater ponds, and marshes. As such, an extremely diverse menagerie of waterfowl calls this area home—if only seasonally. Each year, hundreds of thousands of individual birds representing more than two hundred species visit Farmington Bay for nesting and migration seasons.

15

Frary Peak

Type: Desert; dirt; out-and-back

Season: Fall–Spring

Total Distance: 6.8 miles round-trip

Time: 3–4 hours

Rating: Moderate/Strenuous

Elevation Gain: 2,100 feet

Location: Antelope Island State Park

Maps: USGS ANTELOPE ISLAND US TOPO

Contact: Antelope Island State Park, 4528 West 1700 South, Syracuse, UT 84075; 801-773-2941; www.state parks.utah.gov/antelope-island

Trailhead GPS Coordinates: Frary Peak Parking: N40 59.628 W112 12.160

Comments: Completely devoid of trees (until the very top of the route), this hike offers incredible panoramic views and no shade whatsoever.

OVERVIEW

An airy hike to the tallest point of Antelope Island, the Frary Peak Trail features steady climbing as it travels southward from the trailhead to the island's highest point. With an elevation of 6,596 feet, this mountain stands roughly 2,400 feet–almost 0.5 mile–above the surface of the Great Salt Lake and offers unimpeded views of the lake and its surroundings.

THE TRAIL

The Frary Peak Trail begins at the top of a very steep–yet paved–access road on the eastern edge of Antelope Island. Climbing to the southwest at grades in excess of 20 percent, this short road requires your vehicle to take care of a few hundred feet of ascension for you. In the large parking area at the road's terminus, a topographical map depicts the island and this trail; signs here also remind visitors that this trail is reserved for pedestrian use only.

As the trail leaves the parking lot, it immediately begins dispensing with some of the route's 2,100 vertical feet of ascent. As it climbs the east-facing slopes above the parking lot, the path passes by gnarled boulders reminiscent of an extraterrestrial landscape. Composed of highly metamorphosed quartzite, these dark, twisted rocks are a quintessential component of the otherworldly Antelope Island terrain.

As the trail climbs higher and higher, it offers uninterrupted views across the eastern portion of the Great Salt Lake and the Wasatch Mountains beyond it. From here, it is

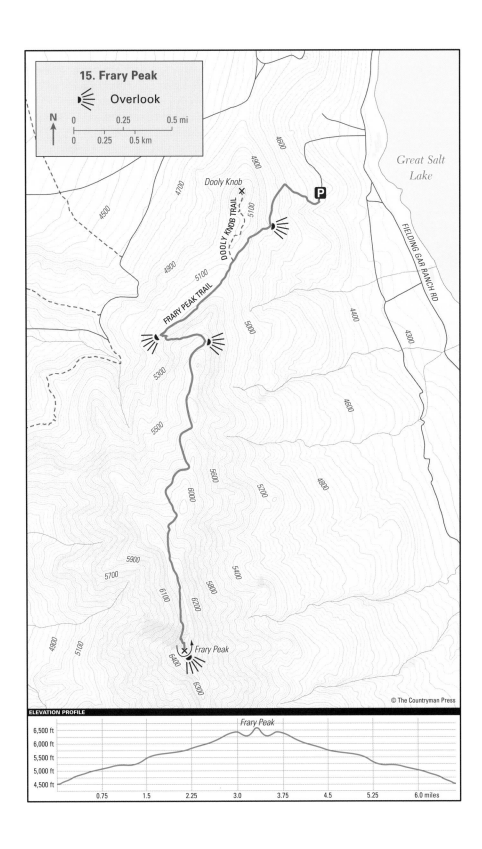

hard to imagine that more than 2 million people reside along the base of this mountain range. Though the distance between the trail and the Wasatch Front metropolis is not more than 15 miles, it does an incredible job of erasing the visual evidence of that population.

The trail, whose distance is marked every 0.5 mile, continues to climb along the eastern slopes of Antelope Island's spine. On either side of the path, grassy slopes are only seldomly interrupted by smatterings of small boulders—but never by any trees.

Just less than 1.0 mile into the hike, the trail reaches a junction. Here the Frary Peak Trail continues to the south, and a separate spur trail heads to the north. This northern route, the Dooly Knob Trail, reaches that peak—elevation 5,278 feet—after about 0.6 mile of climbing. If you wish, you may add this detour to your Frary Peak hike; or you may choose to simply ignore the side route and stick to your primary mission.

Just after passing the Dooly Knob Trail, the Frary Peak Trail reaches the crest of the ridge-line and passes onto the western slopes of the mountains. Though the trail maintains its southerly trajectory, it now features views of the western Great Salt Lake, White Rock Bay (Chapter 14 in this book), and the Stansbury Mountains in the far distance.

After a total of 1.25 miles, the path passes through a field of oversized boulders, squeezing quite closely between some of them. These boulders create literally the only shade you will find until just before reaching the summit of Frary Peak; if you'd like to pause for a snack, this is the place to do it.

After passing through these boulders, the trail switches back to the east and climbs rather steeply for a fraction of a mile before again reaching the crest of the broad and flat ridge, along which it ascends as it turns back to the south. To either side of the trail, the round hillsides fall steeply away, exposing views of White Rock and Stansbury Bays to the west, and Farmington Bay and the Wasatch Mountains to the east. The path climbs higher and higher, cutting through

View from summit of Frary Peak

CHRISTINE BALAZ

View west onto Stansbury Bay from Frary Peak Trail CHRISTINE BALAZ

grassy slopes and exposing ever-higher views of the surrounding landscape.

About 2.3 miles into the route, the trail reaches a false summit. Just 0.6 mile later, it reaches a radio tower. Though on a summit of its own, this radio tower is separated from the route's true summit, Frary Peak, by 0.5 mile and a dip in the trail.

Immediately after passing the radio tower, the trail turns downhill and grows noticeably more rugged. Once broad and even, it becomes loose and fairly rocky. The dryness of the soil makes it quite slippery in spots, requiring focused navigation. During the first few hundred yards, you'll lose about 60 precious vertical feet of elevation before beginning to climb again.

The final 0.1 mile ascent is among the steepest of the entire route. Here the trail degrades and splits into numerous paths that pick their way among the rocks flanking the mountaintop. Rebar and wooden steps reinforce the footing here and there—though more instances of these steps would be handy. It is here you'll encounter the only tree of the route, the occasional Utah juniper. Swarms of grasshoppers take residence in these trees during the summer time. Though they don't bite, they'll certainly startle you as they burst out of the trees en masse.

The actual summit itself is marked with a U.S. Coast and Geodetic Survey marker. Flat rock ledges make for a comfortable place to rest and take in the 360-degree views. If it's too hot, you can retrace your steps and eat lunch in the shade of a tree before returning to your car.

FEES, RESTRICTIONS, AND PERMITS

Dogs and mountain bikes prohibited; this trail closes at night, be sure to check with rangers to learn the exact time of closure; $9 day-use fee required to enter the state park; national parks passes not accepted

16

Little Mountain Summit to Mountain Dell Overlook

Type: Mountain; dirt; out-and-back; side trips and extensions possible

Season: Any; snowy in winter

Total Distance: 4.2 miles round-trip

Time: 1.5–2 hours

Rating: Easy/Moderate

Elevation Gain: 900 feet

Location: Top of Emigration Canyon, east of Salt Lake City

Maps: USGS MOUNTAIN DELL US TOPO

Contact: Wasatch-Cache National Forest: Salt Lake Ranger District, 3285 East 3300 South, Salt Lake City, UT 84109; 801-466-6411; www.fs.usda .gov/uwcnf

Trailhead GPS Coordinates: Little Mountain Summit: N40 46.494 W111 43.119

Comments: A beautiful hike very near Salt Lake City, this is a surprisingly underused trail.

OVERVIEW

This route takes a northeastern path from the top of Emigration Canyon along the ridgeline separating this drainage from Mountain Dell Canyon. Along the way, this bald ridge offers surprisingly beautiful views of the surrounding Wasatch Mountains.

THE TRAIL

This chapter's hike begins where Emigration Canyon Road reaches the ridge at the top of the canyon. From a large parking lot at this summit, the route crosses the road and heads steeply uphill and to the northeast. Though this initial section of the route shocks the system with its severe pitch, the trail soon levels off and assumes a gentle, rolling constitution for the most of the remainder of this route.

Immediately after cresting this initial hill, the trail offers a significantly better set of views than were available at the trailhead. To the east, Mountain Dell Reservoir stretches roughly 1 mile in length; farther afield, the taller peaks lining Parley's Canyon (through which I-80 runs) can be seen. One of the tallest of these, Mount Aire (Chapter 18 of this book), dominates the skyline to the southeast with its summit elevation of 8,621 feet.

Continuing along, the path remains relatively flat for nearly 0.4 mile. During this stretch, the trail continues following the crest of a flat and grassy ridge, allowing for uninterrupted sightseeing. Roughly 0.6 mile from the trailhead, the pitch increases noticeably

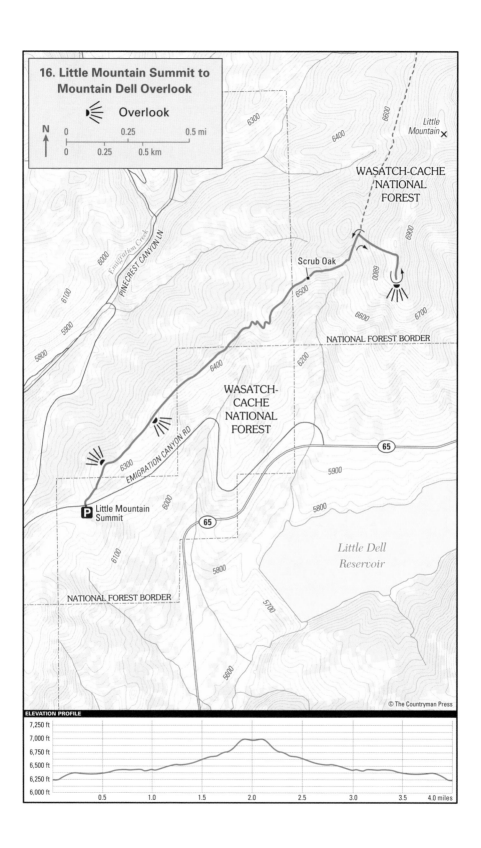

16. Little Mountain Summit to Mountain Dell Overlook

Overlook

N

| 0 | | 0.25 | | 0.5 mi |
| 0 | 0.25 | | 0.5 km | |

Little Mountain ✕

WASATCH-CACHE NATIONAL FOREST

Emigration Creek

PINECREST CANYON LN

Scrub Oak

NATIONAL FOREST BORDER

WASATCH-CACHE NATIONAL FOREST

EMIGRATION CANYON RD

65

65

Little Mountain Summit

Little Dell Reservoir

NATIONAL FOREST BORDER

© The Countryman Press

ELEVATION PROFILE

| 7,250 ft |
| 7,000 ft |
| 6,750 ft |
| 6,500 ft |
| 6,250 ft |
| 6,000 ft |

0.5   1.0   1.5   2.0   2.5   3.0   3.5   4.0 miles

View back to the west and toward Salt Lake Valley

for 0.1 mile, bringing you up to another flat section of ridge. At 0.3 mile later, the path heads through a clump of bushes and loses elevation for a very short distance.

At 1.0 mile from the trailhead, the trail begins climbing once again and, 0.1 mile later, it deviates from its straight, northeast trajectory for the first time since leaving the road. During next 0.2 mile, the trail heads through its first and only series of switchbacks.

After passing through this zigzag section, the path again levels off momentarily before resuming its ascent through the only serious vegetation of the route—a large stand of scrub oak. You remain in this thicket for but 0.2 mile before reemerging onto a bald ridge once again.

The trail heads east along this ridge for another 0.2 mile before curving to the left and pitching uphill quite noticeably. Over the next 0.1 mile, the trail assumes a grade of 20 percent, allowing it to reach a shrub-covered shoulder between two hilly peaks.

From this shoulder, our chapter's route turns right and heads steeply uphill and to the southeast. Aiming for the obvious peak above, the trail climbs at a grade of 25 percent for just 0.2 mile in order to reach the high point of this unnamed mountain. From this summit, the trail bends to the south and descends slightly as it follows the high ridgeline of this mountain for 0.1 mile to its end.

From the trail's terminus, hikers enjoy 360-degree views. Looking to the east across Mountain Dell and Parley's Canyons, hikers see the peaks and ridgelines separating Mill Creek, Big Cottonwood, and Little Cottonwood Canyons. To the southwest, Emigration Canyon leads down toward the Salt Lake Valley. In all directions, the countless peaks of the Wasatch Mountains scrape the sky.

To return to the parking area, you must turn around and follow the same route by which you came—unless you're prepared to embark on a significant extension. Those wishing to extend their trip may return to the shoulder junction (0.3 mile before the trail's terminus), and continue heading northeast and toward Birch Spring Pass. In this direction, the trail network is vast; hikers wishing to continue should carry a map.

FEES, RESTRICTIONS, AND PERMITS

The area east of Little Mountain summit, Mountain Dell Canyon, is a Salt Lake City watershed—no dogs are allowed; this trail tours the ridgeline above this watershed, though dog restrictions on this particular trail are not clear, it is best to leave pets at home; bikes OK

Heading eastward from Little Mountain Summit   CHRISTINE BALAZ

17

Rattlesnake Gulch to Pipeline Trail

Type: Mountain; dirt; out-and-back; side trips possible

Season: All; can be snowy and icy in winter

Total Distance: 3.2 miles round-trip

Time: 1–2 hours

Rating: Easy/Moderate

Elevation Gain: 850 feet

Location: Mill Creek Canyon, east of Salt Lake City

Maps: USGS SUGAR HOUSE US TOPO

Contact: Wasatch-Cache National Forest: Salt Lake Ranger District, 3285 East 3300 South, Salt Lake City, UT 84109; 801-466-6411; www.fs.usda .gov/uwcnf

Trailhead GPS Coordinates: Rattlesnake Gulch Trailhead: N40 41.498 W111 46.149

Comments: Though dogs are allowed in Mill Creek Canyon, dog owners are still responsible for cleaning up dog waste.

OVERVIEW

This short and accessible hike offers excellent views across Mill Creek Canyon and down into the Salt Lake Valley, rendering it quite popular among locals. Climbing steeply at first through Rattlesnake Gulch, the route then joins the Pipeline Trail. This nearly flat path traverses westwardly along the wall of Mill Creek Canyon to an overlook of Salt Lake City.

THE TRAIL

The Rattlesnake Gulch to Pipeline route begins low in Mill Creek Canyon at the canyon's first major pullout. From this parking area on the northern side of the road, the trail heads uphill and past a large signboard. Here you can look at an overview map; dog owners should grab some of the provided plastic bags to clean up solid waste. (Don't worry; the Forest Service also provides a trash can for disposal at the trailhead.)

From the trailhead to the turnaround point, the path remains broad and extremely well-worn. As it climbs uphill, the trail sticks to the bottom of Rattlesnake Gulch, passing in and out of scrub oak stands along the way. Particularly in the warm, sunny patches of trail, you should look out for the gulch's namesake residents—rattlesnakes. Though not overwhelmingly common, these snakes indeed live in Mill Creek Canyon, and typically hang out on its warmer, south-facing slopes. (The author can attest firsthand to their presence.)

At 0.3 mile from the trailhead, the path bends gradually to the northeast just before

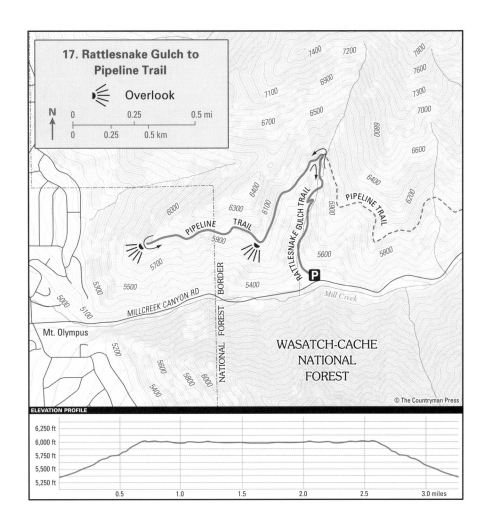

17. Rattlesnake Gulch to Pipeline Trail

Overlook

N

| 0 | 0.25 | 0.5 mi |
| 0 | 0.25 | 0.5 km |

PIPELINE TRAIL

RATTLESNAKE GULCH TRAIL

PIPELINE TRAIL

MILLCREEK CANYON RD

NATIONAL FOREST BORDER

Mt. Olympus

WASATCH-CACHE
NATIONAL
FOREST

Mill Creek

© The Countryman Press

ELEVATION PROFILE

passing an old pipe section and a collection of large boulders. This segment of large-diameter pipe is a throwback to the former water pipeline that used to run the length of today's Pipeline Trail.

At 0.4 mile from the trailhead, you pass a limestone slab and head through a pair of switchbacks that ascend the western side of the gulch. The trail then straightens out, heads back toward the center of the gully, and then crosses to its other side. The route meanders like this for a total of 0.2 mile be-

fore again entering the center of the gulch and heading directly up its bottom.

At 0.7 mile after leaving the parking lot, the Rattlesnake Gulch Trail ends at the Pipeline Trail. Turning left here, this chapter's route joins the Pipeline Trail and immediately transitions from steep to flat. Broad and extremely well-worn, this pedestrian highway cuts a horizontal line along the canyon wall, much like a topographical line on a map. You can now stretch your legs and pick up speed for the remaining portion of the trek.

Low in Rattlesnake Gulch

During the first 0.4 mile on the Pipeline Trail, the trail heads to the southwest and out of the notch created by Rattlesnake Gulch. Slicing across a very steep hillside, this portion of the Pipeline Trail offers excellent and exposed views across Mill Creek Canyon.

At 1.1 miles from the parking lot, the trail bends to the right and heads due west. At this crook, the trail offers its first views of the Salt Lake Valley. As it continues in this direction, the trail travels in and out of tree patches. Following the canyon wall, the path weaves in and out of notches in the hillside. Large, open patches of grass improve the already open vistas.

As it heads farther west, the trail begins offering views into the mouth of Neffs Canyon. Mount Olympus, which forms the southern wall of this canyon's entrance, is easily recognizable by its wall of sheer quartzite slabs. Stretching roughly 900 feet from top to bottom, this low-angle, orange cliff holds numerous easy rock climbs.

After its initial bend to the west, the trail weaves in and out of three small notches on the mountainside before reaching its terminus 1.6 miles from the trailhead. The route's end is easily recognizable by the presence of yet another section of abandoned pipe, as well as the suddenly excellent views of the Salt Lake Valley.

From here, hikers may turn around and retrace their steps to the car. Those wishing to embark on a more serious journey may continue heading east on the Pipeline Trail (past the junction with Rattlesnake Gulch). Doing so leads to numerous other trails and opportunities to summit Grandeur Peak or Mount Aire. However, these trips add significantly more trail miles, elevation gain, and therefore hours and energy required.

Heading west on Pipeline Trail

CHRISTINE BALAZ

$3 day-use fee required of all vehicles in Mill Creek Canyon; in order to share Mill Creek Canyon fairly among mountain bikers and dog owners, dogs must be leashed on all trails on even-numbered days but dogs may be off-leash on odd-numbered days

Pipeline Trail

The Pipeline Trail is an extremely popular pathway that runs the length of lower Mill Creek Canyon—a distance of roughly 5.5 miles. Located high on the south side of the canyon, this nearly flat pathway was originally created to hold a flume that transported water from Elbow Fork (along which the Mount Aire Trail, Chapter 18, ascends) to the Upper Mill Creek power station. When this channel was abandoned, the track it occupied was converted to a recreation trail. Today, this trail is a veritable pipeline of people—connecting Rattlesnake Gulch to Church Fork, Grandeur Peak, Burch Hollow, and Elbow Fork. As such, many people use this pathway to create larger biking and hiking loops within the canyon.

18

Mount Aire

Type: Mountain; dirt; out-and-back

Season: Spring–Fall; possible in winter without excessive snow

Total Distance: 3.4 miles round-trip

Time: 1.5–3 hours

Rating: Strenuous

Elevation Gain: 2,000 feet

Location: Mill Creek Canyon, east of Salt Lake City

Maps: USGS MT AIRE US TOPO

Contact: Uinta-Wasatch-Cache National Forest: Pleasant Grove Ranger District, 390 North 100 East, Pleasant Grove, UT 84062; 801-785-3563; www.fs .usda.gov/uwcnf

Trailhead GPS Coordinates: Mount Aire Trailhead: N40 42.395 W111 41.392

Comments: A short but very steep hike, this packs a lot of views and effort into its distance.

OVERVIEW

Though it stretches just 1.7 miles from bottom to top, the Mount Aire Trail contains an extremely generous amount of elevation gain. As such, it passes through a variety of ecosystems and terrain, and offers lofty views of American Fork Canyon, Parley's Canyon, the Great Salt Lake and Salt Lake Valley, and the Wasatch Mountains.

THE TRAIL

The hike to Mount Aire's summit begins at the floor of American Fork Canyon, where Mill Creek Canyon Road makes a distinct hairpin turn to the south. A kiosk and pit toilet mark the beginning of this trail; here the Forest Service has posted an overview map which depicts the trail network, mountain peaks, campgrounds, picnic areas, and various land demarcations of American Fork Canyon. Though on this route you'll be entirely in Wasatch National Forest, you can see on this map that the canyon is also comprised of Mount Olympus Wilderness and designated watershed areas.

From here, the trail heads north and immediately into the relatively lush forests of the canyon bottom. With a starting elevation of 6,751 feet, the base of this route is significantly cooler and moister than the Salt Lake Valley, merely 5 miles to the west. Even in the peak of summer, the drainage up which the Mount Aire Trail travels remains lush and full of low-lying plants. Moistened by a small stream, wildflowers, grasses, and bushes grow thick here among the deciduous and

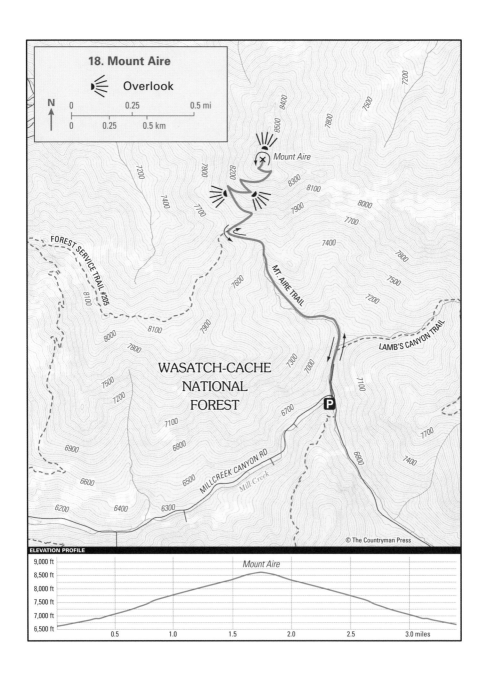

18. Mount Aire

Overlook

N

0   0.25   0.5 mi
0   0.25   0.5 km

Mount Aire

FOREST SERVICE TRAIL #205

MT. AIRE TRAIL

LAMB'S CANYON TRAIL

WASATCH-CACHE
NATIONAL
FOREST

MILLCREEK CANYON RD

Mill Creek

P

© The Countryman Press

ELEVATION PROFILE

Mount Aire

9,000 ft
8,500 ft
8,000 ft
7,500 ft
7,000 ft
6,500 ft

0.5   1.0   1.5   2.0   2.5   3.0 miles

evergreen trees. The trail remains quite near to this water source for the first half of the route.

After just 0.2 miles, the trail splits in two; a separate route, Lamb's Canyon Trail, heads up and over a ridge to the east. This hike's path, the Mount Aire Trail, continues uphill and to the north. Marked by permanent signs, this junction is easy to navigate.

If hiking in summer, you'll pass through gardens of wildflowers including Indian paintbrush, white crane's bill, and firecracker penstemon. Overhead, tall aspen and coniferous trees loom and create just enough spotty shade to make for pleasant temperatures. As the trail climbs higher and higher, the views of the mountain peaks to the south grow better and better. Don't forget to turn around occasionally and witness the Wasatch Mountains as they come into view.

Nearly 1.0 mile into the hike, the trail passes a low-angle limestone slab on the left, and then reaches a ridgeline shoulder. From this saddle, the ridge rises to the east and west, and the mountains fall away to the north and south, exposing glimpses of Mill Creek Canyon and yet unseen views down into Parley's Canyon in the north. At this point, the trail splits. If you were to head west along the unmarked (and unmaintained) Forest Service Trail #205, you would eventually come to Grandeur Peak. However, our route to Mount Aire requires you to take a right here and head eastward and upward to the obvious mountain peak.

After this junction, the trail continues its climb via switchbacks. Though the trail zigzags up its final ascent, its grade actually remains nearly as steep (but not quite as severe) as that of its initial 1.0 mile. Just 0.25

View south onto peaks of Big and Little Cottonwood canyons from Mount Aire CHRISTINE BALAZ

Mount Aire

View looking down Mount Aire Trail in its lush lower section

CHRISTINE BALAZ

mile and two switchbacks above the shoulder, you'll gain your first views of Salt Lake City to the west. Another 0.1 mile along, keep your eyes open to see the great views of the Oquirrh Mountains to the west of Salt Lake City.

About 0.15 mile from the summit at the end of a switchback, you'll be surprised with a totally unexpected view of I-80 in Parley's Canyon, below and to the northeast. After an entire hike full of gorgeous mountain scenery, this bustling interstate highway seems a bit out of place. However, you can ignore it and keep walking the final few minutes to the summit.

The trail makes a turn to the north just before reaching the high point of this route. After passing through a spiny section of trail riddled with orange sandstone blocks, you'll reach a cairn that marks the summit of Mount Aire. From this nearly naked peak, you'll have 360-degree views of the surrounding Wasatch Mountains. To the west, you'll see the Great Salt Lake, Antelope Island, the Oquirrh Mountains and even the Stansbury Mountains in the far distance. To the east, you'll see I-80 climbing toward Park City. And to the south, you'll see many tall peaks of the Wasatch Mountains near Little and Big Cottonwood Canyons.

The hike back to the car follows along the exact same route, but is quite a lot more scenic than the approach hike. Keep your eyes peeled and your camera out.

FEES, RESTRICTIONS, AND PERMITS
$3 fee required for vehicles in Mill Creek Canyon; national parks passes honored; dogs OK off-leash on odd-numbered days but dogs must be leashed on even-numbered days

Moose Alert

Bear in mind: Plants aren't the only life form that appreciates these wet environs. Moose, in particular, also flock to this area. Though docile and rather clumsy in appearance, moose are actually among the most aggressive, temperamental, and unpredictable large animals in North America. Keep your eyes open and ears tuned for these animals; if you see one in the middle of the trail, you'd best retreat and choose another hike for the day (Chapters 17 or 19 of this book). With a weight range of roughly 450–1,500 pounds (the males being heavier), this species is large and full of trampling power.

19

Dog Lake from Upper Big Water

Type: Mountain; dirt; out-and-back; side trips and alternative routes possible

Season: Spring–Fall; possible in winter without excessive snow

Total Distance: 5.2 miles round-trip

Time: 2–4 hours

Rating: Easy/Moderate

Elevation Gain: 1,400 feet

Location: Mill Creek Canyon, east of Salt Lake City

Maps: USGS MT AIRE US TOPO

Contact: Uinta-Wasatch-Cache National Forest: Pleasant Grove Ranger District, 390 North 100 East, Pleasant Grove, UT 84062; 801-785-3563; www.fs .usda.gov/uwcnf

Trailhead GPS Coordinates: Upper Big Water Parking Lot: N40 40.634 W111 38.746

Comments: A very pleasant route characterized by switchbacks and buffed surfaces, this trail is also popular among mountain bikers.

OVERVIEW

This route extends from the very top of Mill Creek Canyon Road to Dog Lake–which stands on the ridge between Mill Creek and Big Cottonwood Canyon. From the Mill Creek side, the approach to this tiny lake is by way of well-maintained singletrack trails that climb at pleasant grades, zigzagging through aspen and evergreen forests.

THE TRAIL

This hike begins at the very top of Mill Creek Canyon Road. From the top of the canyon, numerous interconnected trails lead to Dog Lake. Our trail itself departs from the south side of a large parking lot there. As soon as you leave the parking lot, you step into a lush forest–lush, that is, for Utah anyway. Located on a north-facing slope, these high-elevation hillsides are full of grass, flowers, shrubs, and trees.

At 0.3 mile into the hike, the trail reaches its first junction. Here our path merges with the Big Water Trail, and both run together toward Dog Lake. At this point in the journey, the forest is thick enough to provide some shade, but not so thick as to completely obstruct views of the surrounding Wasatch peaks.

About 0.9 mile later the trail forks; from here, the Big Water Trail heads to the right and takes a slightly longer route to the next junction. Our route, the Upper Big Water Trail, heads to the left and takes the most direct route uphill. At 0.1 mile after this junction, the Great Western Trail splits off to the left; stay off of this route unless you want to take a long detour; the Great Western Trail does not

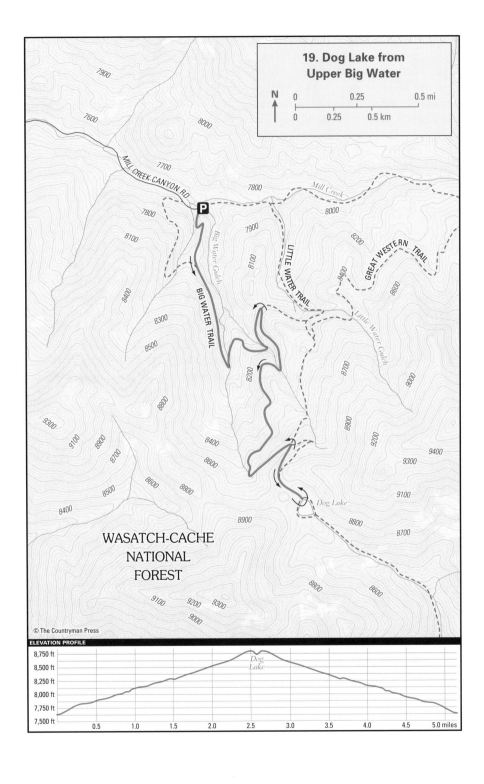

19. Dog Lake from Upper Big Water

N
0   0.25   0.5 mi
0   0.25   0.5 km

MILL CREEK CANYON RD.

Mill Creek

Big Water Gulch

LITTLE WATER TRAIL

GREAT WESTERN TRAIL

Little Water Gulch

BIG WATER TRAIL

Dog Lake

WASATCH-CACHE
NATIONAL
FOREST

© The Countryman Press

ELEVATION PROFILE

Dog
Lake

take you to Dog Lake. In fact, if you took this trail, you could theoretically hike to Canada.

The middle section of this hike is characterized by pleasant switchbacks through groves of coniferous trees and occasional, large patches of tall, moderately spaced aspen. Through these trees, views to the north and across Mill Creek Canyon are occasionally possible. Keep your eyes tuned to the northwest and try to catch a glimpse of the tall, pyramidal Mount Aire (Chapter 18 in this book).

After 2.3 miles of hiking, the Upper Big Water Trail encounters yet another junction. From here, you're just 0.2–0.3 mile to Dog Lake itself, depending on the route you take. Just before reaching the lake, the trail levels off and dips down. The tiny, round body of water that is Dog Lake appears suddenly through a thin grove of tall aspen trees. Our route ends at the lake. To return to your car, retrace your steps and follow signs for the Upper Big Water parking area. You can tailor your return hike's distance by electing to take the longer or shorter trail options at each junction.

FEES, RESTRICTIONS, AND PERMITS
$3 fee required for vehicles in Mill Creek Canyon; national parks passes honored; dogs OK off-leash on odd-numbered days but dogs must be leashed on even-numbered days

Big Water, Upper Big Water, and Little Water Trail Network

The three main trails in the area—Big Water Trail, Upper Big Water, and Little Water Trail—all lie roughly parallel to each other, and all lead to the same destination: Dog Lake. These trails form an interconnected network, occasionally merging and running together. Our route, the Big Water Trail, is one of two departing from this uppermost parking area.

Though the trail system at the top of Mill Creek Canyon can seem complicated and convoluted, it really isn't so difficult to navi-

gate. Route-finding is easy, and all trail junctions are clearly labeled with their destinations; if your goal is Dog Lake, simply follow signs for Dog Lake at each junction. You'll even have the option of selecting longer or shorter routes to Dog Lake. If this all sounds confusing, take a look at the overview map located at the trailhead; or better yet, take a digital photograph of this map, and carry it with you on your hike.

Great Western Trail

The Great Western Trail, like the famous Appalachian and Pacific Crest Trails, stretches from the southern end of the United States to its northern border—and this chapter's hike shares 1.0 mile with this vast trail. However, unlike the very well developed Appalachian Trail, the Great Western Trail is a complicated, somewhat rudimentary system of interwoven trails. Nevertheless, many hikers tackle large sections of this trail—and a few brave souls even manage to complete the route in its entirety every year. From the Upper Big Water parking lot, the Great Western Trail heads east and reaches Guardsman Pass Road in Park City after 12.8 miles—and eventually Canada after more than 2,000 miles.

Hike to Big Cottonwood Canyon

Though our route ends at Dog Lake, the trail continues southward and downhill into Big Cottonwood Canyon. Though you'd hike only another 2.5 miles from Dog Lake down to the Mill D Trailhead of Big Cottonwood Canyon, you'd end up more than 23.6 road miles away from the Upper Big Water parking lot in Mill Creek Canyon. This is because though the trail must only hike up and over a narrow ridgeline to span the two parking areas, the paved route between the two stretches down Big Cottonwood Canyon, across the Wasatch foothills, and back up the entirety of Mill Creek Canyon.

Dog Lake peeking out from behind the aspens

20

Willow Heights to Willow Lake

Type: Mountain; dirt; out-and-back

Season: Spring–Fall; possible in winter without excessive snow

Total Distance: 2.0 miles round-trip

Time: 1–2 hours

Rating: Moderate

Elevation Gain: 750 feet

Location: Big Cottonwood Canyon, east of Salt Lake City

Maps: USGS PARK CITY WEST US TOPO

Contact: Wasatch-Cache National Forest: Salt Lake Ranger District, 3285 East 3300 South, Salt Lake City, UT 84109; 801-466-6411; www.fs.usda .gov/uwcnf

Trailhead GPS Coordinates: Willow Heights Trailhead: N40 37.816 W111 36.287

Comments: Be aware of the plentiful moose in the area; though docile in appearance, these animals can be extremely unpredictable and dangerous.

OVERVIEW

The hike from Willow Heights Trailhead to Willow Lake is a short yet steep journey through a vast forest of tall aspen trees. Once at the lake, hikers enjoy excellent views across Big Cottonwood Canyon to the peaks of Solitude Mountain Resort, to the south. Framed by the aspen forests and lake, this vista of high Wasatch peaks is easily worth the effort.

THE TRAIL

The trail to Willow Lake departs from the north side of Big Cottonwood Canyon Road (UT 190); from the pullout on the roadside, an engraved boulder renders the trail relatively easy to spot. After leaving the Willow Heights Trailhead, you have less than 0.1 mile of moderately graded warm-up before the trail turns uphill and assumes a grade of 20–30 percent for 0.5 mile. Though this hike's pitch is rather severe, the trail's beautiful environs do a good deal to distract hikers from their aching legs.

Leaving the road, you immediately enter into a magical forest of lofty aspen trees. In this very first section of the route, numerous shortcut trails form a network with the actual trail. Easy to identify, the main trail is the most well-worn of the bunch; stay on this one in order to minimize hiker impact on the area. Less than a minute into the hike, the trail passes by a sign with an overview map and area restrictions.

As the trail climbs, it offers scattered views of the surrounding mountainsides

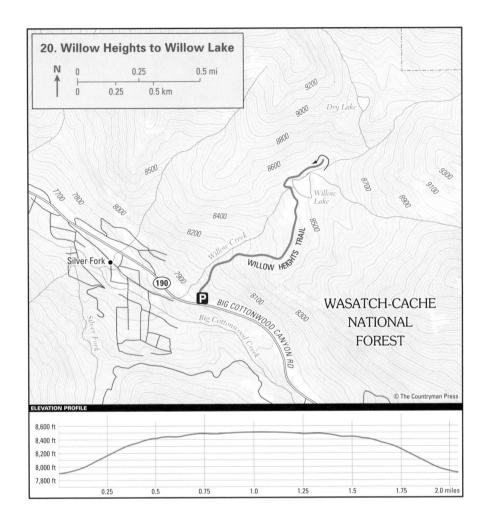

20. Willow Heights to Willow Lake

N
0   0.25   0.5 mi
0   0.25   0.5 km

9200
9000
Dry Lake
8800
8600
8500
8728
9300
9100
8900
8400
8200
Willow Creek
Willow Lake
WILLOW HEIGHTS TRAIL
8500
7700 7800
8000
7900
Silver Fork
190
P
BIG COTTONWOOD CANYON RD
8100
8300
Big Cottonwood Creek
Silver Fork
WASATCH-CACHE NATIONAL FOREST

© The Countryman Press

ELEVATION PROFILE

8,600 ft
8,400 ft
8,200 ft
8,000 ft
7,800 ft

0.25   0.5   0.75   1.0   1.25   1.5   1.75   2.0 miles

through thin spots in the aspen canopy. To the left, the ridgeline separating Mule Hollow from the Willow Creek Drainage dominates the skyline. To the right, hillsides lead up to a high ridgeline that forms the boundary between Salt Lake and Summit Counties.

Roughly 0.5 mile from the trailhead, you find yourself finally leaving the seemingly infinite aspen forest. Though the trees don't disappear altogether here, they do thin noticeably as the trail finally eases off in grade. Entering into a fairly flat and open field, the path here levels

off almost completely and cuts across a grassy expanse. In this field, you should look to the left and enjoy the long views down the length of Big Cottonwood Canyon.

After crossing this short field, the trail heads up one final—short and gradual—step before reaching the southern shore of Willow Lake. The higher the trail climbs, and the closer it nears the lake, the better the views it offers of Solitude Mountain Resort.

Once at the lake, the path forks. Here the trail becomes a 0.5-mile loop that wraps

View south and across Big Cottonwood Canyon from just beneath Willow Lake CHRISTINE BALAZ

around the shores of Willow Lake. In the interest of better views, this chapter's route heads left and toward the western, tree-free shore of this lake. Be aware that, in wet conditions, portions of this trail become impassable.

After taking a left at this junction, you should make note of yet another faint trail heading back down the mountainside (roughly parallel to and west of the Willow Creek Trail). This unnamed trail also heads back toward UT 190, but stops just short of the highway in a small neighborhood. Hikers wishing to remain on this chapter's route should avoid this trail and return to their car by way of the Willow Creek Trail—lest they must complete their journey with a stretch of some road- and highway-walking.

Walking around the open, western shore of the small, teardrop-shaped Willow Lake, hikers get excellent views of the lake itself and surrounding hillsides, as well as the route's best vistas of the high peaks of Solitude Mountain Resort—topping out at 10,500 feet. Before returning to your car, you can enjoy a picnic in the sun here, or move on to the lake's shady eastern shore if shade is preferable.

FEES, RESTRICTIONS, AND PERMITS
No fees; Big Cottonwood Canyon is a Salt Lake City watershed, so no dogs are allowed in the canyon; snow chains or four-wheel drive required of all vehicles during the winter months

The never-ending aspen forests along the trail to Willow Lake   CHRISTINE BALAZ

21

Silver Lake Loop

Type: Mountain and wetland; boardwalk and dirt; loop; extensions possible

Season: Spring–Fall; Solitude Nordic area closed to foot traffic during ski season

Total Distance: 0.9 miles round-trip

Time: 0.5–1 hour

Rating: Easy

Elevation Gain: 150 feet

Location: Silver Lake, Solitude Mountain Resort, Big Cottonwood Canyon, east of Salt Lake City

Maps: USGS BRIGHTON US TOPO

Contact: Wasatch-Cache National Forest: Salt Lake Ranger District, 3285 East 3300 South, Salt Lake City, UT 84109; 801-466-6411; www.fs.usda .gov/uwcnf: or Solitude Mountain Resort, 12000 Big Cottonwood Canyon Rd., Solitude, UT 84121; 801-534-1400; www.skisolitude.com

Trailhead GPS Coordinates: Solitude Mountain Resort Nordic Center: N40 35.212 W111 35.080

Comments: A short and extremely pleasant stroll on boardwalks and single-track trails, this nature trail is very popular among families; if you wish to avoid crowds, visit early or late in the day–or during the work week.

OVERVIEW

The Silver Lake Trail is a large system of boardwalks and dirt paths that form a loop through and around the wetlands, marshes, and forests surrounding Silver Lake. Because of its tranquil atmosphere, pleasant scenery, and general ease, this leisurely route is perfect for the very young and very old. Along the way, numerous signs point out and explain various components within the Silver Lake ecosystem. Those with extra time and energy can easily connect to other area trails, extending the route.

THE TRAIL

The Silver Lake Loop Trail departs from a sizeable parking lot adjacent to the Solitude Mountain Resort Nordic Center. The most popular trail in Big Cottonwood Canyon, this is fittingly well signed and maintained. Those wishing to learn more about the area before heading out on the trail may stop in at the Nordic Center for no charge. Inside, various exhibits explain Silver Lake's history and ecosystem.

Silver Lake lies west of the Nordic Center, and the Silver Lake Loop Trail originates on the northern side of the building. This chapter's route arbitrarily takes the loop in a clockwise direction, heading left from the Nordic Center.

The first section of trail cuts to the west and across a long section of wetland. In this initial segment, the trail consists of a broad boardwalk that meanders lazily around bushes growing above the rushes. Numer-

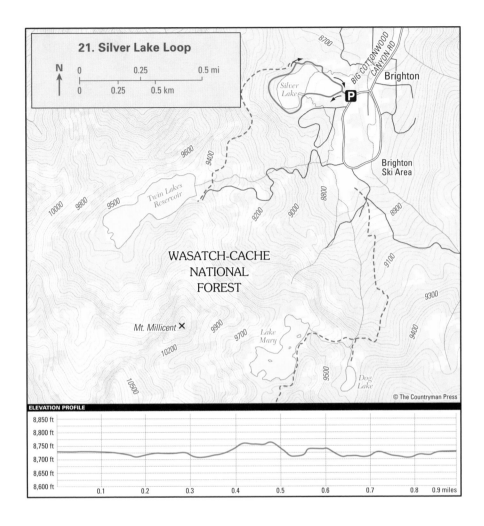

21. Silver Lake Loop

N

| 0 | 0.25 | 0.5 mi |
| 0 | 0.25 | 0.5 km |

8700

BIG COTTONWOOD CANYON RD

Brighton

Silver Lake

P

Brighton Ski Area

9600

9400

10000

9800

9500

Twin Lakes Reservoir

9200

9000

8800

8900

9100

WASATCH-CACHE NATIONAL FOREST

9300

Mt. Millicent ✕

9900

9700

Lake Mary

10200

9500

Dog Lake

9400

10500

© The Countryman Press

ELEVATION PROFILE

8,850 ft
8,800 ft
8,750 ft
8,700 ft
8,650 ft
8,600 ft

0.1   0.2   0.3   0.4   0.5   0.6   0.7   0.8   0.9 miles

ous interpretive signs stand adjacent to the path in this first section of trail; these discuss natural phenomena, from beavers' ability to alter wetland habitat to frog species that have gone missing from the area.

At 0.2 mile from the parking area, the trail finally approaches Silver Lake, coming very near to its extremely clear waters. Here it crosses over a stream and curves to the south. About 0.1 mile later, the boardwalk deposits you onto a plank-lined gravel path in a forest. Now on the western shore of this lake, the trail bends to the northwest as it weaves through tall conifer trees. Roughly 0.3 mile from the trailhead, the path comes quite near the shores of Silver Lake, offering ample views of Big Cottonwood Canyon's peaks to the east.

After about 0.2 mile in the forest, the trail climbs a bit and curves to the east. Here it passes through an open, grassy field and beneath an aspen grove. This relatively high point offers the route's best perspective on Silver Lake and its surroundings. During the

Boardwalk leading through wetlands surrounding Silver Lake

summer months, this field is dominated by the colorful blossoms of wildflowers such as fireweed, shooting star, columbine, bluebell, and Richardson's geranium. In fall, the aspen groves to the immediate west and the distant east of the lake display brilliant colors of fall foliage.

At 0.6 mile into the hike, the trail reaches a signed junction; to continue following this chapter's route, stay straight here. The path leading left and to the northwest from here splits again shortly after this junction, sending various branches toward Lake Solitude, Twin Lakes Reservoir, and Mount Evergreen (elevation 9,840 feet). Those wishing to venture into this rather complex trail network would be well-advised to do so with a detailed trail map in hand.

After passing the junction, the Silver Lake Loop Trail bends to the east and climbs for a few hundred yards before descending again. After this drop, the gravel path gives way to a boardwalk as the trail reenters the wetlands surrounding Silver Lake. The most scenic section of trail thus far, this portion of the hike offers the best views of Solitude's craggy peaks looming above Silver Lake. Clayton Peak, the tallest of these, tops out at 10,721 feet.

Hikers see the Solitude Mountain Resort Nordic Center well before they reach it. This center marks the end of this chapter's route. Those wishing to further their tour of Big Cottonwood Canyon may drive uphill to the

Trail above the shores of Silver Lake   CHRISTINE BALAZ

Brighton ski area and hike to Dog Lake and Lake Mary (Chapter 22 of this book).

FEES, RESTRICTIONS, AND PERMITS
No fees; Big Cottonwood Canyon is a Salt Lake City watershed, so no dogs are allowed in the canyon; snow chains or four-wheel drive required of all vehicles during the winter months; hiking within Solitude Mountain Resort boundaries only permitted outside of ski season

22

Brighton to Dog Lake and Lake Mary

Type: Mountain; dirt; out-and-back; extensions possible

Season: Spring–Fall; Brighton ski area closed to hiking during ski season

Total Distance: 2.4 miles round-trip

Time: 2–4 hours

Rating: Moderate/Strenuous

Elevation Gain: 800 feet

Location: Brighton ski area, Big Cottonwood Canyon, east of Salt Lake City

Maps: USGS BRIGHTON US TOPO

Contact: Wasatch-Cache National Forest: Salt Lake Ranger District, 3285 East 3300 South, Salt Lake City, UT 84109; 801-466-6411; www.fs.usda .gov/uwcnf: or Brighton Resort, 8302 South Brighton Way, Brighton, UT 84121; 801-532-4731; www.brighton resort.com

Trailhead GPS Coordinates: Brighton Resort Center: N40 35.896 W111 35.054

Comments: This hike is just a sampling of Brighton and Solitude's interconnected trail network; hikers interested in exploring the network more thoroughly should carry a map in hand.

OVERVIEW

This hike begins in the heart of Brighton resort, ascends its slopes, and visits two lakes. Along the way, it passes underneath chairlifts, past meadows and rock outcrops, and over streams. A popular hiking route, this trail is well-worn and well-signed. Its short distance and relatively mild amount of climbing, combined with its multiple trailside lakes, makes this route well-suited for families.

THE TRAIL

The hike from Brighton to Dog Lake and Lake Mary originates at the Brighton resort center, where a large and obvious sign marks the trailhead. From the gravel parking lot, it follows the Lake Mary/Catherine Pass Trail, originating immediately adjacent to and south of the base area lodge. Here, the Forest Service has posted restrictions pertaining to the area, as well as a trail map and other information.

From the trailhead, the route heads uphill and directly past the lodge. In its first few hundred feet, the path consists of a timberlined, gravel walkway. Shortly above the immediate resort base area, the gravel walkway turns into a proper dirt trail. Where the trail's surface changes, a small sign confirms your correct path.

Gaining elevation at a steady rate, the Lake Mary/Catherine Pass Trail heads roughly due south for 0.2 mile. There it zigzags briefly, and then resumes its southern trajectory. Along the way, its surroundings consist mostly of grassy fields strewn with

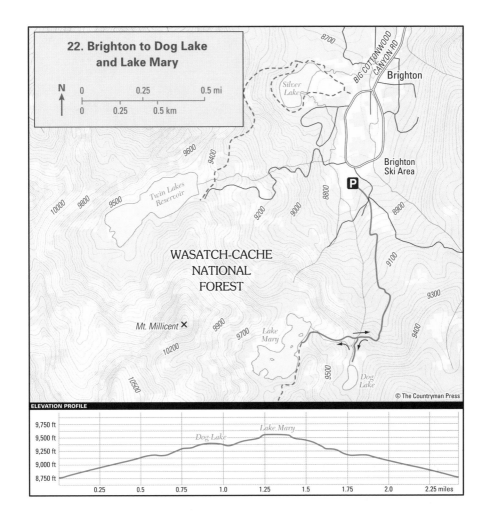

white quartz monzonite boulders and random tree patches. Because of the low-lying nature its surrounding vegetation here, the trail provides its travelers with ample views down onto Brighton and Big Cottonwood Canyon.

At 0.4 mile from the parking area, the trail comes to a service road. You should stay straight here to remain on this chapter's route. Shortly after this intersection, the trail bends slightly to the west and then to the south again—right before encountering the service road again. This chapter's route stays straight here, and continues heading south and uphill.

After passing the service road for its second time, the trail assumes a fairly mellow grade for 0.1 mile before arcing to the west and pitching steeply uphill for a similar distance. At 0.8 mile from the trailhead, the route forks at a well-signed junction. This chapter's route takes the left fork and heads to Dog Lake.

The detour to this small lake consists of just 0.1 mile of rather flat trail. Hikers quickly

Lake Mary

arrive at Dog Lake, a natural body of water that sits at the base of a cliffy and lightly forested cirque. To the south, Pioneer Peak is the tallest point along the visible ridgeline. With an elevation of 10,450 feet, this stands just more than 1,000 feet above Dog Lake.

From Dog Lake, this route heads back to the north 0.1 mile along the same trail to return to the junction from which it just came. Returning to this intersection, you have traveled just more than 1.0 mile. Rather than turning right and returning to the parking area, this chapter's route instead turns left and continues heading west toward Lake Mary.

Soon after passing this junction, the trail crosses a bridge, climbs a slope, and enters a steep and narrow gully. On either side of the trail, short and steep rocky hillsides rise. Here the trail passes through an aspen grove as it climbs over white quartz monzonite boulders. Following the plumbline of the gully, the trail gains elevation rather abruptly.

Lake Mary becomes obvious to hikers well before they reach it. More aptly called Mary Reservoir, this body of water is pent up by a dam, under which the trail passes. However unnatural the dam, the lake itself is actually quite scenic to behold by those standing on its shores. Walled with evergreen forests on its southeastern side and with white cliffs, talus, and boulders on its northwestern side, this lake could readily pass for a natural high-Wasatch body of water.

From Lake Mary, this chapter's route retraces its steps back to the parking area—omitting the Dog Lake detour. From the lake, the return hike stretches just 1.1 miles. Hikers wishing to further explore this corner of the Wasatch Mountains can do so by continuing along the trail as it passes by Lake Mary and toward Catherine Pass. In fact, hikers continuing beyond Catherine Pass leave Big Cottonwood Canyon and descend into the top of Little Cottonwood Canyon through Albion Basin (Chapter 25 of this book), finding themselves at Alta Ski Area after roughly 3.5 miles.

Hikers wishing to remain in Big Cottonwood Canyon while extending their trip can return to the trail junction near Dog Lake, and follow signs toward Silver Lake. Hikers following this route will encounter a number of trail junctions and associate loops within the Brighton/Solitude area. Anyone wishing to embark on such a mission would be well-suited to carry a detailed trail map in hand.

FEES, RESTRICTIONS, AND PERMITS
No fees; Big Cottonwood Canyon is a Salt Lake City watershed, so no dogs are allowed in the canyon; snow chains or four-wheel drive required of all vehicles during the winter months; hiking within Brighton Resort boundaries only permitted outside of ski season

Brighton's lifts: empty and still during summer   CHRISTINE BALAZ

23

Red Pine Lake

Type: Mountain; dirt; out-and-back; side trips possible

Season: Spring–Fall; may be hot in summer

Total Distance: 6.6 miles round-trip

Time: 3–4 hours

Rating: Moderate/Strenuous

Elevation Gain: 1,900 feet

Location: Little Cottonwood Canyon, east of Salt Lake City

Maps: USGS DROMEDARY PEAK US TOPO

Contact: Wasatch-Cache National Forest: Salt Lake Ranger District, 3285 East 3300 South, Salt Lake City, UT 84109; 801-466-6411; www.fs.usda .gov/uwcnf

Trailhead GPS Coordinates: White Pine Trailhead: N40 34.538 W111 40.888

Comments: Though this trail begins in national forest, roughly half of it lies within the Lone Peak Wilderness.

OVERVIEW

The Red Pine Lake Trail leads from the White Pine Trailhead up the southern wall of Little Cottonwood Canyon to Red Pine Lake via the Red Pine Fork drainage. The trail shares its first, fairly flat mile with the White Pine Lake Trail, then branches off and grows much steeper in its second half. This trail offers fantastic views up and down the length of the U-shaped Little Cottonwood Canyon, as well as of the picturesque Red Pine Lake and it surrounding high-mountain cirque.

THE TRAIL

Little Cottonwood Canyon—home of the famous Snowbird and Alta resorts—is one of the most striking canyons in the entire Wasatch Mountains. A deep and steep gouge in the Salt Lake City–area Wasatch, this canyon is walled with white quartz monzonite cliffs. Closely resembling granite, these cliffs were scoured into their distinctive U shape by glaciers.

The hike to Red Pine Lake begins at White Pine Trailhead, a large parking area on the south side of Little Cottonwood Canyon Road. From the parking area, the trail heads south and downhill to a bridge. You pass over Little Cottonwood Creek here, then begin ascending the canyon wall gradually in a southward direction. The path, broad and flat here, is surrounded by a dense forest of tall aspen trees.

After leaving this stand of aspen 0.3 mile from the trailhead, the path enters into a mixed forest of deciduous and evergreen

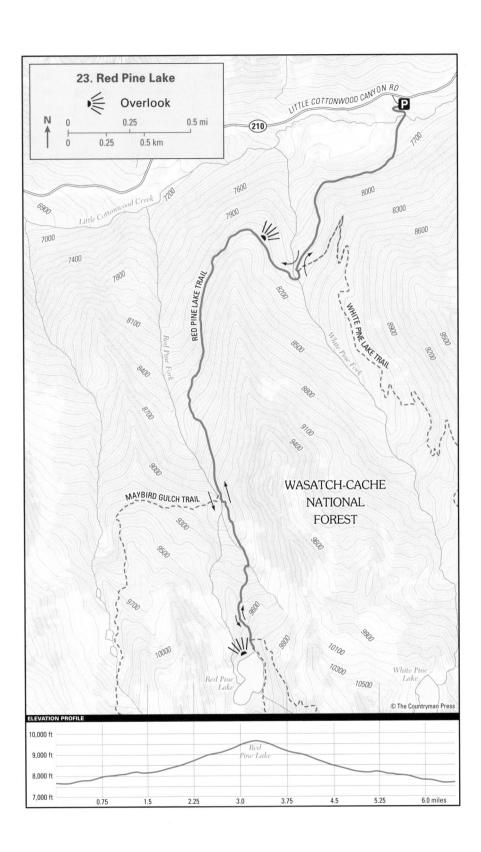

23. Red Pine Lake

Overlook

N

| 0 | 0.25 | 0.5 mi |
| 0 | 0.25 | 0.5 km |

LITTLE COTTONWOOD CANYON RD

210

7700

8000

8300

8600

6900

Little Cottonwood Creek

7200

7600

7900

7000

7400

7800

8100

8400

8700

RED PINE LAKE TRAIL

Red Pine Fork

8200

8500

8800

9100

9400

WHITE PINE LAKE TRAIL

White Pine Fork

8900

9200

9500

WASATCH-CACHE
NATIONAL
FOREST

9000

MAYBIRD GULCH TRAIL

9300

9500

9700

10000

9600

9600

9800

9900

10100

10300

10500

Red Pine
Lake

White Pine
Lake

© The Countryman Press

ELEVATION PROFILE

10,000 ft							
9,000 ft					Red		
8,000 ft					Pine Lake		
7,000 ft							
	0.75	1.5	2.25	3.0	3.75	4.5	5.25	6.0 miles

trees and hooks to the west. Heading west, it becomes much steeper for a short section. At 0.7 mile from the trailhead, the trail flattens out and bends to the south as it heads through stands of midsized aspen. Hikers enjoy views down through the mouth of the canyon before entering a fold in the mountainside.

At 1.0 mile into the route, the trail comes to a signed fork. Here, the White Pine Lake and Red Pine Lake Trails divide. Though they indeed split here, both trails actually head to the left. The Red Pine Lake Trail (this chapter's route) is recognizable as the higher and the smaller of the two paths—the one that climbs above the junction sign; the White Pine Lake Trail is the lower and wider of the two. During summer months, this junction is simple to navigate; however, with any snow cover, finding the right trail can be tricky.

Just after this junction, the Red Pine Lake Trail arcs back to the right and crosses over the fern-lined White Pine Fork by way of a footbridge. After crossing the stream, you head back to the northwest and work back out of this drainage. Along the way, you enjoy good views eastward and into upper Little Cottonwood Canyon before entering the Lone Peak Wilderness, 0.3 mile past the junction. Roughly 0.2 mile into the wilderness, the trail enters a clearing in the forest and offers excellent down-canyon views.

Just after this clearing, the trail wraps around the hillside and back to the left, where it enters into another fold of the mountainside—this one carved by Red Pine Fork. Once you come into the crease of this drainage—roughly 1.6 miles from the trailhead—the path becomes markedly steeper as it heads south and directly uphill. The trail's incline, once 5 percent, increases to 18 percent for the next 1.5 miles.

Roughly 2.3 miles from the trailhead, the Red Pine Fork drainage narrows noticeably, and 0.3 mile later, the trail and creek come very near to each other. Shortly afterward, you encounter a junction. To remain on this chapter's route, stay straight; the right fork of this junction leads to Maybird Gulch after 1.1 miles.

Just beyond the junction, the trail passes beneath a large tailings pile from an old mine. Here, the nearby stream causes the trail to be wet in almost any season. After about 0.2 mile of stone-hopping, you pass beneath a huge talus field. Beyond this scree zone, the trail grows even steeper. Here it maintains an average grade of roughly 30 percent for 0.2 mile as it climbs through an evergreen forest. Rounding off noticeably, the trail offers a much mellower grade for the final 0.3 mile approach to Red Pine Lake, elevation 9,680 feet.

This chapter's route ends at the southern shore of Red Pine Lake, and returns to the White Pine Trailhead by the same path. However, hikers here have the option of continuing 0.5 mile and ascending another 400 vertical feet to Upper Red Pine Lake, elevation 10,040 feet. Extremely eager hikers could add the 2.2-mile, round-trip journey to Maybird Gulch; an eastward, backcountry bushwhack up and over the ridgeline to White Pine Lake; or the 8.2-mile, round-trip trek into White Pine Lake from the low trail junction.

FEES, RESTRICTIONS, AND PERMITS
No fees; Little Cottonwood Canyon is a Salt Lake City watershed, so no dogs are allowed in the canyon; roughly half of this trail lies within the Lone Peak Wilderness, so no wheeled vehicles (including bikes) are allowed; snow chains or four-wheel drive required of all vehicles during the winter months

View north and across Little Cottonwood Canyon from Red Pine Lake Trail   CHRISTINE BALAZ

View west and down Little Cottonwood Canyon from Red Pine Lake Trail   CHRISTINE BALAZ

The Wasatch

The Wasatch Mountains have a length of approximately 160 miles, and stretch from southern Idaho to beyond and south of Provo. Running north-south, they mark the end of the Great Basin to the west and the beginning of the Rocky Mountains to the east. An imposing range, these mountains rise more than 7,000 feet above the valley floors—making for an incredibly steep incline. Within this range lie uncounted canyons and peaks—and trails that explore them.

24

Snowbird to Hidden Peak

Type: Mountain; dirt; out-and-back; alternative routes possible; free tram ride from summit to base when in operation (call or check online for details)

Season: Late Spring–Midfall; Snowbird Ski & Summer Resort closed to hiking during ski season

Total Distance: 3.2 miles from base to top

Time: 2–4 hours

Rating: Strenuous

Elevation Gain: 2,900 feet

Location: Snowbird Ski & Summer Resort, Little Cottonwood Canyon, east of Salt Lake City

Maps: USGS DROMEDARY PEAK US TOPO

Contact: Wasatch-Cache National Forest: Salt Lake Ranger District, 3285 East 3300 South, Salt Lake City, UT 84109; 801-466-6411; www.fs.usda .gov/uwcnf: or Snowbird Ski & Summer Resort, UT 210, Snowbird, UT 84092; 801-933-2222; www.snowbird.com

Trailhead GPS Coordinates: Snowbird Ski & Summer Resort Center/Entry Two: N40 34.596 W111 39.227

Comments: There is no charge to ride the tram down the mountain; however, hikers wishing to ride it to the top must pay $16 (when in summer operation). The aerial tram cannot operate in the presence of excessive winds.

OVERVIEW

This in-bounds route provides the rare opportunity to hike to the top of a mountain and skip the knee-hurting descent. During the summer season, hikers may park at the base of Snowbird Ski & Summer Resort, hike to the summit of Hidden Peak, and ride the aerial tram back to the base area for free. Along the way, the route offers excellent views of Little Cottonwood Canyon, Mount Superior, and the Pfeifferhorn. From the summit of Hidden Peak, the various summits of Big Cottonwood Canyon, Park City, and American Fork Canyon are visible. Bring a warm jacket and hat in order to stay warm while savoring the sights at the usually windy summit of Hidden Peak.

THE TRAIL

Snowbird Ski & Summer Resort doesn't hibernate in the off-season. On the contrary, this world-class ski area morphs into a vibrant summer playground. In addition to a base area filled with amusement park–style attractions, the mountain itself offers a network of crisscrossing trails for hikers and mountain bikers alike.

This chapter's route follows hiking-only trails whenever possible to travel from the resort center to the Ridge Trail—which it takes to the summit of Hidden Peak. Bear in mind that the route-finding nearest the bottom of the mountain is the trickiest and most convoluted; the important thing is that you aim for and eventually connect with the Peruvian Gulch Trail, which lies east of, and roughly parallel to, the Peruvian Lift.

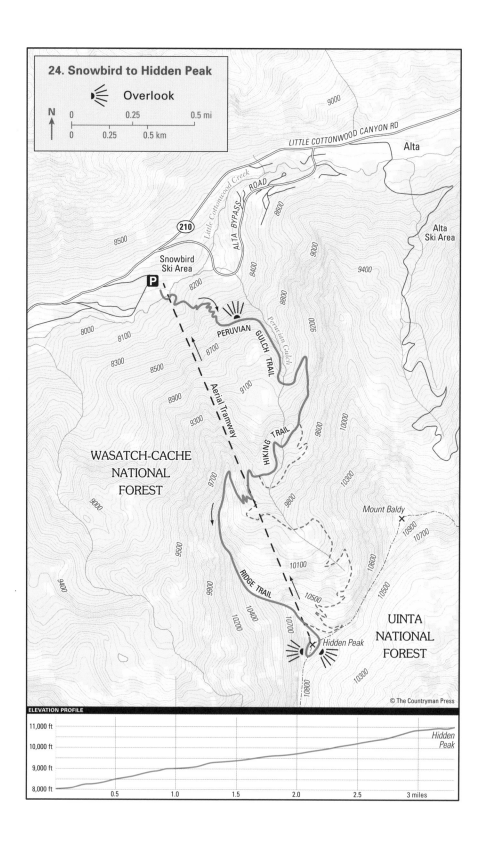

24. Snowbird to Hidden Peak

Overlook

N

| 0 | | 0.25 | | 0.5 mi |
| 0 | 0.25 | | 0.5 km | |

9000

LITTLE COTTONWOOD CANYON RD

Alta

Little Cottonwood Creek

ROAD

8600

Alta
Ski Area

210

8500

9000

9400

Snowbird
Ski Area

P

8200

8400

8800

9200

9026

PERUVIAN

Perution Gulch

GULCH TRAIL

8000

8100

8700

8300

8500

9100

8900

Aerial Tramway

9300

HIKING TRAIL

9600

10000

9700

10300

Mount Baldy
×

10900

10700

WASATCH-CACHE
NATIONAL
FOREST

9000

8800

9500

10100

10600

10500

9400

9900

RIDGE TRAIL

10500

10300

10200

10400

10700

Hidden Peak
×

UINTA
NATIONAL
FOREST

10800

10300

© The Countryman Press

ELEVATION PROFILE

11,000 ft							Hidden Peak
10,000 ft							
9,000 ft							
8,000 ft							
	0.5	1.0	1.5	2.0	2.5	3 miles	

To locate the beginning of this route, you must find and get to the top level of the resort center with its spacious patio. Leaving the large deck on its south side, this route enters onto the mountainside and nears the base of the Peruvian Lift. From here, a paved road leads uphill and to the west.

After climbing this road just a few hundred feet, a steep, signed connector trail braches off and leads toward the Peruvian Gulch Trail. This leads uphill and slightly to the left, crossing under the Peruvian Lift, before connecting with the Peruvian Gulch Trail.

Once on the Peruvian Gulch Trail, hikers enter a section of short, tight switch-backs lasting 0.2 mile. Just afterward, the trail straightens out to the east, offering good views of the Hellgate of Little Cottonwood Canyon. Located between Alta and Snowbird, this distinctive pair of white-and-grey limestone cliffs nearly pinches together at the base of the canyon, forming a gate of sorts. Hailing back to the early mining days of Alta, the name "Hellgate" expresses exactly what the late 19th century Salt Lake City Mormons thought of Alta's mining population—with their breweries, gambling, and such.

Moving along, the trail bends toward the south and offers the first view of Hidden

View east and onto the Hellgate Cliffs from low on Snowbird's Slopes   CHRISTINE BALAZ

Looking north and across Little Cottonwood Canyon from Hidden Peak's summit ridge

CHRISTINE BALAZ

Peak roughly 0.8 mile from the resort center. About 0.1 mile later, you come into a large open area, which holds the junction of many ski runs and summer trails. Signs point the way to the Peruvian Gulch Trail (which this chapter's route continues to follow), a large dirt road at this point.

From this intersection, the path arcs to the left before making a sharp right-hand turn 0.1 mile later. After passing through this switchback, you stay on the dirt road 0.3 mile before encountering a signed junction with the Hiking Trail. From here, both the Peruvian Gulch and Hiking Trails lead in the same direction, and both work to reach the Ridge Trail. This chapter's route takes the more pleasant, singletrack Hiking Trail; however, the dirt-road Peruvian Gulch Trail is a perfectly acceptable alternative.

Heading west 0.3 miles through a broad, tree-lined gulch, the Hiking Trail crosses over the Peruvian Gulch Trail once again. Shortly afterward, it heads under the aerial tram and meets up with the Ridge Trail at a signed intersection—1.9 miles from the base area.

The initial section of the Ridge Trail is comprised of a series of short switchbacks ascending the basinlike mountainside. Toward the end of the zigzags, you pass an old tailings pile. The trail then straightens out to the north, offering elevated views down onto the slopes of Snowbird. At 0.2 mile beyond the tailings pile, the trail makes a hairpin turn back to the south, and 0.1 mile after that, it gains the Peruvian Ridge.

The Ridge Trail then follows the crest of this ridge as it leads southward and directly to the Hidden Peak summit. Though you appear to be near the summit here, you must still walk 1.0 mile and gain just more than 1,000 feet of elevation to get there. However arduous, this final section of the journey is also the most scenic. While on the ridge, the trail offers spectacular views of the mountains surrounding Snowbird, including those of the long Mount Superior, directly to the north and across Little Cottonwood Canyon, and eventually those of the distinctive Pfeifferhorn to the southwest.

Once at the summit, hikers have incredible, 360-degree views in all directions. To the south, the peaks of American Fork Canyon soar; to the west and north, Little Cottonwood Canyon stretches; and to the northeast, the mountains of Park City and Big Cottonwood Canyon can be seen. Take the time to enjoy these views, but be prepared for windy and chilly conditions at the top—even on the warmest of summer days.

To return to the base area, hikers can take any number of trails or ride the tram for no cost. Trams depart from the summit every 20 minutes, weather permitting.

FEES, RESTRICTIONS, AND PERMITS

No fees; Little Cottonwood Canyon is a Salt Lake City watershed, so no dogs are allowed in the canyon; snow chains or four-wheel drive required of all vehicles during the winter months; hiking within Snowbird Ski & Summer Resort boundaries only permitted outside of ski season

The Not-So-Bad Complications of Inbounds Hiking

Many trails begin at the Snowbird Ski & Summer Resort Center and make their way to the top of Hidden Peak. The resulting plethora of trails and junctions can be confusing to navigate. It is therefore recommended that you visit Snowbird's Web site and print a "Summer Hiking and Biking Trails" map before departing, or simply snap a digital photo of one at the base area. Because Snowbird performs a good deal of mountain maintenance during the summer months, you should also be prepared to encounter trail closures and be willing to adjust your route to Hidden Peak.

25

Albion Basin to Catherine Pass

Type: Mountain; dirt; out-and-back; side trips and extensions possible

Season: Late Spring–Fall; Alta Ski Area closed to hiking during ski season

Total Distance: 3.0 miles round-trip

Time: 1–2 hours

Rating: Easy/Moderate

Elevation Gain: 950 feet

Location: Alta Ski Area, Little Cottonwood Canyon, east of Salt Lake City

Maps: USGS BRIGHTON US TOPO

Contact: Wasatch-Cache National Forest: Salt Lake Ranger District, 3285 East 3300 South, Salt Lake City, UT 84109; 801-466-6411; www.fs.usda .gov/uwcnf: or Alta Ski Area, UT 210, Alta, UT 84092; 801-359-1078; www .alta.com

Trailhead GPS Coordinates: Catherine Pass Trailhead: N40 34.974 W111 37.107

Comments: A relatively short yet beautiful hike in the upper reaches of Albion Basin, this gives hikers a taste of the alpine Wasatch without requiring much effort.

OVERVIEW

The hike from Albion Basin to Catherine Pass is perfect for those wishing to experience the high-elevation Wasatch without having to embark on a serious or strenuous mission to do so. This route begins near the top of Little Cottonwood Canyon Road and climbs toward the ridgeline of Albion Basin. On the way, it winds through open fields, past trees, and through a meadow, offering excellent views down Little Cottonwood Canyon and across Alta Ski Area.

THE TRAIL

The Catherine Pass Trail originates at its own trailhead near the very end of Little Cottonwood Canyon Road. The trailhead itself is marked by a fairly large parking area, pit toilet, and sign. From the parking area, the trail departs to the east, crossing the road and then heading up the slopes of Alta.

The path begins as a well-worn single-track trail that quickly passes underneath the Albion Lift. At 0.2 mile from the parking area, the trail merges with a dirt service road and passes the top of the lift 0.1 mile later.

After passing the lift, this dirt lane bends to the southeast. As it winds up the gently sloped hillsides of Alta, the trail's meanders provide excellent down-canyon views of Mount Superior. Open fields surround the trail, dotted by occasional tree patches. Small, white quartz monzonite boulders are strewn about the high-elevation vegetation of grass and low-lying shrubs.

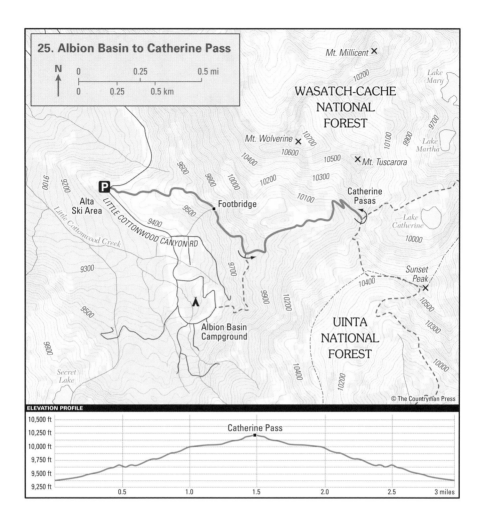

25. Albion Basis to Catherine Pass

N

0   0.25   0.5 mi

0   0.25   0.5 km

Mt. Millicent ✕

10200

Lake Mary

WASATCH-CACHE
NATIONAL
FOREST

Mt. Wolverine ✕
10700
10600

10400

10200

10500

10300

✕ Mt. Tuscarora

Lake Martha

9700

10100 9900

9600

9800

10000

P

Alta
Ski Area

LITTLE COTTONWOOD CANYON RD

Footbridge

Catherine
Pasas

10100

Lake Catherine

10000

9100

9200

Little Cottonwood Creek

9400

9500

9700

9300

9500

9900

10200

Albion Basin
Campground

UINTA
NATIONAL
FOREST

Sunset
Peak
✕

10400

10500

10300

10000

9600

Secret
Lake

10400

10200

© The Countryman Press

ELEVATION PROFILE

		Catherine Pass			

10,500 ft
10,250 ft
10,000 ft
9,750 ft
9,500 ft
9,250 ft

0.5   1.0   1.5   2.0   2.5   3 miles

At 0.5 mile from the trailhead, you pass over a small footbridge, and then skirt past a limestone outcrop. Facing south at this point, the trail showcases Devil's Castle–the set of limestone cliffs crowning Albion Basin. Though rather rotten, these cliffs actually hold a handful of rock climbing routes that lead from the base all the way to the top.

At 0.7 mile into the hike, the trail passes over a tailings pile and almost immediately comes to a signed junction with a trail leading to the Albion Basin Campground. To stay on this chapter's route, head left here.

Once past this intersection, the trail turns to the east again and ascends rather steeply for 0.3 mile before delivering you into a basin. With a meadow occupying its bottom, and steep hillsides all around it, this basin is completely hidden from Alta's base area. The trail stays in this basin for 0.2 mile before resuming its ascent.

Alta's lifts: quiet during summer

CHRISTINE BALAZ

View west and across Albion Basin CHRISTINE BALAZ

The trail ascends rather steeply for its final 0.3 mile. As it does, it enters a forest of tall evergreen trees and passes through three switchbacks that alleviate the steepness of the route. Without warning, the trail reaches the crest of Catherine Pass. Beyond the ridge lies Lake Catherine and the Brighton ski area.

This chapter's route ends here at Catherine Pass, and sends hikers back to the car on the trail by which they arrived. However, it is possible to continue hiking down to Catherine Lake, 0.3 mile away—and even farther to Lake Mary and Dog Lake (Chapter 22 of this book). Few people complete this extension, though—doing so would require retracing their steps back to the top of Catherine Ridge. The alternative shuttle car option is rather impractical, as the road distance between the Albion Basin and Brighton Trailheads is nearly 30 very steep and winding miles.

FEES, RESTRICTIONS, AND PERMITS

No fees; Little Cottonwood Canyon is a Salt Lake City watershed, so no dogs are allowed in the canyon; snow chains or four-wheel drive required of all vehicles during the winter months; hiking within Alta boundaries only permitted outside of ski season

26

Tibble Fork Loop

Type: Mountain; dirt; loop; extensions possible	
Season: Spring–Fall	
Total Distance: 4.2 miles round-trip	
Time: 2–3 hours	
Rating: Moderate	
Elevation Gain: 1,100 feet	
Location: Tibble Fork, American Fork Canyon, east of Highland	
Maps: USGS TIMPANOGOS CAVE US TOPO and USGS ASPEN GROVE US TOPO	
Contact: Uinta-Wasatch-Cache National Forest: Pleasant Grove Ranger District, 390 North 100 East, Pleasant Grove, UT 84062; 801-785-3563; www.fs.usda.gov/uwcnf	
Trailhead GPS Coordinates: Tibble Fork Dam: N40 28.870 W111 38.823	
Comments: This trail passes through multiple junctions; be sure to study a map (or bring one with you) in order to complete the route without problems.	

OVERVIEW

This hike forms a loop, combining the parallel Tibble Fork and Mill Canyons and a connector trail spanning the two. Forested for nearly its entire length, this trail offers plenty of shade and is therefore a reasonable option for summer hiking. Along the way, it passes through patches of scrub oak, groves of aspen, forests of conifer, and occasional grassy fields. These fields and the trees outlining them frame the surrounding peaks of American Fork Canyon handsomely.

THE TRAIL

Parking for the Tibble Fork Loop is best done in one of the small pullouts along Tibble Fork Road near the dam of Tibble Fork Reservoir. However, if these lots are full, you may park in the much larger lot on the northern side of the reservoir, and walk the short distance to the dam. From the road, you cross over the dam on foot to reach the trailhead. Marked by a small kiosk and Forest Service trail sign, this is hard to miss.

Following signs to the right, hikers turn to the southeast and immediately begin climbing. Almost immediately, the trail enters a section of switchbacks that ascends the scrub oak–covered hillside. At 0.4 mile from the dam, the trail straightens out and continues heading southeast. On this next stretch of trail, the taller vegetation largely recedes, exposing some of the hike's longer-distance views.

At 0.9 mile from the trailhead, you pass into a stand of aspen and, 0.1 mile later, you

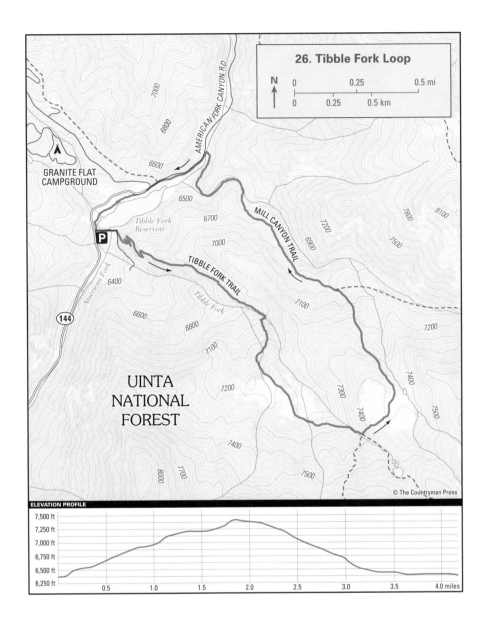

26. Tibble Fork Loop

N
0   0.25   0.5 mi
0   0.25   0.5 km

GRANITE FLAT
CAMPGROUND

7000

6800

6600

AMERICAN FORK CANYON RD.

6500

Tibble Fork
Reservoir

6700

MILL CANYON TRAIL

7200

6900

7800

8100

7500

P

7000

TIBBLE FORK TRAIL

American Fork

6400

Tibble Fork

7100

7200

144

6600

6800

7100

7300

7400

7500

UINTA
NATIONAL
FOREST

7200

7400

7400

8000

7700

7500

© The Countryman Press

ELEVATION PROFILE

7,500 ft
7,250 ft
7,000 ft
6,750 ft
6,500 ft
6,250 ft

0.5   1.0   1.5   2.0   2.5   3.0   3.5   4.0 miles

cross by a large gulch. The trail then pitches uphill rather steeply for a short section and heads through mixed areas of aspen groves and grassy clearings. One of the uppermost clearings is also one of the largest on this section of trail; you should pause and turn around here to behold the picturesquely framed White and Red Baldy to the north (Chapter 23 of this book). These peaks are some of the tallest on the ridge that separates Little Cottonwood Canyon to the north from American Fork Canyon to the south.

View through scrub oak early in the Tibble Fork Loop

At 1.8 miles from the beginning of the route, the trail reaches a four-way junction. To stay on this route, turn left to follow the sign for Mill Canyon Trail. After this junction, the trail ascends to its high point, elevation 7,516 feet, after just 0.1 mile. It then drops down into a large meadow that sometimes holds a small lake. Another faint trail heads right and east across this meadow; stay straight and head north along the main trail to remain on this chapter's route.

Leaving this clearing, the trail passes through mixed aspen and evergreen forest. At 0.5 mile after this junction—and 2.5 miles from the parking area—it encounters a signed junction. Turn left here to follow the Mill Canyon Trail and head toward Tibble Fork Reservoir.

Shortly after passing through this junction, the trail enters its last large clearing. Here you enjoy one final view of the ridgeline separating American Fork and Little Cottonwood Canyons before plunging downhill.

For the next 0.5 mile, the trail essentially heads directly down the gullet of Mill Canyon, descending very steeply in places. At the bottom of this steepest section, the trail comes near the stream, even crossing it. In this lower portion of the Mill Canyon Trail, you also pass near a few orange-red sandstone outcroppings.

Once at the bottom of the hill, you run into the cobble-bottomed Tibble Fork Stream. From here, hikers have two options: They can either pick their way along the southern shore of Tibble Fork Reservoir and back to the car—or they may turn right, cross Tibble Fork by way of a bridge, and then walk back to the parking area on the road and northern shore of this reservoir. Though both options are fine, this chapter's route takes the northern option due to its more open views.

Back at the car, hikers may choose to lounge on the shores of Tibble Fork Reservoir, or to possibly tack on another nearby hike. Going 2.0 dirt road miles uphill from Tibble Reservoir, a beautiful trail leads from Silver Lake Flat to Silver Lake (Chapter 27 of this book); back in the main fork of American Fork Canyon, the Pine Hollow Trail (Chapter 28) offers another possibility.

FEES, RESTRICTIONS, AND PERMITS
$6 day-use fee is required of all vehicles entering American Fork Canyon; pets OK

View across high meadow of Tibble Fork Loop
CHRISTINE BALAZ

27

Silver Lake Flat to Silver Lake

Type: Mountain; dirt; out-and-back; extension possible

Season: Spring–Fall

Total Distance: 4.6 miles round-trip

Time: 2–4 hours

Rating: Moderate/Strenuous

Elevation Gain: 1,500 feet

Location: Tibble Fork, American Fork Canyon, east of Highland

Maps: USGS DROMEDARY PEAK US TOPO

Contact: Uinta-Wasatch-Cache National Forest: Pleasant Grove Ranger District, 390 North 100 East, Pleasant Grove, UT 84062; 801-785-3563; www.fs .usda.gov/uwcnf

Trailhead GPS Coordinates: Silver Lake Flat: N40 30.418 W111 39.388

Comments: This hike takes place in bear country; hikers should consider carrying bear spray.

OVERVIEW

Though short and only moderately strenuous, the trail from Silver Lake Flat to Silver Lake tours some of American Fork Canyon's most gorgeous high-elevation terrain. Beginning at the Silver Lake Flat Reservoir, this hike leads up Silver Creek Basin to the natural Silver Lake, which stands beneath White and Red Baldy—both of which have an elevation well over 11,000 feet. Along the way, this route offers stunning views of its glaciated surroundings as well as of the lofty peaks of the Mount Timpanogos Wilderness—including those of the namesake mountain itself.

THE TRAIL

The parking area for the Silver Lake Trail is located on the far northern side of the Silver Lake Flat Reservoir. Standing at this point, you have already accomplished a good portion of the climbing toward Silver Lake—with vehicular assistance.

The trail itself originates on the northern side of the large parking area. Adjacent to a pit toilet and large signboard, the path is easy to locate. On this signboard, the Forest Service has posted information regarding the area, including a topographical overview map. From here, the trail heads due north and into a large stand of aspen trees.

During its opening section, the path splits numerous times. However, the "real" trail here is easy to recognize as the broadest and most well-worn of the bunch. (These side trails lead to open areas where families tend to picnic.) At 0.2 mile from the trailhead,

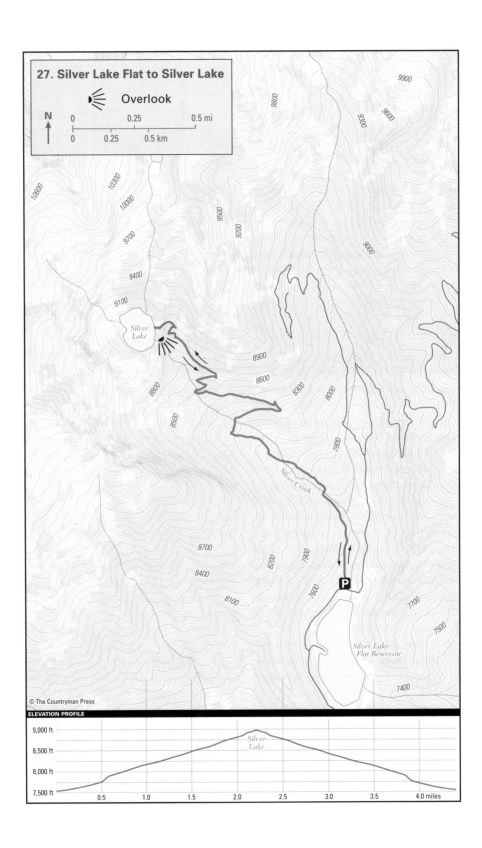

27. Silver Lake Flat to Silver Lake

Overlook

N

| 0 | 0.25 | 0.5 mi |
| 0 | 0.25 | 0.5 km |

9900
9800
9300
9600
9000
10300
10000
9700
9500
9200
9400
9100
Silver Lake
8900
8600
8800
8500
8300
8000
7800
Silver Creek
8700
8200
7900
8400
7600
8100
P
7700
7500
Silver Lake Flat Reservoir
7400

© The Countryman Press

ELEVATION PROFILE

9,000 ft
8,500 ft
8,000 ft
7,500 ft

Silver Lake

0.5   1.0   1.5   2.0   2.5   3.0   3.5   4.0 miles

Early glimpse of White Baldy Peak from Silver Lake Trail   CHRISTINE BALAZ

you pass through a cluster of bright white quartz monzonite boulders. Afterward, the trail curves subtly to the northwest and offers its first glimpses of the surrounding mountain before passing over a small stream by way of a log bridge.

At 0.5 mile from the trailhead, you enter the Lone Peak Wilderness. Marked by a sign, this border cannot be missed. After crossing into the wilderness, the trail continues climbing to the northwest at a steady rate. At 0.1 mile into the Lone Peak Wilderness, you enter a small clearing and once again enjoy views of the surrounding peaks.

At 0.9 mile from the trailhead, the path bends sharply to the right, and 0.1 mile later it encounters another stream crossing. After this crossing, the path continues eastward and uphill for 0.2 mile, climbing out of the drainage and onto the mountainside above it. It then makes a hairpin turn to the left.

Heading west for 0.4 mile, the trail continues rising above the drainage, passing a large quartzite outcrop, and then entering a section of four tight switchbacks. After these, the trail again cuts to the northwest. Remaining on this south-facing mountainside for its entire second half, the path offers better and better views of the Silver Creek Basin, below, as well as of the peaks of the Mount Timpanogos Wilderness to the south. The best views of all, though, are of White Baldy's rocky and pointy summit to the northwest.

At 0.3 mile from Silver Lake, the trail enters a final section of switchbacks. All persons should attempt to minimize human impact here by staying on the main trail and avoiding shortcuts.

Standing on the shores of Silver Lake, you are surrounded in all directions by a tall cirque of peaks. The tallest of these, White

50 Hikes in Utah

Silver Lake and White Baldy

CHRISTINE BALAZ

Baldy, dominates the skyline to the northwest at an elevation of 11,321 feet. Believe it or not, at this point, you stand hardly more than 1.0 mile due south from Little Cottonwood Canyon's Red and White Pine Lakes (Chapter 23 of this book). If a trail went to the top of White Baldy, you could look directly down onto these bodies of water.

From Silver Lake, an unmaintained trail leads to the north and eventually to a smaller body of water called Silver Glance Lake. At 0.6 mile beyond and 880 vertical feet above Silver Lake, this lake requires a good bit of effort to reach. However, this small alpine lake rewards those committing to the effort with solitude and even more spectacular alpine scenery, given its intimate nearness to Red and White Baldy.

FEES, RESTRICTIONS, AND PERMITS

$6 day-use fee is required of all vehicles entering American Fork Canyon; wheeled vehicles not allowed; pets OK; much of this hike falls within the Lone Peak Wilderness, so please familiarize yourself with wilderness restrictions before entering

Rough Road Ahead

Though the road leading up to Tibble Fork Reservoir is paved and of a mellow grade, the road above this reservoir is dramatically different. Turning to dirt beyond Tibble Fork Reservoir, the road becomes very steep and winding in places—and riddled with washboards and rough stones. The distance between Tibble Fork Reservoir and this chapter's trailhead, Silver Lake Flat, is less than 2.0 miles; but the journey is fairly rough. Though the road should be manageable for most passenger vehicles, it can be dubious at times for those with two-wheel drive and/or low clearance. In any case, this road is never recommended for vehicles pulling trailers.

28

Pine Hollow

Type: Mountain; dirt; out-and-back; side trips and extensions possible

Season: Spring–Fall

Total Distance: 3.6 miles round-trip

Time: 1.5–2 hours

Rating: Moderate

Elevation Gain: 1,250 feet

Location: American Fork Canyon, east of Highland

Maps: USGS TIMPANOGOS CAVE US TOPO and USGS ASPEN GROVE US TOPO

Contact: Uinta-Wasatch-Cache National Forest: Pleasant Grove Ranger District, 390 North 100 East, Pleasant Grove, UT 84062; 801-785-3563; www.fs .usda.gov/uwcnf

Trailhead GPS Coordinates: Pine Hollow Trailhead: N40 26.970 W111 38.614

Comments: This hike follows a stream for much of its length. A natural habitat for wild animals, this hollow is the site of numerous animal sightings—from deer to cougars and bears. Hikers on this route should be alert so as to avoid an incident.

OVERVIEW

The Pine Hollow Trail leads up a long, cool drainage and through pleasant forests and aspen groves. Meeting up with the Great Western Trail for its final pitch, this route leads up to a beautiful, open meadow with unbeatable views of Mount Timpanogos. Starting at an elevation of nearly 6,700 feet, climbing to over 7,900 feet, and offering shade for most of its length, this is a good option for summer hikers.

THE TRAIL

The Pine Hollow Trail originates at the top of the westernmost S-curve on the Alpine Scenic Highway (UT 92) in American Fork Canyon—at the cleverly named Pine Hollow Trailhead. This trailhead serves as the jumping-off point for a large and complicated network of trails surrounding the Great Western Trail. Quite spacious and marked with a pit toilet and large kiosk, this parking area cannot be missed. Already in the parking area, you enjoy generous views of the massive Mount Timpanogos, immediately to the south.

The Pine Hollow Trail leaves the parking area by heading east and directly past the pit toilet. After just a few steps, you must cross the road, and pick up the trail on its opposite side. This path—popular, well-worn, and marked with a sign—should be easy to spot.

From the road, the trail leads directly uphill and almost immediately encounters a junction. Stay right here to remain on this chapter's route. After this junction, the trail

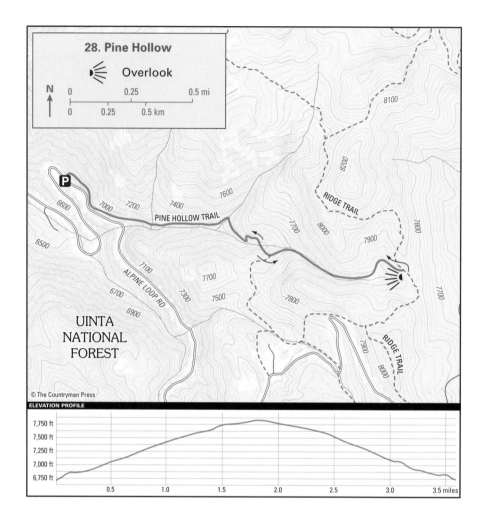

28. Pine Hollow

Overlook

N

0   0.25   0.5 mi

0   0.25   0.5 km

8100

8200

RIDGE TRAIL

P

6600   7000 7200 7400   7600

PINE HOLLOW TRAIL

7700   8000   7900   7800

6500

7100

ALPINE LOOP RD

7700

6700

7300   7500

6900

7800

7700

**UINTA
NATIONAL
FOREST**

7900

RIDGE TRAIL

8000

© The Countryman Press

ELEVATION PROFILE

7,750 ft							
7,500 ft							
7,250 ft							
7,000 ft							
6,750 ft							

0.5   1.0   1.5   2.0   2.5   3.0   3.5 miles

heads up-canyon and roughly parallel to the road, climbing across a scrub oak–covered hillside. After a short distance, the trail curves subtly to the south to face Mount Timpanogos. The vegetation stands just low enough here to offer uninterrupted views of this mountain once again.

At 0.4 mile from the trailhead, you overlook the road one final time as it disappears around a bend. About 0.2 mile later, the trail itself enters Pine Hollow and is swallowed up by a dense conifer forest. During this section, the path assumes the steepest grade of its entire length. At 0.7 mile into the hike, the evergreens momentarily give way to an aspen grove, and shortly afterward, the trail crosses through a stony gully and veers sharply to the right.

Just after this abrupt turn, the trail enters a clearing on a steep hillside. Here it remains for 0.2 mile, passing through a short set of switchbacks. This open area, covered only with grass, sagebrush, and scrub oak, provides you with the opportunity to look down the length of American Fork Canyon for the first time on this trip.

Leaving this clearing, the trail reenters the forest, crosses a stream, and climbs into a small clearing. At 1.2 miles from the parking area, the trail reaches another junction. Go left here to follow signs for the Ridge Trail. After passing through this junction, the trail enters a lighter forest than before and heads more or less to the east. The path slowly arcs to the southeast and comes quite near a stream just 0.2 mile later.

On its final stretch, the trail flattens out a good deal as it leads eastwardly through aspen trees. At 1.6 miles from the trailhead, you enter a large rolling clearing, lined on all sides with aspen trees. About 0.2 mile later, the trail reaches a junction. Though an infinite number of extensions can be had from this point, this chapter's route stops here and heads back to the trailhead. Turning around here to face the southwest, you will immediately understand why this clearing is the destination of the route. From this meadow, the views of Mount Timpanogos cannot be beaten.

From here, the most direct return trip to the Pine Hollow Trailhead is along the same trail. Given the many other connector trails in the area, it is naturally possible to take an

Mount Timpanogos from ridge about Pine Hollow

CHRISTINE BALAZ

alternative route. However, any such deviation would require hikers to walk along UT 92 to return to the Pine Hollow Trailhead. Those wishing to freestyle here would naturally be helped immensely by carrying a detailed trail map.

FEES, RESTRICTIONS, AND PERMITS

$6 day-use fee is required of all vehicles entering American Fork Canyon; pets OK; check with Utah Department of Transportation for seasonal road closures

Mount Timpanogos

Mount Timpanogos, though not the tallest in the Wasatch Mountains, is arguably the most iconic and famous peak in this range. With an elevation of 11,749 feet, this actually ranks as the second-tallest peak—behind the less dramatic Mount Nebo, elevation 11,928 feet. Rising 5,269 feet—nearly a vertical mile—above the Utah Valley, this beautifully glaciated alpine mountain is surrounded by knife-blade ridges, limestone cliffs, and U-shaped drainages.

29

Stewart Falls from Sundance

Type: Mountain; dirt; out-and-back; side trips and extensions possible

Season: Spring–Fall; Sundance Resort closed to hiking in winter

Total Distance: 3.5 miles round-trip

Time: 1.5–2 hours

Rating: Easy/Moderate

Elevation Gain: 650 feet

Location: Sundance Resort, Alpine Scenic Loop

Maps: USGS ASPEN GROVE US TOPO

Contact: Uinta-Wasatch-Cache National Forest: Pleasant Grove Ranger District, 390 North 100 East, Pleasant Grove, UT 84062; 801-785-3563; www.fs .usda.gov/uwcnf: or Sundance Resort, 8841 North Alpine Loop Road, Sundance, UT 84604; 1-866-259-7468; www.sundanceresort.com

Trailhead GPS Coordinates: Sundance Resort Base Area: N40 23.478 W111 34.641

Comments: To those unfamiliar with it, the Sundance Resort base area is like a maze; don't be shy about asking for directions.

OVERVIEW

This leisurely hike begins at the Sundance Resort and climbs westwardly toward Stewart Falls (sometimes called Stewart Cascades). Located on the eastern slopes of the enormous Mount Timpanogos, these falls drain a massive basin on the mountain's east face called Cascade Cirque. Composed of two tiers, this cascade—more than 200 feet tall—flows perennially.

THE TRAIL

Unless staying at the Sundance Resort, hikers should park at one of the two large resort-center parking lots reached immediately after leaving the Alpine Highway. Despite Sundance's openness to hikers and bikers during the summer months, there is a surprising lack of trail-related signs to be found in the base area. Due to this lack of signage, locating the trailhead is the trickiest part of the entire route. Further complicating matters, there are actually multiple ways to access the Stewart Falls Trail from the resort. Given the potential trickery of the route-finding, this chapter describes the simplest and most surefire way to reach the trail—via its access point at Mandan Knoll.

From the southwestern corner of Mandan Knoll, the trail heads uphill and into the forest. Marked by a small boulder engraved NATURE TRAIL, this path shouldn't be too tricky to find. From the moment it leaves the pavement, the path remains well-worn and easy to follow.

In its initial section, the trail heads southwest, across a hillside covered in scrub oak.

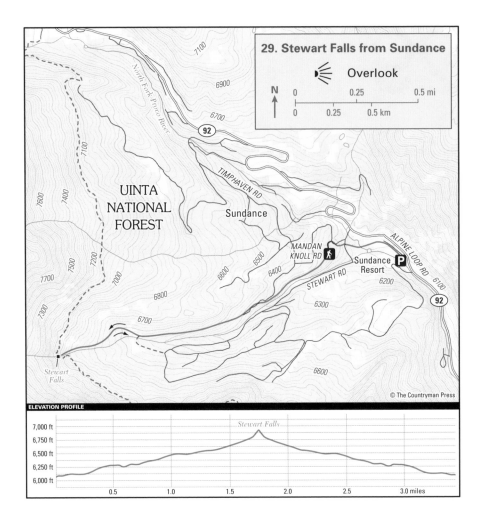

29. Stewart Falls from Sundance

◖≶ Overlook

N

0   0.25   0.5 mi

0   0.25   0.5 km

7100

North Fork Provo River

6900

6700

92

7100

TIMPHAVEN RD

UINTA
NATIONAL
FOREST

Sundance

7600 *7400*

7500 *7200*

6500

MANDAN
KNOLL RD

Sundance
Resort   P

ALPINE LOOP RD

7700

7000

6600

6400

STEWART RD

6200

6100

6800

6300

92

6700

Stewart
Falls

6600

© The Countryman Press

ELEVATION PROFILE

| | | | | *Stewart Falls* | | | |

7,000 ft
6,750 ft
6,500 ft
6,250 ft
6,000 ft

0.5   1.0   1.5   2.0   2.5   3.0 miles

At 0.2 mile from Mandan Knoll, the trail encounters its first junction; to stay on this chapter's route, continue heading straight. (The other trail heads downhill back to the Sundance Resort.)

After this junction, the trail curves slowly to the right. Here it enters a long section of light aspen forest. Interspersed only occasionally with evergreen trees, these aspen let in ample light, filtering it pleasantly.

About 1.0 mile from the parking area, the trail reveals its first glimpses of Mount Timpanogos. By this point, the path has curved to face due west. During this next section of trail, the trees all but disappear, giving way to low-lying shrubs and grasses. Revealing increasingly open views, this lower vegetation and almost arrow-straight trajectory allows you to clearly understand the surroundings—a massive drainage beneath an even more substantial cirque on Mount Timpanogos. On this stretch of trail, Stewart Falls reveals itself to hikers for the first time.

Mount Timpanogos, Cascade Cirque and Stewart Falls

At 1.3 miles into the hike, the trail comes to a junction marked with the number 23. Stay straight here to follow this chapter's route. Just after this intersection, the trail bends slightly to the left and leads gently downhill for a short section. After passing into a small clearing, the trail runs into yet another intersection 0.2 mile beyond the previous one. Continue walking due west here and toward the falls.

After this final junction, the trail comes quite near the creek leading away from the falls. As such, it enters a section of thicker vegetation. Just before reaching the falls, the path opens up significantly, offering up-close views of this two-tiered cascade pouring over banded, moss-covered limestone cliffs. When the water flow is low, hikers can even climb to a natural platform at the top of the first cascade.

From the cascade, you must turn around and retrace your steps to reach the Sundance Resort. Those wishing to extend the journey may follow a trail leading uphill and to the south. This trail requires roughly 400 feet of climbing to reach Dry Lake, 1.0 mile beyond the falls. From Dry Lake, a number of other trails lead back to the base of Sundance Resort; carrying a detailed map would be wise of any hiker attempting to include this extension in their trip.

Stewart Falls   CHRISTINE BALAZ

FEES, RESTRICTIONS, AND PERMITS
Pets OK, but they should be leashed in the Sundance Resort base area; bikes not allowed on the Stewart Falls Trail

Locating Mandan Knoll
From the main parking lot, your goal is to reach Mandan Knoll, a cul-de-sac standing uphill and due west from the resort center—approximately 0.4 mile as the crow flies. To get there, you must head west through both large parking lots, continuing west as these give way to a small road. This passes the Foundry Grill, Art Studio, and Sundance Gallery. Staying just south of, but parallel to, UT 92, the road ends and immediately turns into a zigzagging foot path. This paved trail crosses over Stewart Road, and then runs parallel to Timphaven Road. Still heading west, this footpath runs directly into Mandan Knoll Road. Turn left onto this road and walk the short distance to its terminus. All told, the walking distance from the lowest parking lot to Mandan Knoll is just less than 0.5 mile; if you've walked farther than that, it'd be a good idea to find someone and ask for directions.

30

Lakes Country Loop

Type: Mountain; dirt; lollipop-shaped; side trip possible

Season: Summer

Total Distance: 7.5 miles round-trip

Time: 2–4 hours

Rating: Easy/Moderate

Elevation Gain: 1,100 feet

Location: Mirror Lake Highway (UT 150), western Uinta Mountains

Maps: USGS MIRROR LAKE US TOPO and USGS ERICKSON BASIN US TOPO

Contact: Uinta-Wasatch-Cache National Forest: Kamas Ranger District, 50 E. Center St., Kamas, UT 84036; 435-783-4338; www.fs.usda.gov/uwcnf

Trailhead GPS Coordinates: Lily Lake Trailhead, Trial Lake Recreation Area: N40 40.907 W110 57.784

Comments: A long and nearly flat tour of the western Uintas, this trail allows hikers to cover a lot of distance with relatively little effort.

OVERVIEW

This lollipop-shaped route heads due west from the Lily Lake Trailhead, a popular recreation access point along UT 150. Given its long distance, this trail sees noticeably fewer hikers than other trails in the area, rendering it an excellent option for those who prefer solitude. Though lengthy, this route is quite flat, allowing for speedy exploration of this lake-filled alpine area at the base of Long Peak.

THE TRAIL

The trail for the Lakes Country Loop is the westernmost of two departing from the same parking lot. Marked clearly, the correct trail should be easy to locate as it heads due west and away from the pavement. Broad and flat at its origin, this path was once a roadway leading to the northern shores of Crystal Lake. Though its width narrows after reaching this lake, the initial section of this trail nevertheless offers open views of the pyramidal Mount Watson.

After just 0.2 mile of very gradual uphill walking, a small trail branches off to the north and toward Cliff Lake (Chapter 31 of this book). Stay straight here to follow this chapter's route. About 0.3 mile later, the trail dips slightly and crosses a stream, just before heading into the longest climb on the route—a 0.7-mile, 300-vertical-foot ascent. The top of this rise is marked by a sign denoting Mount Watson to the north. Here, with the hike's largest and longest climb already behind you, you can trust in the true ease of this route.

At 1.6 miles after leaving the parking lot, the trail encounters a signed Y junction; this marks the beginning of this hike's loop portion. Arbitrarily, this chapter's route takes the left fork toward Weir and Duck Lakes, walking the loop in a clockwise direction.

Beyond the junction, the initial stretch of trail passes uncounted small lakes as it descends gradually through lush meadows filled with wildflowers. Dozens and dozens of species are represented in these wet, alpine flatlands. Those with white blossoms include fringed grass of Parnassus, alpine bog swertia, and false hellebore—a member of the lily family with white and green blossoms. Common yellow species such as alpine poppy and goldeneye can be seen aside the pink and lavender flowers of various lupines and the deep red blossoms of Indian paintbrush. Leaving these meadows, the trail enters into thick forests and it descends past short cliffs to the north.

After about 2.25 total miles, you enter another open section of meadows. Here small,

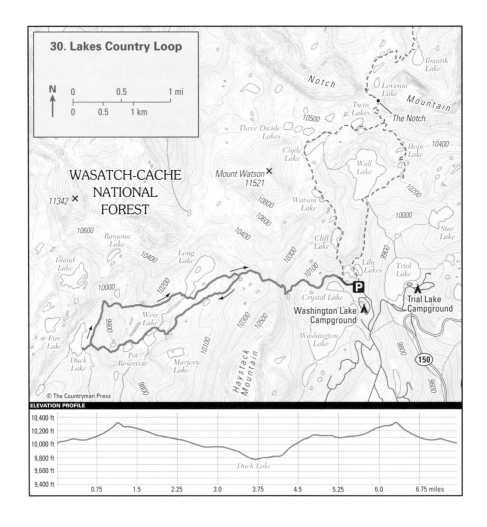

Afternoon thunderstorms roll in over the Lakes Country Loop

alpine streams carve dark, loopy paths into the otherwise totally flat, green meadows. To the north, buttresses of quartzite protrude into these wet flatlands. Wooden footbridges ensure dry passage through the wet areas. Mount Watson, still visible to the northwest, towers above isolated patches of evergreen trees.

At 2.7 miles into the hike, a side trail splits off to the left and toward Marjorie Lake; stay straight here. In another 0.3 mile, the trail passes directly past the signed Weir Lake. To stay on this chapter's route, follow signs toward Duck Lake. Continuing westward, the trail descends even more, entering into thick forests once again.

About 0.6 mile farther along, the trail arrives at yet another junction. This chapter's route takes the 0.1-mile spur trail toward Duck Lake, the westernmost point of this elongated lollipop. Trees line most of the lake's shore; cliffs rim its western sides.

Retracing this short spur trail returns you to the main loop. Once back on this trail, you should head north (left) to continue clockwise travel along this route. The trail continues along a rather linear trajectory for nearly 0.5 mile, descending at first. The trail then suddenly turns east and climbs before arriving at yet another junction. Here, another optional spur trail heads north. Though not included in this chapter's route, this 0.5-mile

Quartzite outcrop in front of Long Peak   DAVID SJÖQUIST

side trail leads to yet another body of water, Island Lake—a popular destination for backpackers and fishermen.

After passing this junction, the trail climbs rather steeply for 0.3 mile. Leveling off, it descends nearly 1.0 mile as it continues its due east track. Along the way, it passes through stands of evergreen trees, thick stands of wildflowers, and bare quartzite slabs.

Shortly before the loop section of this route ends, the trail nears the shores of Long Lake. Signed and easily recognizable as this hike's largest lake, Long Lake offers great views of Long Mountain to the northwest and Mount Watson to the northeast.

Just after passing Long Lake, the loop portion of this trail ends. From here, about 0.5 mile of climbing and 1.1 miles of descending lead back to the parking lot and the end of this route.

FEES, RESTRICTIONS, AND PERMITS

Dogs and bikes permitted; a Mirror Lake recreation fee is required of all those who park and recreate along UT 150; day-use passes cost $3, and other options are available

31

Wall Lake and
Notch Mountain Trail

Type: Mountain; dirt; loop with side-spur; side trips possible

Season: Summer

Total Distance: 5.7 miles round-trip

Time: 2–4 hours

Rating: Moderate

Elevation Gain: 1,000 feet

Location: Mirror Lake Highway (UT 150), western Uinta Mountains

Maps: USGS MIRROR LAKE US TOPO

Contact: Uinta-Wasatch-Cache National Forest: Kamas Ranger District, 50 E. Center St., Kamas, UT 84036; 435-783-4338; www.fs.usda.gov/uwcnf

Trailhead GPS Coordinates: Lily Lake Trailhead, Trial Lake Recreation Area: N40 40.907 W110 57.784

Comments: Beware afternoon thundershowers, which seem to arrive like clockwork in this range.

OVERVIEW

A high-country loop in the Uinta Mountains, this hike is rich with expansive views and passes uncounted lakes. En route, the trail ascends gradually upward through forests and past rock slabs toward the skirts of Notch Mountain and eventually Mount Watson before again descending toward the trailhead. Along the way, it passes through thick fields of wildflowers and over large wet meadows via numerous footbridges.

THE TRAIL

The Uinta Mountains are an enormous, tall, and dominant range in northeastern Utah. Yet, given their lofty altitude, these mountains are nevertheless quite accessible to hikers—even casual day hikers. Along the Mirror Lake Highway this range, though giant and punctuated with craggy peaks, is relatively flat and somewhat plateaulike. The Notch Mountain Trail, like many other hiking trails along UT 150, is therefore pleasant and relatively long—with little elevation gain considering its alpine environment. This particular route tours the broad, lake-filled basins and ledges beneath Notch Mountain and Mount Watson. Avoiding the summits of these mountains, this trail enjoys rather mellow topographical relief.

As you leave your car, look for the signed Notch Mountain Trail, the easternmost of two paths departing from the northern end of this large parking area. On the sign marking the trailhead, you should see that you are just 1.0 trail mile from Wall Lake.

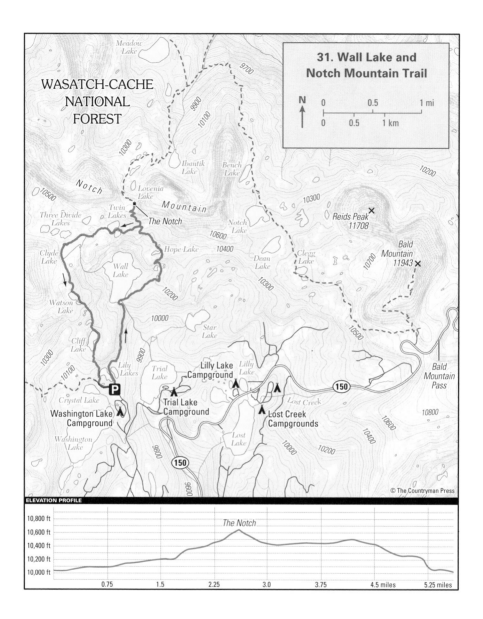

31. Wall Lake and Notch Mountain Trail

N 0   0.5   1 mi
   0   0.5   1 km

WASATCH-CACHE NATIONAL FOREST

Meadow Lake

Ibantik Lake

Bench Lake

Notch Mountain

Reids Peak 11708 ✕

Bald Mountain 11943 ✕

Three Divide Lakes

Twin Lakes

Lovenia Lake

The Notch

Notch Lake

Clegg Lake

Clyde Lake

Hope Lake

Dean Lake

Wall Lake

Watson Lake

Star Lake

Cliff Lake

Lily Lakes

Trial Lake

Lilly Lake

Lilly Lake

Bald Mountain Pass

Crystal Lake

Lily Lake Campground

Lost Creek

Trial Lake Campground

Washington Lake Campground

Lost Creek Campgrounds

Lost Lake

Washington Lake

© The Countryman Press

ELEVATION PROFILE

The Notch

10,800 ft
10,600 ft
10,400 ft
10,200 ft
10,000 ft

0.75   1.5   2.25   3.0   3.75   4.5 miles   5.25 miles

As soon as you leave the pavement, you'll understand immediately that this is a popular route. Wide and well-worn, this path is used by fishermen, backpackers, horse packers, and day hikers en route to the several dozen lakes and numerous hiking paths accessed by this trailhead. After just a few minutes of

walking, the trail passes its first lakes, threading through a narrow gap between two small bodies of water called Lily Lakes.

After passing these lakes, the trail enters its least eventful stretch, characterized by relatively thick evergreen forests and only occasional glimpses of the surrounding Uinta

Fields of wildflowers cover the Uintas in summer   DAVID SJÖQUIST

peaks. However, as the trail continues north-ward toward Wall Lake, it climbs steadily (though gradually). Doing so, it gains higher ground and earns better views for the re-mainder of the hike to come.

Suddenly the trail emerges from the woods, bringing hikers face-to-face with the large, cliff-lined Wall Lake and the extremely open views it creates. To the north, Notch Mountain dominates the skyline. It doesn't take much imagination to see how this moun-tain came into its name. From this vantage point, it is also easy to understand that this hike will be a relatively flat one; its high point, the notch of Notch Mountain, is really not that high at all—at least relative to the hike's starting point at 10,032 feet.

The trail passes Wall Lake—which is ac-tually a reservoir—by crossing the earthen dam on its southeastern side. Just after crossing the dam, the Trial Lake Trail merges with the Notch Mountain Trail from the south;

stay straight (north) at this junction to remain on this chapter's route. After this, the trail stays relatively close to the eastern shores of Wall Lake for about 0.3 mile.

After passing Wall Lake, the path bends toward the east and threads through another set of lakes, the largest of which is called Hope Lake. Here the definition of "lake" blurs, as many of these are quite small, and others have evaporated into lush meadows. As it works its way through these lakes of various sizes, the trail gradually curves north again and then west. Eventually it meets the base of a castlelike quartzite cliff band and then picks its way upward and to the top of it by way of stone steps.

Atop this cliff band is a flat, grassy plateau rich with small lakes and open views off to the south. Mount Watson, which you soon will walk beneath, can be seen domi-nating the skyline to the southwest. Despite the beauty of the views here, it is important to keep your eyes focused on the trail so as to stay on route.

At 2.25 miles into the hike, the trail reaches a faint, easy-to-miss junction marked by numerous cairns clustered atop quartzite slabs. To follow this chapter's route, take the side spur trail that heads north (right) and directly into the notch of Notch Mountain. Doing so will take you uphill for about 0.3 mile. Once in the notch, you'll enjoy some of the route's most spectacular views. From here, backcountry trails continue northward (including the trail in Chapter 32 of this book). Our route, however, turns around and retraces the 0.3 mile spur trail to regain the main Notch Mountain Trail.

Once back at the loop trail, take a right at the easy-to-miss junction mentioned earlier. Heading west, this portion of the hike is characterized by a very faint trail—a trail that often splits and fades out as it navigates among numerous small lakes. Many people camp along the lakes in this region, and many side trails lead from campsites to the lakes themselves, making this portion of the hike rather confusing. Though the trail often splits and disappears in this section of the hike, you can nevertheless navigate this stretch of the route successfully by trending southwest and toward the obvious, dome-shaped Mount Watson to your southwest.

After passing numerous lakes, including Twin Lakes and John Lake, you'll walk directly past sizeable quartzite slabs left of the trail before reaching the long northern shoreline of Clyde Lake. It is here that the trail again becomes well-worn and obvious. At 0.8 mile after the junction with the Notch Mountain

Looking west toward Notch Mountain and Wall Lake

DAVID SJÖQUIST

Wall Lake and Notch Mountain Trail

Trail, another side route splits away to the Three Divide Lakes to the west; stay straight here, hugging the shores of Clyde Lake as the trail bends gradually left and toward the south.

After passing Clyde Lake, the trail climbs briefly again before descending past Watson, Linear, Petite, and Cliff Lakes. The last of these, Cliff Lake, should be obvious in name. Here Utah rock climbers often can be seen enjoying the relative coolness afforded by the Uintas' high elevation.

At 1.7 miles after the junction at Clyde Lake, the trail merges with the Lakes Country Trail (Chapter 30 of this book). You'll want to go left here and head southeast along this trail–a veritable highway at this point. From here, just 0.2 mile of extremely easy hiking leads back to your car.

FEES, RESTRICTIONS, AND PERMITS

Dogs and bikes permitted; a Mirror Lake recreation fee is required of all those who park and recreate along UT 150; day-use passes cost $3, and other options are available

Rock Climbers

The Uinta Mountains are an extremely popular summer recreation area for the residents of Utah. Because of its consistently high elevation, this range offers pleasant temperatures that no other place in the region can during July and August. Ridden with quartzite cliff bands, this range is also popular among rock climbers. And because Salt Lake City is home to one of the nation's largest populations of climbers, you'll more than likely see some enjoying the routes during the height of summer.

32

Notch Mountain Trail: Bald Mountain Pass to Lily Lakes Trailhead

Type: Mountain; dirt; point-to-point; side trip possible

Season: Summer

Total Distance: 9.8 miles one-way

Time: 3–5 hours

Rating: Moderate

Elevation Gain: 1,000 feet (and 1,600 feet lost)

Location: Mirror Lake Highway (UT 150), western Uinta Mountains

Maps: USGS MIRROR LAKE US TOPO

Contact: Uinta-Wasatch-Cache National Forest: Kamas Ranger District, 50 E. Center St., Kamas, UT 84036; 435-783-4338; www.fs.usda.gov/uwcnf

Trailhead GPS Coordinates: Bald Mountain Pass: N40 41.353 W110 54.276

Comments: A shuttle car is required for the 5.2-mile return trip to the first parking area, unless hikers are willing to complete journey on foot.

OVERVIEW

A long and relatively flat tour of the back-country in the Uinta Mountains' Mirror Lake region, this point-to-point hike begins at the highest point of the Mirror Lake Highway, Bald Mountain Pass—with an altitude of 10,715 feet—and cuts a northwestern path down into the backcountry behind Reids Peak. Roughly halfway through, the trail bends back to the southwest and climbs up to and through the notch of Notch Mountain before descending again and terminating at the Lily Lakes Trailhead.

THE TRAIL

The Notch Mountain Trail offers a point-to-point journey into a lesser explored portion of the western Uintas. Perhaps because of its length—nearly 10 miles—or because of its shuttle car requirement, this trail receives vastly less traffic than many nearby hikes. The farther away from the trailhead it ventures, the thinner the path becomes. And though route-finding should not become an issue, hikers will certainly notice the difference in the size and clarity of this trail compared to that of the more popular ones. Though all trail junctions are marked with Forest Service signs, you'd be wise to carry a map in hand. Hikers will want to remain attentive in the middle portion of the route, so as to avoid veering off onto a game trail.

The hike begins on the western end of the large Bald Mountain parking area, near a pit toilet and kiosk. Less than 0.1 mile from the parking lot, the trail to Bald Mountain (Chapter 33 in this book) forks off to the right at a signed junction; stay left.

As it heads west and then north, the trail descends slowly, skirting the flanks of Bald Mountain. At 1.3 miles into the hike, the trail passes by its first tiny lake. About 0.4 mile later, it meets the southwestern shores of Clegg Lake. Looking northeast across the waters of this flat, glacially carved lake, hikers can see the cone-shaped Reids Peak. At 11,708 feet, this mountain stands just a touch shorter than the 11,943-foot Bald Mountain.

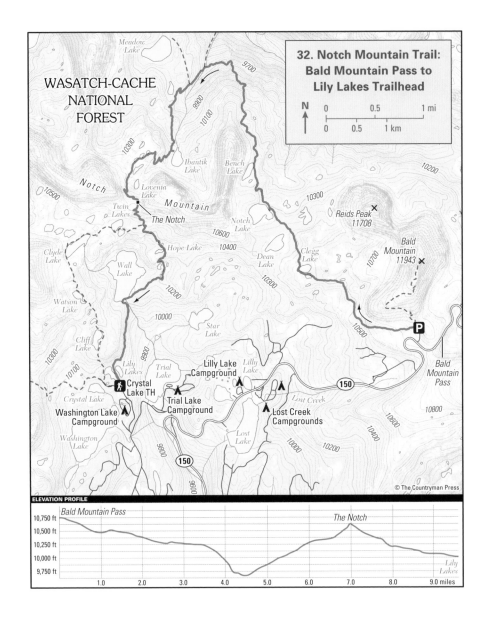

32. Notch Mountain Trail:
Bald Mountain Pass to
Lily Lakes Trailhead

Notch Lake

CHRISTINE BALAZ

After passing Clegg Lake, the trail encounters a series of rather sizeable glacial lakes. Of these, Dean, Notch, and Bench Lakes are the largest the trail directly passes; all are signed. Bench Lake, the most scenic of all, offers open views of Notch Mountain's cliffy, northwesternmost ridgeline directly behind it and to the west.

After passing Bench Lake, the trail continues downhill and to the north for another 1.5 miles. Hikers here will notice the trail grow markedly fainter, as the trailside lakes—which attract fishermen and backpackers—disappear for the next 2.0 miles or so.

Beyond Bench Lake, the gradual downhill grade remains fairly constant for nearly 1.0 mile. After this, the path descends much more steeply for 0.8 mile to reach the low point of this route—elevation 9,740 feet. Here the trail curves to the west and arrives at a signed junction with the Weber River Trail. Stay left and follow signs for Meadow Lake.

The trail begins climbing again and just 0.3 mile later it reaches yet another junction. Here a 0.4-mile spur trail branches to the right (north) and toward Meadow Lake. This presents an easy addition to this chapter's hike; however, to stay on the primary route, hikers should stay left and follow signs for Wall and Trial Lakes.

After this junction with the Meadow Lake spur trail, the Notch Mountain Trail rounds over to the south and continues reclaiming lost elevation. As the trail nears Notch Mountain once again, it passes a broad area of pale quartzite slabs just before reaching Ibantik Lake. The open areas created by these provide expansive views of the mountain's very rugged north face—which is composed almost entirely of sheer quartzite cliffs.

Hikers reaching the shores of Ibantik Lake will have travelled 5.8 miles, and will have just entered the route's most scenic section. As the trail continues to climb toward the notch in Notch Mountain, it gains ever better views of this rocky peak, passing glacial lakes along the way. Above, the elongated mountain forms an imposing cirque. Behind (and to the north), the mountainous, lake-filled basin falls away.

On the final ascent into the notch, the trail passes numerous small lakes and thick fields of wildflowers. Just before the actual saddle, flat rock slabs provide excellent lookout points from which to enjoy the generous views to the north. About 1.3 miles after passing Ibantik Lake, the route reaches its high point, 10,655 feet—just 50 feet higher than the Bald Mountain parking area.

After crossing over the notch, the trail begins to descend again. In just a few hundred yards, it encounters a faint, unsigned junction. Stay left and follow the more obvious trail to continue southeast and toward Wall Lake. (Hikers failing to notice this junction will stay on the correct route.) About 1.5 miles before the end of the hike, the trail curves to the west and kisses the shores of this large body of water.

Just after passing Wall Lake, the trail forks. If you've left your vehicle at the Lily Lakes Trailhead, follow signs and stay right to reach it after just 1.0 mile of hiking. How-

Rain jackets: always a good idea in the Uintas
CHRISTINE BALAZ

ever, if the car is at the Trial Lake Trailhead, take the left fork to reach that parking lot after just 1.3 miles.

FEES, RESTRICTIONS, AND PERMITS
Dogs permitted; a Mirror Lake recreation fee is required of all those who park and recreate along UT 150; day-use passes cost $3, and other options are available

33

Bald Mountain

Type: Mountain; dirt and rock; out-and-back; extension possible

Season: Summer; not to be hiked in bad weather

Total Distance: 2.8 miles round-trip

Time: 1–2 hours

Rating: Moderate (high elevation)

Elevation Gain: 1,200 feet

Location: Mirror Lake Highway (UT 150), western Uinta Mountains

Maps: USGS MIRROR LAKE US TOPO

Contact: Uinta-Wasatch-Cache National Forest: Kamas Ranger District, 50 E. Center St., Kamas, UT 84036; 435-783-4338; www.fs.usda.gov/uwcnf

Trailhead GPS Coordinates: Bald Mountain Pass: N40 41.352 W110 54.249

Comments: A spectacularly lofty hike to a high summit in the western Uintas, this is not to be hiked if bad weather (wind, rain, snow, lightning) threatens. To best avoid bad weather, do this hike in the morning; afternoon thunderstorms regularly form in the Uintas during the summer months.

OVERVIEW

Departing from Bald Mountain Pass, this trail begins at 10,715 feet above sea level. It climbs steadily—though manageably—to the top of Bald Mountain, elevation 11,943, in just 1.4 miles. Properly named, this mountain is almost completely devoid of trees, allowing for birdlike views down onto the surrounding alpine mountainscape.

THE TRAIL

The Bald Mountain Trail originates at the obvious trailhead on the northern side of the Mirror Lake Highway at Bald Mountain Pass. In clear weather, the mountain itself is clearly visible from the parking area.

The hike begins on the northwestern edge of the parking lot, near the pit toilet and kiosk. From here, the trail heads due north into a forest of tall evergreen trees. Though numerous false trails leave the parking lot, the broad and well-worn main trail is easily identifiable.

Less than 0.1 mile from the parking lot, hikers encounter a fork in the trail. The Notch Mountain Trail (Chapter 32 of this book) heads left; to remain on this chapter's route, go right. Immediately beyond this junction, the path begins its steady ascent to Bald Mountain's summit. Shortly afterward, it enters a series of switchbacks trending to the northwest.

As the trail climbs ever higher on the south-facing slope of this massive mountain, the surrounding vegetation grows ever sparser and shorter. As such, the trail offers improving views of nearby landforms. To the south, the plateaulike Mount Murdock, elevation 11,212 feet, dominates the skyline. North and west of Murdock, UT 150 forms looping meanders through the high-altitude landscape. As it travels southwest, this scenic highway weaves through the gap between Lost and Teapot Lakes.

At 0.3 mile into the trip, the trail enters a long, west-trending switchback as it rises above the tree line and enters a section marked by pale blocks of quartzite. About 0.6 mile into the hike, the trail veers sharply to the northeast and begins ascending the rounded shoulder of the mountain. At 0.1 mile beyond this hairpin turn, hikers pass a

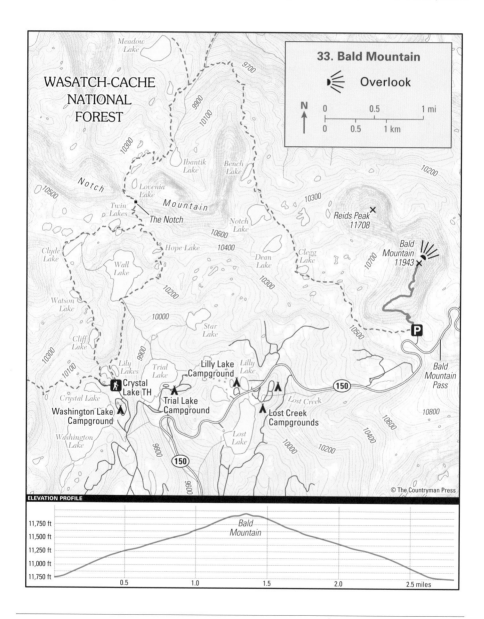

View down onto the high Uintas from the even higher Bald Mountain Trail   CHRISTINE BALAZ

short cylinder of these quartzite stones—presumably constructed in the interest of blocking the strong winds ever-present at 11,400 feet above sea level.

After heading more or less straight up this rounded, talus-covered shoulder for roughly 0.3 mile, the trail wraps around to the eastern side of the mountain. Here hikers experience airy views down onto the S-curves of UT 150 and Moosehorn Lake just north of them, as well as the large Mirror Lake farther to the northeast. After this brief section, the trail makes a sharp switchback to the left as it picks its way to the south and then west up through terraced rock ledges.

After this rocky section, the path wraps around the southern side of the summit ridge and bends to the north. Here it joins the summit ridge itself for the remaining 0.3 mile of the hike. If the sky is clear, this section of trail offers 360-degree views onto the surrounding High Uintas Wilderness landscape. To the northwest, Reids Peak, elevation 11,708

feet, stands less than 1.0 mile away. Odds are good, however, that clouds will swarm the peak, blocking all views—but nevertheless adding an element of high-altitude sensation.

Generally flat and broad, the ridge nevertheless pinches down to a thin spine just before the final summit. The peak itself is rather indistinct, and can be recognized by an impressive array of cairns. Hikers here have the feeling of being on top of the world as, in every direction, the landscape slopes down and away from Bald Mountain.

This chapter's route ends here, returning hikers to the parking lot by way of the same trail. However, the trail indeed continues to the north from the summit of Bald Mountain, down off the mountain, and then to the northeast. It joins the Weber Canyon Trail just before arriving at the Mirror Lake Highway near Pass Lake after roughly 2.0 additional trail miles. Those adding this stretch of hike should be advised that the trail north of the

Clouds moving in on Bald Mountain's exposed summit ridge DAVID SJÖQUIST

summit sees vastly less traffic than the route to this point, making it difficult to follow in parts. Additionally, the hike toward Pass Lake requires a shuttle vehicle or a 3.0 mile walk on roads to return hikers to the Bald Mountain Pass parking lot.

FEES, RESTRICTIONS, AND PERMITS
Dogs OK, but trail is too steep for bikes; a Mirror Lake recreation fee is required of all those who park and recreate along UT 150; day-use passes cost $3, and other options are available

34

Amethyst Basin

Type: Mountain; dirt and rock; out-and-back; side trips possible

Season: Summer

Total Distance: 10.9 miles round-trip

Time: 4–5 hours

Rating: Moderate/Strenuous

Elevation Gain: 2,000 feet

Location: Mirror Lake Highway (UT 150), western Uinta Mountains

Maps: USGS CHRISTMAS MEADOWS US TOPO and USGS HAYDEN PEAK US TOPO

Contact: Uinta-Wasatch-Cache National Forest: Kamas Ranger District, 50 E. Center St., Kamas, UT 84036; 435-783-4338; www.fs.usda.gov/uwcnf

Trailhead GPS Coordinates: Christmas Meadows Road: N40 49.352 W110 48.047

Comments: A significant amount of this hike falls within the High Uintas Wilderness; educate yourself about the rules and regulations regarding this area.

OVERVIEW

A long hike originating at a relatively low elevation (8,900 feet) in the Uinta Mountains, this trail climbs steadily into higher country, past open meadows, rocky waterfalls, and evergreen forests. As it nears its endpoint, Amethyst Lake, the trail enters a beautiful basin of the same name surrounded by gorgeous mountain peaks.

THE TRAIL

The trail leading to Amethyst Basin, Stillwater Fork Trail, departs from the end of Christmas Meadows Road—a popular access point among horse packers, backpackers, and day hikers. Heading due south from this road, it travels about 2.0 miles southward through the Uinta-Wasatch-Cache National Forest before entering the High Uintas Wilderness. Though a single trail at its origin, the path soon branches into numerous trails that explore the area's various basins.

Immediately after leaving the parking area, the trail passes by a kiosk. Posted there are current fire and wildlife advisories. Also at the kiosk is a large map depicting the High Uintas Wilderness, as well as the trails and mountain peaks within it. If you're unfamiliar with the restrictions particular to designated wilderness areas, take a moment to read the sign and learn about the rules in the area.

The first 2.5 miles of trail stick to the bottom of the Stillwater Fork Drainage. This flat and relatively open canyon bottom is characterized by large meadows lined with stands of tall evergreen and aspen trees.

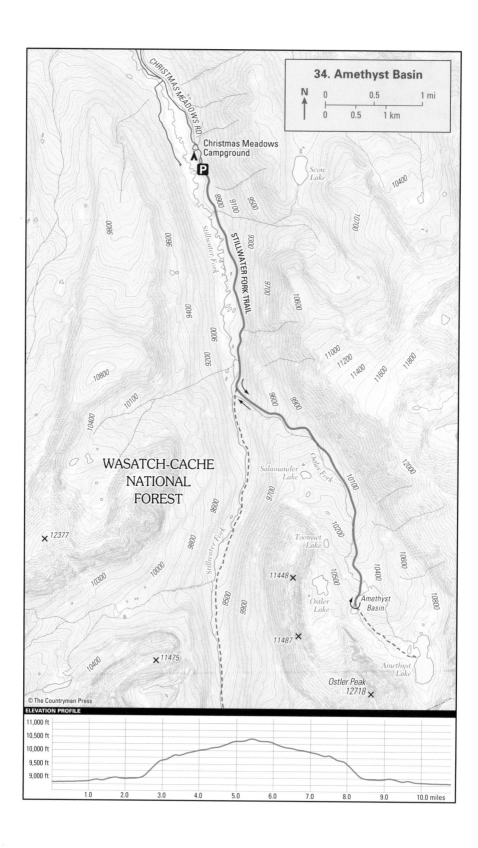

34. Amethyst Basin

N

| 0 | 0.5 | 1 mi |
| 0 | 0.5 | 1 km |

CHRISTMAS MEADOWS RD.

Christmas Meadows
Campground

P

Scow
Lake

STILLWATER FORK TRAIL

Stillwater Fork

WASATCH-CACHE
NATIONAL
FOREST

× 12377

Salamander
Lake

Ostler Fork

Toomset
Lake

11448 ×

Stillwater Fork

Ostler
Lake

Amethyst
Basin

11487 ×

Amethyst
Lake

× 11475

Ostler Peak
12718 ×

© The Countryman Press

ELEVATION PROFILE

	11,000 ft									
	10,500 ft									
	10,000 ft									
	9,500 ft									
	9,000 ft									
	1.0	2.0	3.0	4.0	5.0	6.0	7.0	8.0	9.0	10.0 miles

Like the drainage itself, the trail, too, is quite flat; however, due to rocky and often wet surface conditions, the path nevertheless mandates a fairly slow walking pace.

As the trail goes in and out of these meadows, it offers open views of the surrounding, tree-covered hillsides. Early in the hike, the tall spires of the Uintas are still hidden. However, toward the end of this flat section of trail, the taller peaks of this giant range begin to emerge in the distance.

Roughly 2.0 miles into the hike, the trail enters the High Uintas Wilderness. Marked by a sign, this boundary is impossible to miss. At 0.5 mile later, the trail enters a forest and splits in two. Our route into Amethyst Basin takes the left fork; the right fork continues south in the Stillwater Fork Drainage, and into West and Middle Basins.

Immediately after this signed junction, the trail to Amethyst Basin heads east and embarks on the steepest grade of its entire length. Hikers must endure 0.5 mile with a grade in excess of 21 percent. However steep this section of the route, it is made more enjoyable by nearness to a parallel stream cascading over broken slabs of quartzite. Called Ostler Fork, this small river forms numerous small waterfalls here as it drains the waters of Ostler and Amethyst Lakes.

As the trail climbs, it passes over many bare rock slabs itself. However, due to wear from foot traffic, the route remains easy to follow. On this steep ascent, the impressive Ostler and Spread Eagle Peaks come into better view, dominating the skyline to the southeast and south, respectively.

After roughly 3.0 miles of total walking, the trail rounds over and flattens out significantly. Though much less steep than in its previous section, it retains a grade of approximately 7 percent for the next 2.0 miles. During this section, the trail again bends to

the south as it maintains a course roughly parallel to Ostler Fork. Hikers here have attained a significantly higher elevation, and the trail's environs reflect that as it heads up the final, pitched bench leading into Amethyst Basin.

To either side, the massive mountains rimming the basin can be seen through the fir, spruce, and pine trees flanking the trail. The tree line here is readily apparent–and not

Christmas Meadows en route to Amethyst Basin   CHRISTINE BALAZ

Amethyst Lake and Ostler Peak

much higher than the hiker—as the mountains on all sides of the basin are lined with uninterrupted talus slopes and cliffs. Even in summer, these slopes carry large patches of snow.

Just before coming to Amethyst Lake, the trail passes by a large, wet meadow through which Ostler Fork meanders. Though it is tempting to assume this is the lake itself, it is not. Continue southward along the path just another few minutes and you'll reach the shores of the unmistakable Amethyst Lake. Directly behind the lake, imposing cliffs of orange quartzite tower above scree fields of their own creation. The summit of Ostler Peak, elevation 12,718 feet, stands just to the south of and behind these cliffs.

To return to your car, you have only to turn around and retrace your steps. Though other side trips are possible (at the junction 2.5 miles south of the parking area), these too are lengthy hikes in and of themselves—equal to or greater than the hike to Amethyst Lake in elevation gain and distance.

FEES, RESTRICTIONS, AND PERMITS

Dogs OK, but bikes not permitted within the High Uintas Wilderness (the majority of this route); groups larger than 14 persons and camping within 200 feet of a trail are also prohibited; a Mirror Lake recreation fee is required of all those who park and recreate along UT 150; day-use passes cost $3, and other options are available

35

Fisher Towers

Type: Desert; dirt; out-and-back

Season: Spring, Fall

Total Distance: 4.3 miles round-trip (sign at parking lot says 4.6 miles round-trip)

Time: 2–4 hours

Rating: Moderate

Elevation Gain: 750 feet

Location: Castle Valley, east of Moab

Maps: USGS FISHER TOWERS US TOPO

Contact: Bureau of Land Management: Moab Office, 82 E. Dogwood, Moab, UT 84532; 435-259-2100; www.blm.gov /ut/st/en/fo/moab.html

Trailhead GPS Coordinates: Fisher Towers Recreation Site: N38 43.489 W109 18.537

Comments: This trail offers up-close views of Utah's most bizarre collection of sandstone towers with a distant background of the famous Castle Valley and its formations.

OVERVIEW

The Fisher Towers Trail offers a unique opportunity to view awesome towers on a well-established, yet remote, trail with generous views of the famous Castle Valley and its soaring Wingate sandstone towers. The trail to the towers extends south from the parking area, descending at first, then steadily climbing to the base of the towers. Keep an eye out for rock climbers on the Fisher Towers; though composed of relatively muddy stone, they are popular among climbers for their very novel shapes. The trail continues nearly 1.0 mile beyond the towers, and ends at a rather arbitrary spot. The return hike offers an entirely new set of views, making the walk beyond the towers worth the effort.

THE TRAIL

The Fisher Towers Trail begins at the Fisher Towers Recreation Site, a BLM-operated primitive campground. Simply driving to this recreation area is a visual treat, with plentiful, wide-open views of the towers soaring high above the sagebrush-covered desert. Though the hike to the base of the towers is fairly significant, the road brings you as close as the terrain allows. Where the land becomes too rugged for vehicular travel, the BLM has constructed a well-defined parking lot with a pit toilet.

Here the landscape has deceptive qualities; though it seems that the towers are quite near, they actually stand more than 1.0 mile and a solid hiking effort away. From the parking lot, the trail departs in a southerly

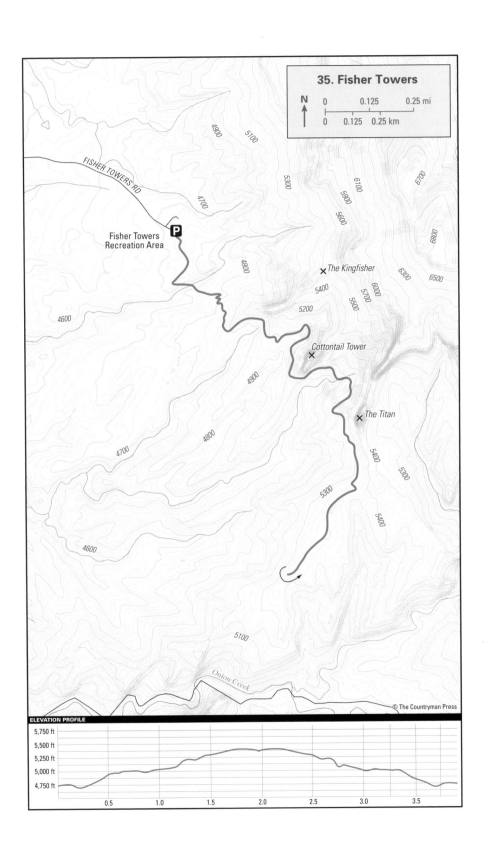

Approaching the corkscrew that the rock-climbing route, Ancient Art, ascends   DAVID SJÖQUIST

direction, heading downhill briefly. That the journey will be a longer than it first appeared immediately becomes clear, as the trail winds down and into a fairly complex system of gulches. Around 0.25 mile, the trail begins a steady ascent that remains rather consistent for the remainder of the hike.

The trail emerges from these ravines, and reaches the base of the towers rather quickly. It remains close to the Fisher Towers—sometimes near enough to touch them—for about 0.5 mile. The many rows of towers reveal themselves as the trail zigzags from one to the next. About 1.5 total miles of hiking brings you to the base of the Titan. At 900 feet in height, this is the largest and most dominant of all the towers. Allow yourself some time to stand beneath this proud feature and rubberneck. Its sheer walls and staggering height will amaze you, especially given its muddy appearance. Of all the Fisher

Towers, this was the first tackled by rock climbers—all the way back in 1962.

While standing beneath the Titan, look back to the north and try to spot any rock climbers that might be ascending the corkscrew-looking tower. The route ascending this feature, Ancient Art, is actually fairly moderate in difficulty (5.11-); this fact, its nearness to other rock climbing destinations, and the feature's utterly unique shape make it a goal for climbers around the world.

After the trail has passed by the towers, it continues working uphill and to the south. About 0.25 mile before its terminus, the grade eases up a good deal. Take advantage of this reprieve, and enjoy the views of Castle Valley's towers to the southeast. The trail's end is clearly marked with a faded wooden sign. Once there, turn around and enjoy a completely different perspective on the towers on the way down.

Looking north past the Fisher Towers toward the Colorado River from the trail's terminus

Fisher Towers

FEES, RESTRICTIONS, AND PERMITS

No fees or restrictions beyond standard BLM regulations; dogs OK; there is a pit toilet at the parking lot, but no garbage service—remove all trash

Westerns Galore: Local Film History

Even if you've never been to the area, you will surely recognize some of its features. Unless you are a rock climber, this is surely due to the area's rich silver screen history. More than two dozen major Hollywood movies have been shot in and around the Fisher Towers and Castle Valley. The more than six decades of movies filmed here include *Rio Grande, Warlock, Cheyenne Autumn, Against a Crooked Sky,* and *Nurse Betty.* Film buffs would greatly appreaciate a stop at the nearby Red Cliffs Lodge Movie Museum (Mile Marker 14 on UT 128, Moab, UT; 435-259-2002; www.redcliffslodge.com/museum) afterward. Admission is free, and it shares its location with a lodge, hotel, and local winery.

Rock or Mud?

Though by all appearances the Fisher Towers seem to consist of nothing more than mud drippings, they are in fact composed of sandstone belonging to the Cutler formation's Organ Rock Tongue, and are topped by a layer of Moenkopi sandstone. Formed by sediment deposition in an ancient floodplain, this rock sat atop significant salt beds. When the weight of overlying layers became too great, these underlying salt fields liquified and collapsed, causing the overlying layers to warp and crack as their base destabilized. The fissures formed by this event exposed the sandstone to erosive forces which, over time, carved these bizarre features. Those familiar with the geology of Arches National Park will recognize that this process is nearly identical to that which caused the crazy, mostly Navajo sandstone formations of that area. For 50 years, rock climbers have been scaling the faces of these towers and, despite their muddy appearance, the underlying rock is much sturdier than you would think.

36

Delicate Arch from Wolfe Ranch

Type: Desert; dirt and rock; out-and-back

Season: Any; beware of snow and ice on rock slabs

Total Distance: 3.1 miles round-trip

Time: 1–2 hours

Rating: Easy/Moderate

Elevation Gain: 550 feet

Location: Arches National Park, north of Moab

Maps: USGS THE WINDOWS SEC-TION US TOPO and USGS BIG BEND US TOPO

Contact: Arches National Park, 4 miles north of Moab on US 191; 435-719-2299; www.nps.gov/arch

Trailhead GPS Coordinates: Wolfe Ranch: N38 44.141 W109 31.256

Comments: This single hike is one of the most popular and iconic in the entire state. If you prefer to avoid crowds, consider doing this hike during the winter or very early in the morning from spring to autumn.

OVERVIEW

The Delicate Arch Trail offers a relatively short yet moderately challenging hike to the state's most famous landform. Along the way, it passes directly by a late 19th century ranch and quite near a petroglyph panel. In its short distance, the trail passes through a diverse collection of terrain, including a marshy wash, an extensive section of slickrock slabs, and a miniature canyon—all of this before popping over a rock spine and into plain view of Delicate Arch itself. This viewpoint—with the arch in the foreground, the La Sal Mountains in the far distance, and tilted desert strata in between—is one of the most jaw-dropping and unique in all of Utah.

THE TRAIL

Arches National Park currently sees more than 1 million visitors each year. This park has a limited road system and no shuttle buses. If you are like most people, you'll probably visit the park during the spring, summer, or fall. That said, if you arrive at the Wolfe Ranch parking lot in the middle of the day, you may very well not find a spot for your vehicle. If you wish to do this hike, beat the crowds by visiting in the off-season or arriving very early in the morning.

The Delicate Arch Trail originates at Wolfe Ranch, in the east-central portion of Arches National Park. Before even breaking a sweat (even on a hot day!), hikers immediately pass by the remains of this historic ranch, which stands near the junction of several meandering washes—a relative oasis in this otherwise

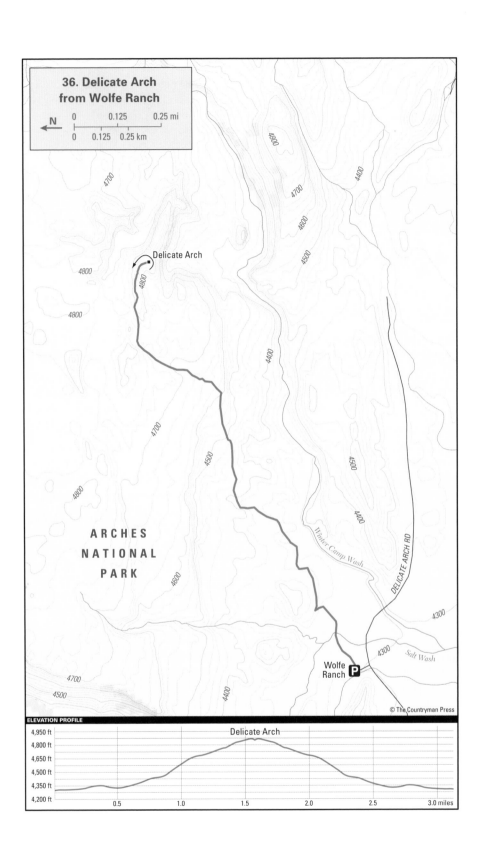

36. Delicate Arch from Wolfe Ranch

N

0   0.125   0.25 mi

0   0.125   0.25 km

4800

4700

4700

4400

4600

4500

Delicate Arch

4800

4800

4800

4400

4700

4500

4500

4800

4400

4600

4600

ARCHES
NATIONAL
PARK

Winter Camp Wash

DELICATE ARCH RD

4300

4700

4300   Salt Wash

4500

4400

Wolfe
Ranch P

© The Countryman Press

ELEVATION PROFILE

Delicate Arch

4,950 ft
4,800 ft
4,650 ft
4,500 ft
4,350 ft
4,200 ft

0.5   1.0   1.5   2.0   2.5   3.0 miles

ultradry environment. Hikers may approach, but not enter, the old cabin.

From here, the broad dirt trail climbs very gradually and then descends briefly into a miniature riparian zone. The path crosses over the marshy Salt Wash by way of a foot-bridge. If you're interested in seeing petro-glyphs, keep your eye out for a side trail to your left (north). A brief detour leads to rock art created by indigenous Ute peoples. This well-preserved panel clearly depicts a hunting scene consisting of more than a dozen figures, including bighorn sheep, dogs, and other animals, as well as horseback riders.

At about 0.5 mile into the hike, the trail begins its most serious ascent, making a beeline up a domed slickrock slab. During peak tourist season, staying on the trail is as simple as looking for, and following, other people. However, if you find yourself here alone, keep your eyes open and look for cairns and faint discoloration of the slabs caused by foot traffic. As you climb higher and higher, you'll gain increasingly open views of the Winter Camp Wash and the small valley it has created.

The slab section of the trail, with its unim-peded views and moderately steep (roughly 12 percent) incline, may seem strenuous. Don't rush, and take your time. Add your own switchbacks if necessary. With very little warning, the trail pops atop the slab and into a miniature canyon adorned with Utah ju-niper, sagebrush, Mormon tea, blackbrush, and various grasses. These plants have rooted themselves in small sandbars in the deepest parts of this bowllike sandstone basin.

The route to Delicate Arch, marked by cairns, continues making its way east

Slickrock ridge across from Delicate Arch

DAVID SJÖQUIST

Delicate Arch from Wolfe Ranch

Delicate Arch: Utah's most iconic rock formation

through this feature, and eventually works its way up toward the southern canyon rim and a fin of rock atop it. A small arch, Frame Arch, forms a hole in this fin. Through Frame Arch, Delicate Arch is visible; take a sneak peak if you'd like. Otherwise, keep walking along the path, noticing the handful of appetizer arches in front of you and to your left. A natural, sidewalklike ledge forms the final stretch of walkway as the trail makes its way past a view-occluding rock fin and into plain view of Delicate Arch.

This incredible feature stands 65 feet tall. An impressive sculpture in and of itself, Delicate Arch is greatly enriched by its surroundings. Beneath it, a sculpted and slanting basin of Navajo sandstone forms a smooth base. This falls away sharply behind the arch, yielding to distant layers of cliff bands, each tilting in a different direction. Behind it all, the La Sal Mountains form a gorgeous panoramic backdrop. This volcanic range, which stands just southeast of Moab, has a top elevation of 12,721 feet at its high-

50 Hikes in Utah

est point, Mount Peale. Even more impressive, this range stands nearly 8,700 feet above the town of Moab—a roughly 1.5 vertical mile rise. Because of its extreme elevation, the La Sal Mountains almost always have some snow cover, rendering them an even more stunning backdrop for this desert rock formation.

FEES, RESTRICTIONS, AND PERMITS

Visitors to Arches National Park must pay $10 for a 7-day pass, federal America the Beautiful passes are accepted; no dogs allowed off-pavement in Arches National Park, so leave dogs at home; to hike with dogs, consider visiting the nearby Dead Horse Point State Park's Rim Trail (Chapter 37 in this book) or the Fisher Towers Trail (Chapter 35 in this book).

The History of Wolfe Ranch

In 1898, Civil War veteran John Wesley Wolfe and his family moved from Ohio to what is now Arches National Park and erected a homestead along Salt Wash. The ranch consisted of 100 acres, a one-room cabin, and a corral. Though surrounded by generally dry and inhospitable lands, this particular locale tempted Wolfe to settle in with its relative wetness. The Wolfes erected a dam across Salt Wash to collect water and were able to raise a few head of cattle at any time. In 1906, the family built a more "modern" cabin with a wooden floor to replace the original; amazingly, this "improvement" is what you see today. The Wolfe family remained in the area just more than a decade before giving up and heading back east toward civilization in Etna, Ohio.

37

Dead Horse Point Rim Trail

*Type: Desert; dirt, rock, and pavement;
loop with several spurs*

Season: Fall–Spring

*Total Distance: 8.4 miles round-trip (about
1.0 mile less if skipping the spurs)*

Time: 2.5–4 hours

Rating: Moderate

Elevation Gain: 150 feet

*Location: Dead Horse Point State Park,
west of Moab*

*Maps: USGS SHAFER BASIN US
TOPO*

*Contact: Dead Horse Point State Park,
end of UT 313 (30 miles from Moab);
435-259-2614; http://stateparks.utah
.gov/parks/dead-horse*

*Trailhead GPS Coordinates: Dead
Horse Point State Park Visitors Center:
N38 29.266 W109 44.159*

*Comments: This scenic hike tours the
edge of the landform around which this
state park is centered; the hike, though
flat, is quite exposed in many places.
Use extra caution in the event of high or
gusty winds.*

OVERVIEW

Dead Horse Point is a portion of high desert plateau that towers 2,000 vertical feet above the Colorado River directly below. Connected to the main mesa by a mere filament, this virtual island is supported on all sides by sheer sandstone cliffs, and offers extremely scenic views down upon the desert canyons beneath it. The Dead Horse Point Rim Trail departs from the state park's visitors center, crosses onto the point, and tours its entire perimeter—often coming quite near to the edge of this lofty island. Within your time constraints and hiking stamina, take as many spur trails as possible, as these afford the route's best views. Be aware that, particularly in the second half of the hike, the trail can be nebulous and somewhat difficult to follow; keep a sharp eye out and follow your instincts to stay on the path. Picking up a free map at the visitors center will help you stay on track and better select which spur trails to take.

THE TRAIL

Dead Horse Point State Park stands almost exactly on the way from Moab to Canyonlands National Park's Island in the Sky district. Requiring but a 5-mile detour, this state park is one of Utah's most photographed areas and easily warrants the additional driving. Day hikers will appreciate this state park perhaps more than Canyonlands National Park; Dead Horse Point's major trail, the Rim Trail, tours a lofty mesa and circumnavigates the entirety of Dead Horse Point, forming a

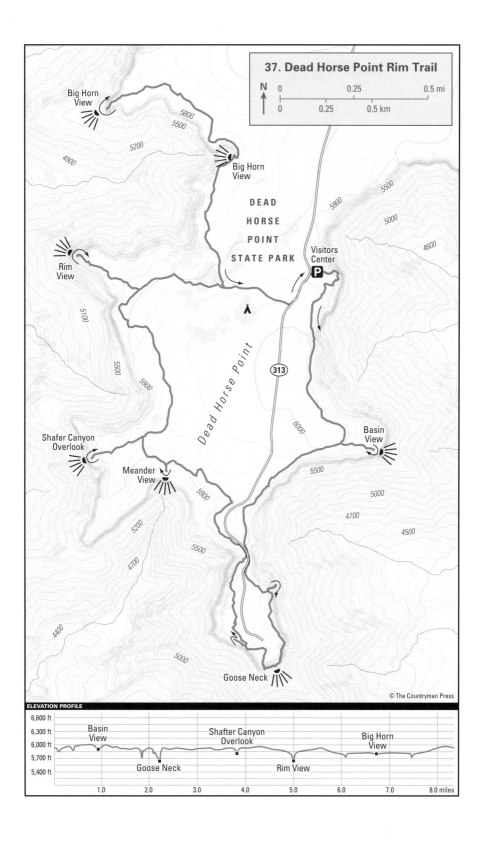

37. Dead Horse Point Rim Trail

N

| 0 | | 0.25 | | 0.5 mi |

| 0 | 0.25 | 0.5 km |

Big Horn
View

5800
5500
5200
4900

Big Horn
View

**DEAD
HORSE
POINT
STATE PARK**

5900
5500
5000
4600

Rim
View

Visitors
Center

P

5100

5500

5900

313

Dead Horse Point

6000

Shafer Canyon
Overlook

Meander
View

Basin
View

5500

5000

4700

4500

5200

5900

4700

5500

4400

5000

Goose Neck

© The Countryman Press

ELEVATION PROFILE

6,600 ft							
6,300 ft	Basin		Shafter Canyon			Big Horn	
6,000 ft	View		Overlook			View	
5,700 ft							
5,400 ft		Goose Neck		Rim View			
	1.0	2.0	3.0	4.0	5.0	6.0	7.0	8.0 miles

Looking east from Dead Horse Point onto the Intrepid Potash, Inc. evaporation ponds   DAVID SJÖQUIST

very natural and incredibly scenic loop around these spectacular features. The Rim Trail, though long, features almost no elevation change, allowing hikers to cover a great distance in a short period of time.

The trail begins at the Dead Horse Point State Park visitors center parking lot. A short, self-guided loop trail can be taken by leaving the parking lot on its eastern side. This hike takes but a minute or two and points out various natural features along the way. The Rim Trail cuts to the south from this loop, and heads across the flat, sandy mesa top, dotted with sagebrush and juniper.

Looking to your right, it would appear that you were walking across an ordinary desert plain. However, looking to the left reveals more than 300 million years of earthy brown and red geology exposed by the 2,000-foot-deep meanders of the Colorado River. Almost otherworldly in appearance, this wild and vast desert canyon landscape and the

space above it creates a great feeling of exposure. The Colorado snakes through the scene in a series of enormous loops, weaving in and out of sandstone towers and fins perched atop tiered pedestals. As if painted by an artist, the colors of the towers fade incrementally from the foreground into the distance.

The trail continues to work its way around the mesa's southeastern edge. Signed spur trails lead to the brink of the plateau, while the main trail works its way across its scenic center. Though the vistas continue to hold the same theme throughout the trail's entire course, each subsequent overlook offers subtly different glimpses of the canyon lands below.

The path continues south, approaches the actual Dead Horse Point, and crosses onto it 1.6 miles into the hike. Because of the extremely narrow width of the land connecting Dead Horse Point to the main plateau, the trail unavoidably joins with the road for a short section before entering the point. Once on the actual point, the trail bends east and away from the road again, entering a very scenic portion of the route that maintains a cliff-edge perspective around Dead Horse Point. Here the point is so small that vistas offer much greater than 180-degree angles of view. Though rock walls protect visitors from the precipitous drop-offs, exercise extreme caution during windy conditions.

The trail reaches its southernmost point, marked by shelters and signs, after 2.25 miles of walking. Though on maps, this appears the to be the rough halfway point of the route, you are realistically only ¼ of the way through the hike at this point; the remaining hike, including all spur trails, stretches about 6.15 more miles. If you do complete the entire route, you will be af-

forded spectacular views from the western half of Dead Horse Point and the plateau to its north. Along the way, Canyonlands National Park's Island in the Sky dominates the views to the west and southwest.

If, however, you do skip the spur trails, you can save yourself about 1.0 mile of hiking on the return trip. Those tired at this point can dramatically shorten the trip by walking back to the visitors center along the road; this option requires just 1.5 miles of hiking.

FEES, RESTRICTIONS, AND PERMITS
Visitors to Dead Horse Point State Park must pay $10 for a day pass, and federal America the Beautiful passes are not accepted; dogs are allowed in Dead Horse Point State Park, but not on the Intrepid Trail—if you plan to hike or bike on that trail, leave dogs at home

Colorado River meanders from Dead Horse Point   DAVID SJÖQUIST

The Gruesome Legend of Dead Horse Point: Fact or Fiction?

From a modern perspective, the landform of Dead Horse Point is a spectacular place from which to view the Colorado River canyons below. However, from a late 19th century standpoint, this place served as an extremely clever place to corral horses; an entire herd could be kept on the point with just 50 feet or so of fencing to barricade the neck of the point, and close it off from the main plateau. According to popular legend, cowboys herded wild mustangs onto the point but, for unknown reasons, deserted the area and left the horses stranded without water. Exposed to the elements, these horses perished. However, some historians say this story was invented as a means to attract tourism, claiming that the real story behind the name is much less brutal. According to this camp, early Mormon pioneers named the plateau Dead Horse Point after a clearly visible rock formation at its base that resembles a dead horse.

What the Heck Is That?

Early in the hike, you won't be able to avoid seeing an enormous, shiny field in the distance. These reflective blue spots on the desert floor are solar evaporative ponds owned and operated by Intrepid Potash, Inc. Millions of years ago, ancient seas covered this land. The seas eventually evaporated, leaving behind enormous fields of potassium chloride, or "potash," salt. Over time these salt beds were covered with subsequent layers of sediments. Today Intrepid Potash pumps water down into the subterranean potash formation, dissolving the salt. The salt water is then brought back to the surface, where it is dyed with blue pigment and spread out on vinyl to hasten its evaporation. Once dry, the potassium chloride is collected, refined, and used as a primary ingredient in plant fertilizer.

38

Cohab Canyon

Type: Desert; dirt; out-and-back; side trips possible

Season: Spring–Fall

Total Distance: 3.4 miles round-trip

Time: 1.5–2.5 hours

Rating: Easy/Moderate

Elevation Gain: 900 feet (450 feet the way out; 450 feet on return trip)

Location: Capitol Reef National Park

Maps: USGS FRUITA US TOPO

Contact: Capitol Reef National Park Visitors Center, intersection of UT 24 and Scenic Drive, Torrey, UT 84775; 435-425-3791; www.nps.gov/care

Trailhead GPS Coordinates: Gifford Homestead: N38 17.048 W111 14.824

Comments: This canyon provides some respite from the heat; however, during summer, when the sun is directly overhead, there is very little shade to be found. Bring plenty of water and sunscreen.

OVERVIEW

This trail tours the length of a small, hidden canyon. It takes a 1.7-mile beeline northeast across the Waterpocket Fold, from the Scenic Drive and the Gifford Homestead to the Fremont River and UT 24. From the trailhead, the path climbs quickly before turning and plunging into the relatively cool, hidden Cohab Canyon. The trail climbs for a total of 0.6 mile before gradually descending toward the Freemont River. Those wishing to cut this hike in half can do so easily by leaving a shuttle car at either end of the trail; conversely, those wishing to add distance may do so by leaving a vehicle at the end of the Grand Wash Road and taking the Frying Pan Trail and the Cassidy Arch Trail into the Grand Wash (recommended with a map).

THE TRAIL

Though this trail can be hiked from either end, this book's version of the hike begins at the Gifford Homestead, as those hiking this route would in all likelihood also enjoy checking out Captiol Reef National Park's Scenic Drive, the historic town of Fruita, and the Gifford Homestead. However, those driving through the park on UT 24 wanting to skip the Scenic Drive detour may just as easily start at the opposite end of the trail.

Our route begins at the Gifford Homestead parking lot and includes 0.1 mile of southerly walking along the Scenic Drive. The trail departs from the road and begins ascending the hillside on the opposite side of the road. The initial climbing is steady and

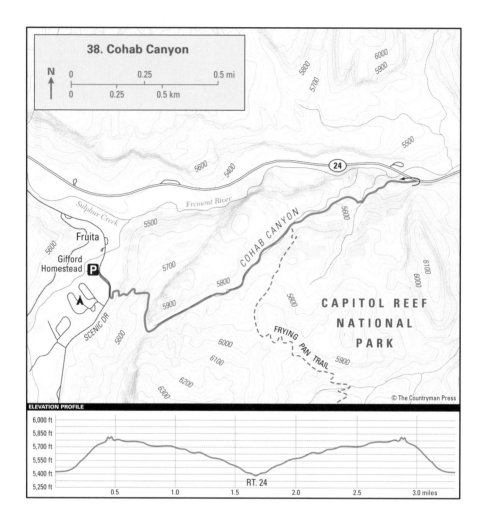

38. Cohab Canyon

N

0   0.25   0.5 mi

0   0.25   0.5 km

Fruita

Gifford Homestead

Sulphur Creek

Fremont River

COHAB CANYON

FRYING PAN TRAIL

CAPITOL REEF NATIONAL PARK

SCENIC DR

© The Countryman Press

ELEVATION PROFILE

6,000 ft						
5,850 ft						
5,700 ft						
5,550 ft						
5,400 ft			RT. 24			
5,250 ft	0.5	1.0	1.5	2.0	2.5	3.0 miles

moderate on switchbacks that cut through deep red soil strewn with peculiar-looking black boulders that quite resemble bowling balls. This is the sunniest, most open portion of the hike, and it lasts about 0.4 mile. Be sure to take your time and enjoy the views afforded by the trail's meanders; from these, the quaint town and green lands of Fruita contrast scenically with the surrounding orange-and-red desertscape.

After its initial climb, the trail nearly reaches the cliff bands topping the hillside and traverses beneath them for a short distance. A total of 0.5 mile of walking brings hikers to a pile of large boulders at the mouth of Cohab Canyon. From these, you can steal one final look back out and down into the Fruita Valley. Rounding these boulders, the path plunges into the canyon. Walled by pale yellow and orange cliffs filled with round pockets, Cohab Canyon is rather narrow and squat at first. Here the trail turns downhill and stays this way until it reaches UT 24. Multiple slot canyons join Cohab Canyon on either side; if you have extra time, walk into these extremely narrow notches and enjoy their refrigeration.

As the trail continues to work its way down the canyon, the cliffs lining it on either side round off and turn from sheer walls into domed slabs. The canyon opens ever more and gains a very sandy bottom. Don't try to hurry through this section, as it will only prove frustrating and unproductive. Take it easy and keep your eyes pointed toward the horizon to steal possible glimpses of resident bighorn sheep. The canyon continues to broaden, and the domed rock slabs give way to terraced hillsides, revealing the grand Captiol Reef landscape in the background.

Suddenly the trail comes to the edge of a hillside overlooking the Freemont River. In just a few minutes' walking, hikers make their way down this embankment and toward UT 24. If you're hot, cross the highway and dip your feet in the river. From here, you can return either the way you came or find the shuttle car you had parked here in advance.

FEES, RESTRICTIONS, AND PERMITS
Visitors to Capitol Reef National Park's Scenic Drive must pay $5 at the self-serve fee tube for a 7-day pass, and federal America the Beautiful passes are accepted; no dogs are allowed off-pavement in Captiol Reef National Park, so leave dogs at home

Historic Fruita

Utah, one of the most rugged, isolated, and arid pieces of land in the United States, didn't see European settlement until 1847, when Mormon pioneers arrived in Salt Lake City. An even more extreme example of craggy and inaccessible landscape, the Captiol Reef area wasn't home to permanent settlers until nearly 40 years later. However, once there, early residents found Fruita's land—located at the confluence of Sulphur Creek and the Fremont River—to be quite fertile. These Mormon settlers were able to grow vegetables, alfalfa, sorghum, and plentiful fruit orchards—to this day, roughly three thousand of these trees still stand. These diverse crops largely supported the economy of the town, despite the intense difficulty of exporting them across the rugged landscape. In 1896, the townspeople erected the one-room schoolhouse that today stands along UT 24. In 1937, Capitol Reef became a national monument, and in 1971 a national park. The National Park Service gradually bought the land from residents and the town of Fruita became extinct.

Gifford Homestead Barn across from western trailhead of Cohab Canyon   DAVID SJÖQUIST

Looking into Cohab Canyon from its western entrance

DAVID SJÖQUIST

The Gifford Homestead

Located along today's Scenic Drive, this homestead is one of the best known structures of historic Fruita. Renovated by the National Park Service and the Capitol Reef Natural History Association, the main house of this farm serves to depict that of late 19th and early 20th century residents of Fruita and, by extension, rural Utah. Built in 1908, this home belonged to Calvin Pendleton, a polygamist—quite an impressive fact, given the structure's size. The namesake Gifford family did not come into ownership until 1928, and they resided in it until 1969, when the National Park Service purchased it and the land. Today you can buy homemade baked goods and jams in the house, check out the smokehouse and barn, and purchase handicrafts.

Frying Pan Trail

After 1.1 miles, the Frying Pan Trail intersects the Cohab Canyon Trail from the south. One of the most scenic routes in the entire park, the Frying Pan Trail requires either a shuttle vehicle or a full day of speedy hiking to complete; this trail stretches 3.0 miles to reach the Cassidy Arch Trail, which is still another 1.0 mile from the trailhead at the Grand Wash. All told, the one-way distance to hike this Cohab/Frying Pan/Cassidy Arch Trail/Grand Wash route would be 5.0 miles with an elevation gain of nearly 1,300 vertical feet; round-trip it would be 10 miles and double the elevation gain. If you're interested in this route, but don't have a second car, consider instead just walking part of the Frying Pan Trail and then turning around.

39

Cassidy Arch

Type: Desert; dirt and rock; out-and-back; side trips possible

Season: Spring–Fall; watch for snow during early spring

Total Distance: 3.3 miles round-trip (National Park Service says 3.5 miles)

Time: 1.5–2 hours

Rating: Moderate

Elevation Gain: 550 feet

Location: Capitol Reef National Park

Maps: USGS FRUITA US TOPO

Contact: Capitol Reef National Park Visitors Center, intersection of UT 24 and Scenic Drive, Torrey, UT 84775; 435-425-3791; www.nps.gov/care

Trailhead GPS Coordinates: End of Grand Wash Road: N38 15.822 W111 12.944

Comments: Do not attempt to reach the parking area for this hike in the event of a significant storm; the trail originates in the Grand Wash and is prone to flash flooding.

OVERVIEW

Located in the center of the main portion of Captiol Reef National Park, this relatively short hike is easily accessible. Featuring views of the beautiful Grand Wash and sturdy Cassidy Arch, this hike offers fantastic views of untainted Wild West landscape. The route begins by descending gradually into the Grand Wash for a short period, then cutting back and uphill, away from the wash bottom. A short section of switchbacks and steady climbing yield quickly to a more gradual section of trail that offers fantastic views of the Grand Wash below. As the route climbs slowly, it traces contour lines around finger canyons before popping out onto its final section of cairn-marked slickrock. The impressive Cassidy Arch itself marks the end of the hike. Those with extra energy before or after this hike might enjoy walking farther down the Grand Wash before returning to the car.

THE TRAIL

The trail begins where the Grand Wash Road ends. From the parking lot, this path begins as a foot trail and then quickly heads down into the obvious wash. From here, two hikes are possible: one into the Grand Wash itself, and the other up toward the Cassidy Arch. To follow this route to the arch, keep a sharp eye out for the Cassidy Arch Trail, which splits off to the left after about 0.2 mile of hiking. Though marked by a permanent sign, the junction itself is nevertheless easy to miss if you're not paying attention.

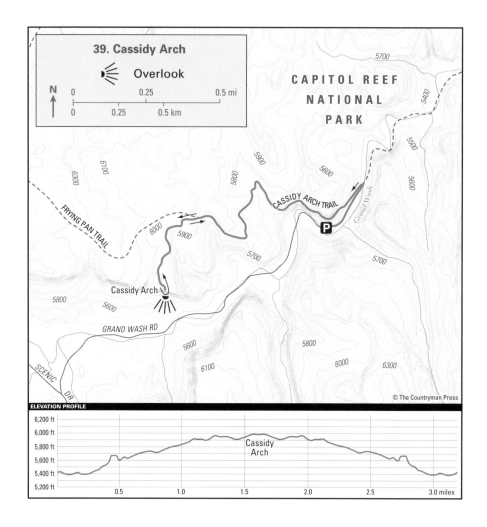

ELEVATION PROFILE

To take the Cassidy Arch Trail, make a sharp left immediately and begin ascending the northern, cliffy walls of the wash. Where the route would otherwise be difficult to pass, the National Park Service has made it more user-friendly with the addition of stone blocks and cut steps. Very quickly the trail reaches the top of the first major cliff band, along which it traces for a while, providing excellent views (and a little exposure!) down into the wash and back toward the west.

After this initial climb of roughly 0.25 mile, the trail becomes significantly less steep, though it does continue to climb gradually. As it continues forward, the trail hugs the hillside, winding in and out of colorful finger canyons and past Utah juniper, pinyon pine, and numerous shrub species, all very thinly scattered along this landscape of stone and sand. As the trail passes through layers of deep red and rich ivory rock bands, keep your eye out to the west to catch early views

50 Hikes in Utah

of the Cassidy Arch, the top of which is level with the top of the wash.

About 1.25 miles into the hike, the trail reaches a junction with the Frying Pan Trail. To stay on this chapter's route, turn left as for Cassidy Arch. At 0.2 mile after this junction, the trail heads out across slickrock slabs. Cairns lead the way across sloping red and white stretches of bald sandstone. Brightly colored and tilted, these are somewhat reminiscent of cartoon scenery. About 0.2 mile later, the trail ends naturally across from the Cassidy Arch. From the trail's terminus, you can see down and through this arch and into the Grand Wash several hundred feet below. Behind it, the wash cuts eastwardly through the brightly colored sandstone of the Waterpocket Fold.

This is the end of the Cassidy Arch Trail. To get back to your vehicle, turn around and return exactly as you came.

FEES, RESTRICTIONS, AND PERMITS

Visitors to Capitol Reef National Park's Scenic Drive must pay $5 at the self-serve fee tube for a 7-day pass, and federal America the Beautiful passes are accepted; no dogs are allowed off-pavement in Captiol Reef National Park, so leave dogs at home; horses not permitted on this trail

Frying Pan Trail Detour: Shuttle Car Advised

From the junction with the Frying Pan Trail, you can continue walking about 3.0 miles to reach Cohab Canyon (a canyon roughly parallel to and north of the Grand Wash); the trail intersects Cohab Canyon Trail (Chapter 38 of this book) about 0.5 mile west of its junction with UT 24, and 1.0 mile east of the Scenic Drive and the Gifford Homestead. One of the most scenic routes in the park, the

Looking east onto Cassidy Arch

Looking west out of the Grand Wash from Cassidy Arch Trail   DAVID SJÖQUIST

Frying Pan Trail requires a lot of elevation gain—nearly 700 additional vertical feet—but rewards its hikers with very little crowding and fantastic scenery. Those wishing to complete this entire journey are advised to bring a map and park a shuttle car at both ends of the route; to complete a round-trip journey on foot would require a huge amount of hiking.

The Grand Wash: An Easy Extension

Once you've descended the entire length of the Cassidy Arch Trail and find yourself back at the bottom of the Grand Wash, you may consider extending your journey by walking yet farther into this scenic gorge. As it gradually descends, the wash grows ever narrower, with is walls becoming sheerer and sheerer. About 2.0 miles from the parking area, the wash enters a section called The Narrows. Here the walls stretch hundreds of feet overhead and stand as close as 15 feet apart. Be warned: This hike is to be avoided at all costs in the event of heavy rain. One of just a few washes cutting through the Waterpocket Fold, this is responsible for draining a huge expanse of land. With featureless, vertical walls, this wash becomes a death trap during flash floods.

40

Golden Throne

Type: Desert; dirt; out-and-back

Season: Spring–Fall; hot in summer

Total Distance: 3.9 miles

Time: 1.5–2.5 hours

Rating: Moderate

Elevation Gain: 700 feet

Location: Capitol Reef National Park

Maps: USGS GOLDEN THRONE US TOPO

Contact: Capitol Reef National Park Visitors Center, intersection of UT 24 and Scenic Drive, Torrey, UT 84775; 435-425-3791; www.nps.gov/care

Trailhead GPS Coordinates: Capitol Gorge: N38 12.580 W111 10.158

Comments: Do not attempt to reach the parking area, located in the Capitol Gorge, during significant precipitation; flash flooding is likely and extremely dangerous.

OVERVIEW

A relatively remote trail for the main section of Captitol Reef National Park, this route traverses across colorful finger canyons of the Waterpocket Fold and high into "dome country." As the trail climbs, hikers are afforded beautiful close-up views of the park's colorful rock bands, as well as far-off glimpses of the Navajo Mountains. Stay on the trail to avoid trampling thick patches of mature cryptobiotic soil found along the way. This trail features steady yet reasonable climbing along its entire length.

THE TRAIL

This route's sightseeing opportunities begin well in advance of the trailhead. Motoring south from the Captiol Reef National Park visitors center, you'll traverse some fantastically colorful scenery along Scenic Drive en route to the Capitol Gorge Road itself. Once on this section of the drive, the road plunges into this namesake gorge in an M. C. Escher–like fashion, cutting through the tilted and uplifted rock layers on either side as it is swallowed up by the mountainous landscape on its eastward descent into the steep Waterpocket Fold.

Departing from the parking area at the end of this road, the trail doubles quickly back to the west, climbing above the Capitol Gorge Road. During its initial ascent, the trail stays near this road, offering ever higher views down into the Captiol Gorge. Quickly, the trail curves to the north and away from the gorge, tracing into a colorful side canyon.

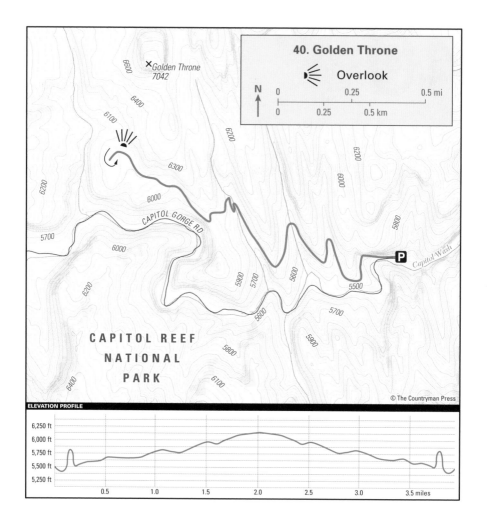

To the hiker's left, a steep sandstone chute eats into the earth. The trail traverses above this and across rust-red soil; ahead, enormous, ivory-colored cliffs tower above the hiker, pinching down on themselves and forming a tight maze in the distance. The trail approaches this labyrinth of walls, but bends left (west) again to traverse around the cliff bands and reveal yet another side canyon. As the trail wraps around this rock mountain, the landscape gradually changes character

again, revealing blocky, orange cliffs in place of wind-buffed ivory walls. Rising ever higher, the path features yet more views down into the Capitol Gorge with increasingly expansive vistas of the surrounding landscape. The underlying structure of the Waterpocket Fold becomes apparent, with parallel layers of tilted stone rising from east to west, visible in all directions. Bands of deep red, bone white, and pumpkin orange rock and soil bear sparse coverings of Utah juniper,

50 Hikes in Utah

pinyon pine, and various cactus species, as well as huge patches of mature cryptobiotic soil. Stay on the trail at all times to avoid destroying this fragile and vital soil guardian!

The trail ends at the fantastic viewpoint of Golden Throne. From the route's terminus, this massive, deep orange dome dominates the skyline. Sitting atop bleached white cliffs and dark red soil skirting them, this dome tops a rainbow of desert features. Looking to the south, you'll notice views of the deep blue, usually snow-covered Navajo Mountains rising in the background. From here, turn around and retrace your steps to arrive back at your car.

FEES, RESTRICTIONS, AND PERMITS

Visitors to Capitol Reef National Park's Scenic Drive must pay $5 at the self-serve fee tube for a 7-day pass, and federal America the Beautiful passes are accepted; no dogs are allowed off-pavement in Captiol Reef National Park, so leave dogs at home

Old Highway through Capitol Gorge

Capitol Reef was given its name by pioneers for the impediment it placed on their travel. Nearly impenetrable, this dramatic, 100-mile-long fold in the earth's crust severely hindered east-west travel in the area. With only five gorges penetrating this formidable

The Golden Throne itself

Golden Throne Trail weaving in and out of side canyons on its ascent   DAVID SJÖQUIST

wrinkle in the earth's crust, early 20th century road makers had very limited choices when selecting their construction sites. Thus, when Capitol Reef was established as a national monument in 1937, very few roads existed in the area—and all were dirt, very rugged, and only passable in summer.

UT 24 was constructed by the Civilian Conservation Corps, and it originally traversed through the Capitol Gorge. However, the constant bombardment by heavy rains and subsequent flash flooding presented enormous headaches to road managers in the form of erosion and massive debris piles. By the late 1950s it became clear that a new route was required, and in the early 1960s construction for a new UT 24 began along the Fremont River. By 1962, the highway was completed in its current location, leaving Scenic Drive as a partial reminder of the old route. Unfortunately, the former location of

the highway exposed many historic petroglyphs to vandals. Today many of the petroglyphs visible in the Capitol Gorge bear unfortunate degradation.

Capitol Gorge: A Casual Addition

Those looking to extend their journey with some easy mileage would be well-served to take a stroll down into the Captiol Gorge from the same parking lot. Extending 1.25 miles into the gorge, this trail features mostly level walking with views of natural water tanks along the way (reached by a short side trail), petroglyphs, and an early Mormon pioneer register. This register features the names of many pioneers carved directly into the walls of the canyon, as well as the dates of these people's passages. Unfortunately, these panels suffered a good deal of vandalism back when UT 24 passed through this gorge. However damaged, they still warrant the walk!

41

Chimney Rock Loop

Type: Desert; dirt; lollipop-shaped; side trips possible

Season: Spring–Fall; hot in summer

Total Distance: 3.5 miles round-trip

Time: 1.5–2.5 hours

Rating: Moderate/Strenuous

Elevation Gain: 900 feet (650 feet the way out; 250 feet on return trip)

Location: Capitol Reef National Park

Maps: USGS TWIN ROCKS US TOPO

Contact: Capitol Reef National Park Visitors Center, intersection of UT 24 and Scenic Drive, Torrey, UT 84775; 435-425-3791; www.nps.gov/care

Trailhead GPS Coordinates: Chimney Rock Trailhead: N38 18.936 W111 18.236

Comments: This is arguably among Utah's most scenic hikes, especially in the desert category. This route is best done around sunset, when the landscape becomes supersaturated in low-angle light.

OVERVIEW

The Chimney Rock Loop offers a lollipop-shaped tour through Capitol Reef National Park. Located immediately off UT 24, this is conveniently located in the no-pay zone of the park. Easily accessible, this single hike is perhaps the most beautiful in the entire park. The trail climbs steeply to overlook Chimney Rock itself, then makes a counter-clockwise loop through hidden backcountry. En route it overlooks the enormous, uplifted feature around which this national park is centered: the Waterpocket Fold. Along the hike you'll see a rainbow of sandstone formations in all different shapes and sizes, sprinkled with a thin covering of desert vegetation including pinyon pine, buffaloberry, and various cactus species.

THE TRAIL

Captiol Reef National Park is one of Utah's most spectacular hidden gems. Tucked in the middle of south-central Utah, and centered around one of its most impassable geological formations, this park is neither on the direct Arches-Canylonlands-Moab circuit, nor in the immediate vicinity of Zion, Bryce, or the Grand Staircase–Escalante National Monument. As such, it is often skipped by those on Utah's tourist circuits and thus offers a deserted, days-of-yore feel that serves only to enhance its striking natural beauty and the impression it bestows upon visitors.

The trail departs from the parking area in a northerly direction, giving hikers a 0.3-mile warm-up of relatively level walking across grass-covered flats before encountering and then ascending a brightly colored hillside. Before you know it, the trail suddenly begins a nearly 1.0-mile climb. However, this is no boring trudge; along the way, the path weaves between boulders; climbs past bands of red, white, purple, and even green soil; and exposes many varied vistas.

At 0.5 mile into the hike (and 0.2 mile into the steep climbing), hikers come to a trail junction. To follow this chapter's route, go right; this puts you on the counterclockwise loop portion of the lollipop-shaped trail. Beyond the junction, the path continues to climb and eventually gains the top of a butte (which you saw from the parking lot below). Staying safely near the edge, the trail provides ever-changing views of the Boulder Mountain Plateau to the southwest and eye-to-eye vistas of the Chimney Rock feature. Looking down from the butte rim, beautiful, fanlike erosion patterns on the bare desert floor below are plainly visible, and the dark

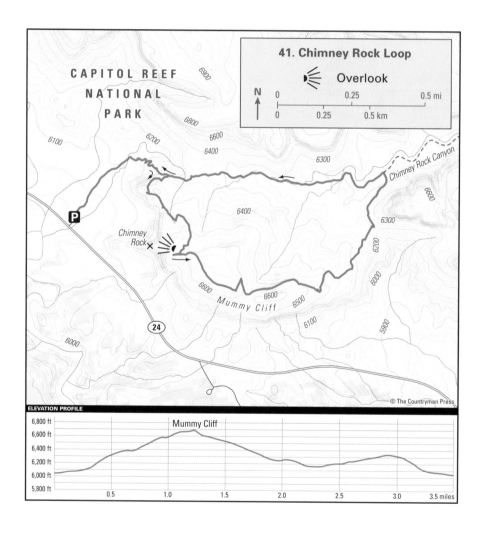

50 Hikes in Utah

Looking west onto UT 24 from Chimney Rock Loop

red earth is speckled with green Utah juniper trees.

Beyond the Chimney Rock overlooks, the trail continues to climb yet higher, with hidden higher terrain ever appearing from behind false summits. The trail eventually reaches its highest point around 1.2 miles into the hike. At this apex, hikers face west and have clear views of the Waterpocket Fold, stretching from the immediate foreground to the distant south, as well as the Henry Mountains peaking out from behind the Waterpocket Fold. Topping out at 11,522 feet, this volcanic range almost always has some snow cover—and is home to a herd of approximately five hundred free-ranging American bison.

For the next 1.0 mile, the trail descends nearly as steeply as it climbed. Staying near to the edge of its resident plateau, it skirts closely to other hillsides, cliffs, and gulches, then through a field of boulders before bottoming out. At this lowest point on the plateau, the trail reaches another junction; to stay on this route, take a left. (If you were to take a right, you would embark on a nearly 8.0-mile, eastwardly hike to UT 24 through Chimney Rock Canyon.)

The trail regains some of its lost elevation, climbing along the floor of a miniature valley for nearly 0.75 mile to reach the stem of the lollipop. If you're here at sunset, don't forget to look back to see the dark red Wingate sandstone cliffs glowing in the sun. From here, you simply retrace your steps for 0.5 mile to reach your car.

FEES, RESTRICTIONS, AND PERMITS

The Chimney Rock Trail stands outside of the Capitol Reef National Park fee zone, no

Capitol Reef: Land of the Sleeping Rainbow   DAVID SJÖQUIST

fees are required; no dogs allowed off-pavement in Capitol Reef National Park, so leave dogs at home

Waterpocket Fold and Its Many Names

Called the Land of the Sleeping Rainbow by indigenous tribes, the Waterpocket Fold is a 100-mile long, dramatic uplift that exposes millions of years worth of sedimentary deposition. Thrust high by tectonic activity 50–70 million years ago, this folding lifted the western layers nearly 1.5 vertical miles higher than the earth on the eastern side. Subsequent erosion has dulled this height difference and exposed a brilliant spectrum of colors. Throughout the feature naturally occurring rounded tanks can be found—hence the name "Waterpocket Fold." Throughout history, these have proved extremely useful to thirsty people and animals. Called a monocline by geologists, this enormous feature runs north-south through south-central Utah. Though the native tribes' name for this feature commented on its brilliant colors, the pioneers dubbed it "Capitol Reef." The "reef" portion of the name originated from what this feature presented to travelers attempting to cross it: a formidable barrier with very few viable ways of passing through it. The "capitol" portion of the name comes from a prominent sandstone feature somewhat resembling that of a capitol building's dome.

42

Calf Creek Falls

Type: Desert; dirt and sand; out-and-back

Season: Spring–Fall

Total Distance: 6.6 miles round-trip

Time: 2–3 hours

Rating: Moderate

Elevation Gain: 400 feet

Location: Calf Creek Recreation Area, Grand Staircase–Escalante National Monument, between Escalante and Boulder

Maps: USGS CALF CREEK US TOPO

Contact: Grand Staircase-Escalante National Monument BLM Field Station, 755 W. Main St., Escalante, UT 84726; 435-826-5600; www.ut.blm.gov /monument

Trailhead GPS Coordinates: Calf Creek Recreation Area: N37 47.644 W111 24.889

Comments: Calf Creek Falls is the single most popular hike in the Grand Staircase-Escalante National Monument.

OVERVIEW

Calf Creek is a tributary of the Escalante River. A perennial stream, it flows only about 7 miles from its headwaters in the north before spilling into the Escalante. This hike follows along the west side of Calf Creek for nearly half of its short journey. Originating in the Calf Creek Recreation Area, the trail quickly passes many campsites, then begins an extremely gradual, rolling ascent toward the natural end of the route: a dead-end amphitheater of cliffs where the creek cascades 126 vertical feet into a pristine pool. Though the route roughly parallels the creek, the trail offers surprisingly little shade or dampness; prepare for full sun exposure on this hike. Though you will be doing very little climbing, the trail is extremely sandy in places, rendering the journey a bit more strenuous than it would otherwise be–particularly for runners. Because of trailside petroglyphs and other points of interest, binoculars are a handy partner for this hike.

THE TRAIL

The parking area for this hike stands on the west side of UT 12, just 1.2 miles north of where the highway crosses over the Escalante River. Signed as the Calf Creek Recreation Area, it is hard to miss. Because of the popularity of this hike, the finite size of the parking lot, and the full sun exposure of the route, an early start is recommended during the summer months. Arriving ahead of the crowds will not only help secure a

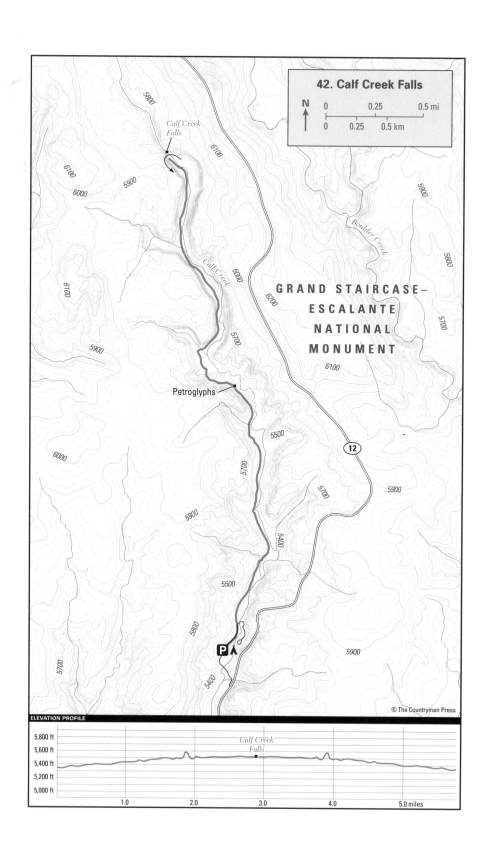

42. Calf Creek Falls

N

| 0 | | 0.25 | | 0.5 mi |
| 0 | 0.25 | 0.5 km | | |

Calf Creek Falls

Boulder Creek

Calf Creek

GRAND STAIRCASE–
ESCALANTE
NATIONAL
MONUMENT

Petroglyphs

12

P

© The Countryman Press

ELEVATION PROFILE

Calf Creek
Falls

5,800 ft
5,600 ft
5,400 ft
5,200 ft
5,000 ft

1.0   2.0   3.0   4.0   5.0 miles

parking space, but will also limit the amount of water you must tote.

As you leave the parking area and head north, you'll walk through the Calf Creek Campground for a few hundred yards before actually joining the trail. Signs make the trail easy to locate; immediately after turning onto the path, look for a box containing information for this self-guided hike. Along the hike, two dozen numbered posts mark points of interest.

On either side of the trail, the canyon's colorful walls change all the time, growing gradually taller and nearer together as the hike progresses. Keeping things interesting, the trail winds and rolls along the lower hills of the canyon side. At times it tours through the underbrush of the canyon floor; other times, it climbs slightly onto the redrock formations of the canyon side, providing slightly more expansive and elevated views of the landscape. About 1.3 miles into the hike, a small granary can be spotted by the observant, occupying a natural cliffside alcove on the eastern side of the canyon. Protected by the overhanging rocks above, and elevated from the ground-dwelling critters below, this structure was used to keep foods dry and safe from animals. Roughly 800–1,000 years old, this granary was either a Fremont or *Anasazi* creation.

Calf Creek Falls

Calf Creek Falls

At 1.4 miles into the journey, an old fence is visible, denoted by Marker #8. Erected by early pioneers, this fence was used to keep weened calves in the natural, box-canyon pasture behind it. As the story goes, this is the reason for the creek and canyon's name. Just a minute farther, at Marker #9 and about 1.5 miles from the parking lot, Fremont-sytle petroglyphs can be seen on the smooth cliff walls on the east side of the canyon. Though somewhat difficult to spot at first, these four human figures are quite large and impressive, even when viewed from afar. Aside from the waterfall itself—and the general beauty of the canyon—these painted figures might be the most impressive singular sight of the hike.

From here, the trail dips quickly through a marshy area and past thick patches of common reed, cattail, and cottonwood trees. It winds into a yet narrower section of canyon whose tall, smooth walls show brilliant water streaking. Here vertical rainbows of black, brown, and orange run nearly the entire height of the walls on the eastern side of the canyon, roughly 300 feet tall. On the western side of the canyon, the walls are much knobbier and do not show the same water streaking; however, these walls feature horizontal striation, with each subsequent layer of sandstone exhibiting a different color of tan, orange, red, or brown.

Without warning, the trail pops into a grove of trees and a sandy, flat alcove at the base of the falls. The route ends at a shallow, frigidly cold pool beneath the 126-foot falls, where adults often dip their feet and brave children fully submerge themselves. A sandy beach lines the attractive, oval-shaped pool, and hikers taking lunch there are cooled by the spray of this impressive waterfall.

From here, the only way out is to retrace your steps. Though the climb was almost imperceptible on the way in, the hike out nevertheless is noticeably easier and faster.

FEES, RESTRICTIONS, AND PERMITS

Dogs are permitted on this trail—however, all dogs must be on a leash, and owners must clean up after their pets; a day fee is required to park at the Calf Creek Recreation Area, and annual national parks passes are accepted

Anasazi and Fremont

The *Anasazi* and Fremont peoples occupied the desert Southwest and therefore the Grand Staircase–Escalante National Monument from roughly 400 to 1400 A.D. These cultures forged a life out of farming and hunting, a lifestyle that often anchored them to the location of their crops. Because of their relatively settled existence, the *Anasazi* and Fremont peoples left behind many permanent structures such as dwellings and granaries, as well as a rich collection of petroglyphs and pictographs. Both peoples disappeared roughly around the same time for unknown reasons—possibly climactic change and reduced precipitation. Though this hike contains just a handful of remnants of these ancient peoples, the Grand Staircase–Escalante National Monument is endowed with uncounted artifacts.

43

Escalante River to Natural Bridge

Type: River canyon; dirt and sand; out-and-back; extension possible

Season: Spring–Fall

Total Distance: 3.7 miles round-trip

Time: 1.5–2 hours

Rating: Easy/Moderate

Elevation Gain: 150 feet

Location: Grand Staircase-Escalante National Monument, between Escalante and Boulder

Maps: USGS CALF CREEK US TOPO

Contact: Grand Staircase-Escalante National Monument BLM Field Station, 755 W. Main St., Escalante, UT 84726; 435-826-5600; www.ut.blm.gov /monument

Trailhead GPS Coordinates: Escalante River Trailhead: N37 46.559 W111 25.169

Comments: This hike contains numerous river crossings, and should be avoided in the presence of spring runoff or whenever flash floods are possible.

OVERVIEW

UT 12 crosses over the Escalante River halfway between the towns of Escalante and Boulder. This hike follows along the colorful, sandy canyon bottom carved by this meandering river. Shady and damp, this route providing visitors with a reprieve from the heat in the middle of the otherwise sunny and dry desert. Heading westward and against the flow of the river, you'll climb very gradually, crossing the Escalante River almost half a dozen times in each direction. Wear sandals (or water-appropriate shoes) and keep your eyes peeled; nearly 1 mile into the hike, it is quite easy to lose the way by missing the trail's second river crossing. The most natural turn-around point for the hike is at the base of Natural Bridge, a massive rock span perched loftily at the top of the cliff band above. However, some people walk all the way from the trailhead to the town of Escalante, a 15-mile journey.

THE TRAIL

If arriving to the trailhead from the town of Escalante, you'll get a glimpse of the hike's first section before you even reach the parking area. Simply pull over into the Escalante River scenic pullout about 0.5 mile before the trailhead to look down upon the squirrelly ribbon of water meandering beneath the surface of the desert. Lined with colorful, wind-buffed, Navajo-sandstone walls, the Escalante has carved its own labyrinthlike path through the earth.

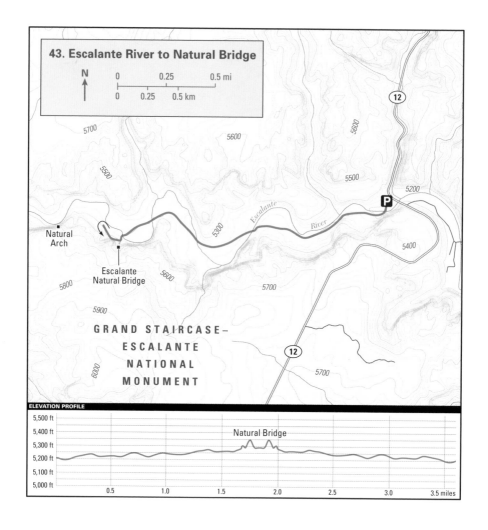

43. Escalante River to Natural Bridge

N

| 0 | 0.25 | 0.5 mi |
| 0 | 0.25 | 0.5 km |

12

5700

5600

5600

5500

5200

Escalante

River

5400

Natural
Arch

5300

Escalante
Natural Bridge

5600

5700

5800

5900

**GRAND STAIRCASE–
ESCALANTE
NATIONAL
MONUMENT**

6000

12

5700

ELEVATION PROFILE

			Natural Bridge			
5,500 ft						
5,400 ft						
5,300 ft						
5,200 ft						
5,100 ft						
5,000 ft						
	0.5	1.0	1.5	2.0	2.5	3.0	3.5 miles

Once at the small trailhead parking lot, the signed path is easy to find. To the southeast, the trail and river lead to Lake Powell after 70 miles. Our route takes the opposite direction and heads west (toward the town of Escalante). Leaving the parking lot, you'll almost immediately cross the Escalante River; you'll know within seconds whether the current is gentle enough for your comfort. In most times of the year, you'll find the water cool and refreshing, and the water level totally reasonable for crossing on foot. How-

ever, high water levels can present problems during springtime after a snowy winter and during particularly fruitful rainstorms.

Once you've completed the first river crossing, you can be sure that the next five won't be any deeper or more severe. For the next 0.8 mile of walking, you can relax on the obvious trail and enjoy the scenery around you. On either side, the route is walled in by sheer yet smooth Navajo sandstone walls standing 100–200 feet in height—visible through the scattered cottonwood trees.

Escalante River and Natural Bridge

CHRISTINE BALAZ

Painted in shades of red, orange, and white, these twisted walls and domes are beautiful to behold.

After approximately 0.8 mile of total hiking, look sharp for an easy-to-miss river crossing. Here a "sucker trail" continues straight and parallel to the river where the main trail bends to the right to cross the water. If you miss the main trail, don't fret; the false trail will quickly fade and become almost unnavigable. After this second river crossing, the proper trail stays easy to find; in many places, it splits into parallel and equally viable options. However, in this sandy, open portion of the journey, the hike's general direction is easy to anticipate. You'll cross the river four more times before reaching the Natural Bridge.

Due to the presence of cottonwood trees and the winding nature of the river, the trail comes into view of the Natural Bridge only shortly before you're actually at its base. This large feature stands on the left side of the river, roughly 130 feet above the trail and nearly as high as the canyon rim. At approximately 100 feet in width, it's hard to miss—even given its camouflaging backdrop of similarly colored sandstone.

Once at the Natural Bridge, you've reached the end of this hike. However, you can continue along another 0.5 mile to cross the river one more time and reach the Escalante Natural Bridge. Much smaller than the Natural Bridge, this feature sits on the south canyon wall and is easy to miss by those not paying close attention. Though an unspectacular feature, it and the scenery en route to it certainly warrant the extension.

FEES, RESTRICTIONS, AND PERMITS

All noncampground, overnight stays in the Grand Staircase–Escalante National Monument require a backcountry permit (obtainable at any of the monument's visitors centers); no fees or dog restrictions

Russian Olive aka Tamarisk: A Weed

Originally from western and central Asia, this nonnative shrub now grows thick along the river banks almost everywhere in southern Utah. Growing as high as 15–20 feet, this small tree can be recognized by its numerous, thin, willowy stems and silvery, narrow leaves. First introduced to North America in the late 1800s, it escaped domesticity and has rampantly taken over river ecosystems. Because of its dense nature, ability to grow in poor soil, resistance to drought, and other properties, it wins territory over native species.

44

Queens Garden/ Navajo Loop/Rim Trail

Type: Desert; dirt and gravel; loop

Season: Late Spring–Early Fall

Total Distance: 3.0 miles round-trip

Time: 1–2 hours

Rating: Moderate/Strenuous

Elevation Gain: 850 feet

Location: Bryce Canyon National Park

Maps: USGS BRYCE CANYON US TOPO and USGS BRYCE POINT US TOPO

Contact: Bryce Canyon National Park, UT 63, Bryce Canyon, UT 84764; 435-834-5322; www.nps.gov/brca

Trailhead GPS Coordinates: Sunrise Point Trailhead: N37 37.861 W112 09.868

Comments: Trail closures caused by snowpack and rockfall are common along the Navajo Loop Trail during shoulder season; however, at least one leg of this loop usually remains open at any given time. If in doubt, inquire with a ranger before embarking on the hike.

OVERVIEW

Part of a larger network of trails exploring Bryce Canyon—or Bryce Amphitheater, as it's most properly called—the Queens Garden/ Navajo Loop/Rim Trail hike includes views of the area's most striking scenery and peculiar formations. Considering its relatively short length of just 3.0 miles, this hike is arguably the best in the park. Taken in a clockwise direction, this loop departs from the rim of Bryce Amphitheater, descends roughly 800 feet by way of gentle switchbacks, meanders through the Queens Garden, and reascends via either arm of the Navajo Loop Trail. Along the way, you'll see more hoodoos, arches, and shades of yellow, orange, and red than you could have imagined.

THE TRAIL

Navigationally speaking, locating the trailhead of this hike is the most difficult task to nail, particularly if you drive your own vehicle. The looping, one-way nature of the roads here can be rather confusing. However you arrive, refer to your Bryce Canyon Trail Map and Guide (free at the entrance station) to help steer you to Sunrise Point, quite near the Bryce Canyon Lodge. As the name suggests, this overlook is, not surprisingly, one of the best places in the entire park to greet a new day. Given its location and orientation, this viewpoint provides excellent views of Bryce Amphitheater's features saturated in the low-angle light of early morning. Regardless of time of day, you can see the Aquarius Plateau, about 15 beeline miles away,

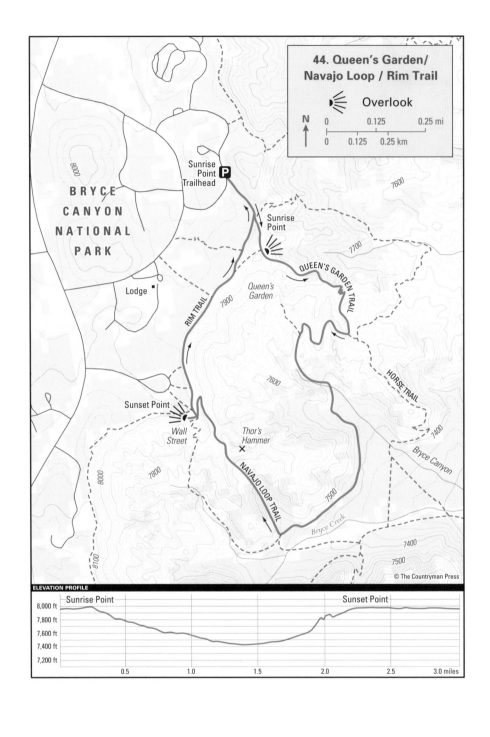

44. Queen's Garden / Navajo Loop / Rim Trail

Overlook

N

| 0 | | 0.125 | | 0.25 mi |
| 0 | 0.125 | 0.25 km |

7600

7700

BRYCE
CANYON
NATIONAL
PARK

8000

Sunrise
Point
Trailhead

P

Sunrise
Point

QUEEN'S GARDEN TRAIL

Lodge

Queen's
Garden

RIM TRAIL

7900

HORSE TRAIL

7400

7600

Sunset Point

Wall
Street

Thor's
Hammer

Bryce Canyon

NAVAJO LOOP TRAIL

7500

8000

7800

Bryce Creek

7400

7500

8100

© The Countryman Press

ELEVATION PROFILE

| 8,000 ft | Sunrise Point | | | | Sunset Point | | |
| 7,800 ft |
| 7,600 ft |
| 7,400 ft |
| 7,200 ft |
| | 0.5 | 1.0 | 1.5 | 2.0 | 2.5 | 3.0 miles |

and Canaan Mountain, just to its south and about 6 miles farther to the east.

From Sunrise Point, follow signs for the Queens Garden Trail, which descends from the rim immediately to the north of Sunrise Point. Given the quick, 0.8-mile, 800-vertical-foot descent of the trail, this portion of the hike is surprisingly gradual and comfortable for the knees. As the broad dirt path zigzags down the hillside, its well-placed corners serve as excellent stopping places for photography and sightseeing. Continuing along the bright dirt slopes of the amphitheater, you'll pass amongst Dr. Seuss–like specimens of Douglas fir and bristlecone pine.

The next section of the hike, the Queens Garden, is definitely the most popular among kids. Here the trail winds among an extremely dense collection of peculiar-looking knobs and fins. At times, it even passes directly through the formations by way of con-structed tunnels and doorways. The trail gradually leaves this natural rock garden, winding into forested lands filled with ponderosa pine, blue spruce, and, if the season is right, wildflowers scattered among a carpet of greenleaf manzanita.

After this short and gentle downhill section, you will encounter the first leg of the Navajo Loop Trail. To stay on this book's suggested route, take this leg of the Navajo Loop Trail to return to the amphitheater rim.

The ascent to the rim via the Navajo Loop Trail is short, steep, and extremely aesthetic. Here the trail squeezes itself between two sheer cliffs, making rapid switchbacks as it ascends the steep chute formed between these pink walls. Though sunlight rarely reaches the trail itself, it causes the cliffs on either side of the trail to glow warmly and vibrantly.

Returning to the rim, you'll find yourself at Sunset Point. If you missed the sunrise at

The characteristic colors of Bryce Amphitheater

The author approaching a manmade doorway in Queen's Garden

Sunrise Point, consider catching the afternoon light here. From Sunset Point, you can see the obviously tilted Sinking Ship formation 3.0 miles to your east and Boat Mesa to the north of the Sinking Ship. Those with tired feet can catch the shuttle bus from here; if you wish to complete the full 3.0-mile loop, follow the Rim Trail to the north; just 0.6 mile of scenic, nearly flat walking will lead you back to the starting place of the hike.

FEES, RESTRICTIONS, AND PERMITS

Visitors to Bryce Canyon National Park must pay $10 for a seven-day pass, and federal America the Beautiful passes are accepted; no dogs are allowed off-pavement in Bryce Canyon National Park, so leave dogs at home

Shuttle Buses

Maybe it's a throwback to childhood, but many people don't take kindly to riding buses. However, the Bryce Canyon National Park shuttle buses come in very highly recommended. Totally free, these buses run at frequent intervals, giving you the flexibility to leave your car outside the park. Best of all, the buses allow you to start and finish hikes at whichever location you wish—a particularly handy freedom in a park full of looping, interconnected trails. Buses are optional, and run only during peak season (i.e., summer).

Amphitheaters versus Canyons

Geologically speaking, Bryce Canyon National Park actually bears a rather incorrect moniker. As any park ranger can tell you, this is because the erosion responsible for this feature is technically different than that which creates a canyon. Whereas a canyon is created by central stream erosion, an amphitheater is actually formed by "headward erosion"—erosion caused by a stream's headwaters eating back into the soil in the reverse direction of water flow. While standing at Sunrise or Sunset Points, be sure look down into the amphitheater and notice the lack of a central stream that would be required to properly dub this feature "Bryce Canyon."

Navigating the Navajo Loop: Frequent Trail Closures

Due to snowfall and frequent threats of rockfall, either leg of the Navajo Loop Trail may be closed at any time, forcing you to take the other leg of the Navajo Loop Trail to the top of the canyon. If this is the case, do not fret; the farther Navajo Loop option only adds about 0.1 mile of total hiking, and each is just as scenic as the other. The worst possible scenario would involve the closure of the entire Navajo Loop Trail; in this case, you must return the same way you came, or by way of the Peek-A-Boo Loop Trail. Returning via the Peek-A-Boo Loop Trail adds approximately 3.0 miles of hiking and delivers you to the amphitheater rim and road at Bryce Point, almost 4.0 road miles south of Sunrise Point. If your time is short, or your fitness limited, be sure to ask a ranger about trail closures before embarking on your journey.

45

Losee Canyon Trail

Type: Desert and canyon; dirt; out-and-back; extensions possible

Season: Spring–Fall; watch for snow up to late spring

Total Distance: 6.0 miles round-trip

Time: 2–3 hours

Rating: Moderate

Elevation Gain: 600 feet

Location: Red Canyon, northwest of Bryce Canyon National Park

Maps: USGS CASTO CANYON US TOPO

Contact: Dixie National Forest: Red Canyon Visitors Center, 3.3 miles east of US 89 on UT 12, Panguitch, UT 84759; 435-676-2626; www.fs.usda .gov/recarea/dixie

Trailhead GPS Coordinates: Red Canyon Losee Canyon Parking: N37 46.177 W112 20.018

Comments: An oft-overlooked and beautiful section of southern Utah, Red Canyon provides nature lovers a chance to escape the infrastructure, crowding, and regulation of the nearby national parks.

OVERVIEW

Red Canyon is a beautiful and colorful recreation area in the 170-million-acre Dixie National Forest. Located just northeast of the US 89 and UT 12 junction, Red Canyon stands between Zion and Bryce Canyon National Parks. This area is extremely easy to access—but nevertheless often ignored by passersby. For those with time, a stop in Red Canyon provides a respite from the sometimes overwhelming crowds and constructed infrastructure of the national parks. The Losee Canyon Trail, open to bikes and pets alike, offers a long and almost imperceptible climb through a quiet and picturesque Wild West canyon. Though it offers no spectacular vistas, the trail is nevertheless surrounded by constant charm and subtly changing beauty.

Note: Don't arrive too early in the year unless you have cross-country skis in hand; with a base elevation of nearly 7,200 feet, this trail is often covered in snow well into spring. The Losee Canyon Trail terminates where it meets the Cassidy Trail, 3.0 miles from the trailhead. From here longer loops are possible; check the map at the trailhead for more information. As you hike, don't be alarmed by bikes and horses you may encounter on the trail.

THE TRAIL

Despite its location in a fairly remote and undeveloped area, the Losee Canyon Trail is nevertheless quite easy to find. Situated along the well-maintained dirt Cohab

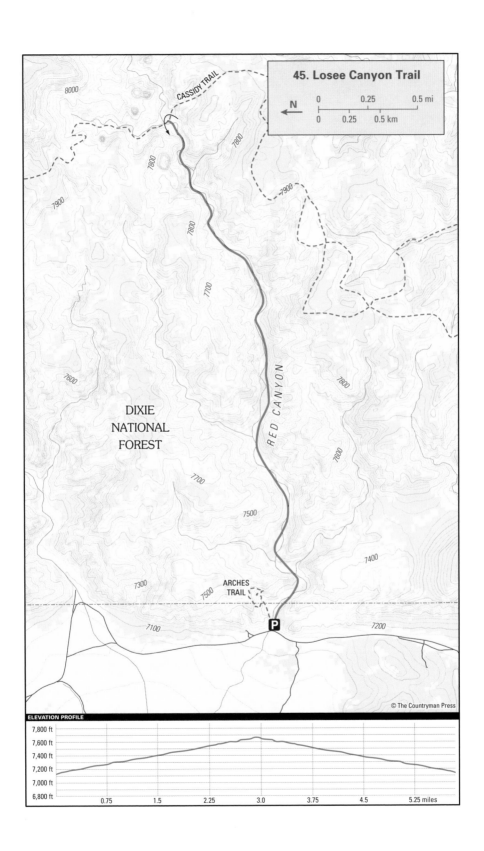

45. Losee Canyon Trail

N ←

| 0 | 0.25 | 0.5 mi |
| 0 | 0.25 | 0.5 km |

CASSIDY TRAIL

8000

7800

7900

7800

7700

7600

RED CANYON

7800

7600

DIXIE
NATIONAL
FOREST

7700

7500

7400

7300

ARCHES
TRAIL

7500

7100

7200

P

© The Countryman Press

ELEVATION PROFILE

| 7,800 ft |
| 7,600 ft |
| 7,400 ft |
| 7,200 ft |
| 7,000 ft |
| 6,800 ft |

| 0.75 | 1.5 | 2.25 | 3.0 | 3.75 | 4.5 | 5.25 miles |

Losee Canyon Trail and the wash it follows

CHRISTINE BALAZ

Canyon Road, with a well-signed parking lot of its own, the Losee Canyon Trailhead boasts its own pit toilet and area overview map. From this small parking area, the trail leads gradually uphill and eastwardly away from the road. As it climbs along the bottom of the namesake canyon, the Losee Canyon Trail more or less follows a wash, crossing or joining it roughly two dozen times en route to its terminus at the Cassidy Trail. Though the seasonal wash is dry by summer, you'll find yourself wading through runoff water and patches of snow if you arrive too early in the season. "Too early" is, of course, dependent on the severity and length of winter every year.

Leaving the parking lot, pick your way northward and downhill (just a few yards) and into the wash to immediately enter the mouth of Losee Canyon. As you begin your almost imperceptible ascent, you'll very quickly begin passing bright orange cliff bands rich with small arches and hoodoods reminiscent of those in Bryce Canyon National Park. Adorned with thin vegetation only, the canyon's sandy, colorful hillsides are readily visible through the limber, bristlecone, and ponderosa pine trees. Though the red and orange sandstone formations strongly resemble those of a hot desertscape, the high-elevation plant life here belongs largely to the alpine category—bestowing the area with an interesting blend of desert-seeming geology and alpine flora.

The Losee Canyon Trail climbs steadily—though extremely gently—through the pleasant, fresh air of this high altitude canyon. The landscape changes only subtly over this distance. After 3.0 miles, the Losee Canyon Trail intersects with the Cassidy Trail in a very nonspectacular way. Marking the junction is handful of wooden Forest Service trail marker signs and a number of hitching posts. From here, loops are possible—either to the south and toward UT 12 and the Red Canyon Trailhead, or to the north and the Casto Canyon Trail. If you wish to continue to the north or to the south, it is best to do so with a map in hand. The trail systems to the north and south of this junction form fairly complicated webs. However, if you follow signs to stay on the Cassidy Trail, you'll make your way to UT 12 (to the south) or the Casto Canyon Trail (to the north).

The end of Losee Canyon Trail and beginning of Cassidy Trail   DAVID SJÖQUIST

FEES, RESTRICTIONS, AND PERMITS

No special restrictions or fees beyond those of Dixie National Forest; be sure to park at the designated Losee Canyon parking lot and not the horse corral, which must be kept clear

Evading Posses in Red Canyon

The Cassidy Trail, which intersects with Losee Canyon Trail at its terminus, is—you guessed it—named after the famous outlaw Butch Cassidy. Born in 1866 as Robert LeRoy Parker in Beaver, Utah, Parker was the oldest of 13 children, and the son of Scottish and British Mormon immigrants. The family moved to a ranch outside of nearby Circleville in 1879, and Butch lived there with his family until 1884. According to local legend, Cassidy got into a fight over a woman at a Panguitch dance during his Circleville residency. Believing he had killed his opponent, he fled to Red Canyon. Though the man actually survived the brawl, a posse was nevertheless sent after Cassidy, who eluded them by hiding along the route of today's Cassidy Trail.

Side Loops via the Cassidy Trail

The Losee Canyon Trail ends where it joins the Cassidy Trail, an 8.9-mile path that extends from the Red Canyon Trailhead on UT 12 northward to the Casto Canyon Trail and a connected system of backcountry pathways. If you wish to extend your hiking trip beyond the Losee Canyon Trail, it is highly suggested that you do so only with a detailed trail map in hand. Though loops to the south and the north are popular, they are lengthy and involve navigating numerous trail junctions. To pick up a map, visit the Red Canyon Visitors Center or download one from the Dixie National Forest's Red Canyon Web site.

46

Arches Trail

Type: Desert; dirt; lollipop-shaped

Season: Spring–Fall; watch for snow up to late spring

Total Distance: 0.75 mile round-trip

Time: 30 minutes

Rating: Easy (with short, steep segments)

Elevation Gain: 200 feet

Location: Red Canyon, northwest of Bryce Canyon National Park

Maps: USGS CASTO CANYON US TOPO

Contact: Dixie National Forest: Red Canyon Visitors Center, 3.3 miles east of US 89 on UT 12, Panguitch, UT 84759; 435-676-2626; www.fs.usda .gov/recarea/dixie

Trailhead GPS Coordinates: Red Canyon Losee Canyon Parking: N37 46.177 W112 20.018

Comments: A short alternative (or addition) to the Losee Canyon Trail, the Arches Trail showcases a huge number of interesting rock formations in a very short distance while also giving excellent views of the surrounding landscape to the southwest.

OVERVIEW

The Arches Trail showcases a very dense collection of natural arches and hoodoos enriched by a scenic backdrop of distant mountains and plateaus to the southwest. Sharing the same parking lot as the Losee Canyon Trail, the Arches Trail makes for either a great addition to the Losee Canyon Trail or a stand-alone adventure with excellent sights-for-effort value—great for those with limited time or fitness. Though short, this trail has a relatively significant amount of climbing and descending; however, the trail is well-maintained and features little unstable footing or exposure, so it can be navigated by nearly any able body.

THE TRAIL

To find the Arches Trail, head northward from the Losee Canyon Trail parking lot. A sign will lead to the stem of this lollipop-shaped trail. Just 0.2 mile of gentle uphill hiking leads to a split in the trail from which a counterclockwise direction of travel is recommended. Less than 0.1 mile later, the trail encounters its first major arch—the largest of the entire hike. Roughly 20 feet wide, this feature cannot be missed. Because this formation stands very near the trail, many visitors have hiked directly to it. Do not be misled by this side trail; the main path hooks to the right at this point, and ascends the canyon's hillside.

The route continues to climb past a number of small arches directly located on either side of the trail. As it ascends, the Arches Trail provides increasingly rewarding views of

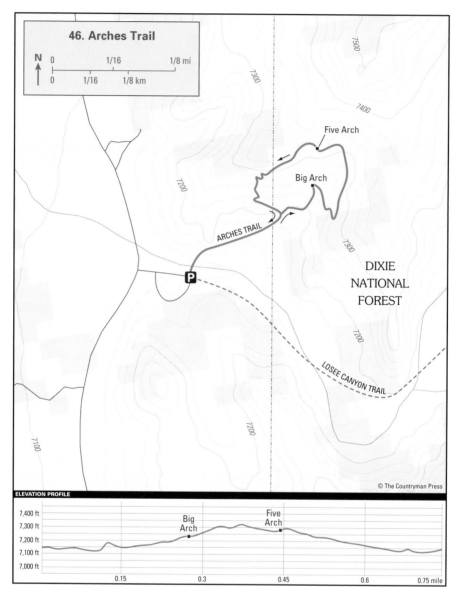

46. Arches Trail

N
0   1/16   1/8 mi
0   1/16   1/8 km

7500
7300
7400
Five Arch
7200
Big Arch
ARCHES TRAIL
7300
DIXIE
NATIONAL
FOREST
P
7200
LOSEE CANYON TRAIL
7200
7100

© The Countryman Press

ELEVATION PROFILE

7,400 ft		Big	Five	
7,300 ft		Arch	Arch	
7,200 ft				
7,100 ft				
7,000 ft				
	0.15	0.3	0.45	0.6 0.75 mile

the nearby red rock landscape and faraway Tushar Mountains to the southwest. These vistas grow better still as the trail reaches the top of the small canyon and bends to the west.

At the northernmost (and highest) apex of the lollipop, the Arches Trail passes through a particularly unique formation composed of adjoined and independent mushroom-shaped hoodoos. This feature alone contains six separate arches, through which the distant landscape can be enjoyed. From here, the reaches of the Grand Staircase can be seen, with views of the lofty Pine Valley and

50 Hikes in Utah

Dense formation at the top of Arches Trail

DAVID SJÖQUIST

Tushar Mountains to the southwest and the Markagunt Plateau to the west.

From here, the trail begins its descent. After just less than 0.4 mile, the loop rejoins the stem of the lollipop. This leads back to the parking lot after 0.2 mile.

FEES, RESTRICTIONS, AND PERMITS

No special restrictions or fees beyond those of Dixie National Forest; be sure to park at the designated Losee Canyon parking lot and not the horse corral, which must be kept clear

47

Watchman Trail

Type: Desert; dirt; lollipop-shaped

Season: Fall–Spring

Total Distance: 3.1 miles round-trip (3.5 miles including the walk from the parking lot to the trailhead)

Time: 1–2 hours

Rating: Moderate

Elevation Gain: 450 feet

Location: Watchman Campground, Zion National Park

Maps: USGS SPRINGDALE EAST US TOPO

Contact: Zion National Park, UT 9, Springdale, UT 54767; 435-772-3256; www.nps.gov/zion

Trailhead GPS Coordinates: Zion Canyon Visitors Center: N37 11.967 W112 59.201

Comments: Due to its location in a broad, open portion of Zion Canyon's bottom, the Watchman Trail offers much warmer hiking than loftier trails like Angels Landing and lush areas like Emerald Pools. During warm weather, this trail is best hiked early or late in the day.

OVERVIEW

With its trailhead hidden amid the busy Zion Canyon Visitors Center and Watchman Campground complex, the Watchman Trail might at first seem unappealing. However, this is one of the best, most overlooked—and therefore quiet—hikes in the park. The trail follows the Virgin River briefly before ascending gradually into a warm desert bowl. A gentle, yet steady, switchback section offers increasingly better cross-canyon views to the south and west before delivering the trail to a round plateau. The trail then splits into a loop that tours the plateau's edge, offering sweeping views of Zion Canyon and the surrounding mountains and cliffs. Though many other trails in the park offer up-close views of these formations, the Watchman Trail provides unique, withdrawn perspective, allowing you to piece them together in your mind, placing each formation in context.

THE TRAIL

To hike the Watchman Trail, you must park (or get off the bus) at the Zion Canyon Visitors Center. You'll notice immediately that the visitors center and Watchman Campground, sitting right next to each other, form a confusing complex of roads, buildings, and signs. If you drive your car, you'll be forced to park in the visitors center parking lot, on the building's western side. If you're not pressed for time, consider checking out this impressive, eco-friendly building. Not only will you take in some information about the park and surrounding area, but you can also learn about the building's state-of-the-art, self-sustaining features.

Though the relative chaos of this mandatory parking area might seem like a turnoff, don't let it deter you; you'll be safely away from all the hubbub in just a few minutes (and 0.2 mile) of walking. Think of this as a bonus: this brief period of nontranquility filters out many would-be Watchman Trail hikers, rendering the remaining 95 percent of the trail much calmer and less crowded than it would otherwise be.

Once you've successfully located the trail, follow it north along the sandy shores

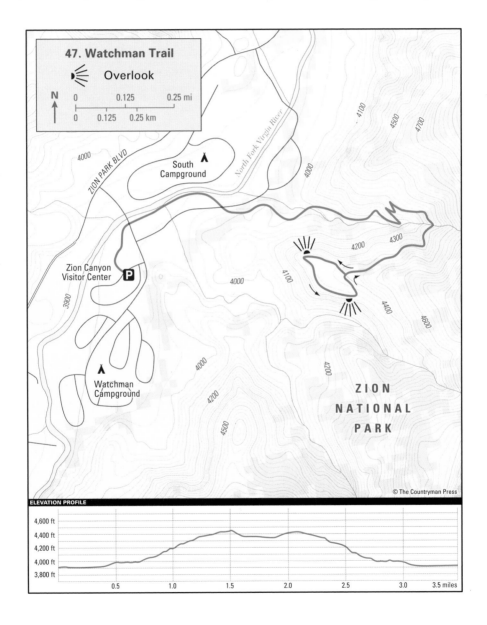

and cottonwood trees of the Virgin River. The trail sweeps gradually to the right, crosses a paved service road (0.25 mile from the start of the trail), passes somewhat near employee housing, and begins ascending into a scooped mountainside. If you do this hike in the springtime, you will find the mountainside rife with yucca plants, thick patches of sagebrush, and numerous wildflower species—including larkspur, goldenrod, and blood-red Indian paintbrush.

The trail climbs steadily, but gently. Notice as the flowers and willows yield to pinyon and numerous species of cactus. It passes through several switchbacks, zigzagging along the walls of the hillside, providing varied and increasingly open views of lower Zion Canyon. Eventually the trail bends south and pops up onto a plateau south of Bridge Mountain. To the east, the Hepworth Wash separates this plateau (and increases the contrast) between it and the staggeringly tall mountains beyond.

You'll soon find yourself at the end of the lollipop's stem, and at the beginning of a loop. This 0.5-mile path traces along the edges of a circular plateau, providing even better views of the surrounding landscape, including Springdale to the south and the Towers of the Virgin to the west.

Once you've completed the loop, retrace your steps to the Zion Canyon Visitors Center. If you have time, stop at the Virgin River and treat your feet to a dip in the cold water.

FEES, RESTRICTIONS, AND PERMITS
Visitors to Zion National Park must pay $25 for a seven-day pass, and federal America the Beautiful passes are accepted; no dogs are allowed off-pavement in Zion National Park, so leave dogs at home

Ascending through switchbacks on the Watchman Trail   DAVID SJÖQUIST

50 Hikes in Utah

Views north across Zion Canyon from Watchman Trail

Locating the Watchman Trail from the Visitors Center Parking Lot

To locate the Watchman Trail without hassle, it's best to start looking for signs before you even leave the car (or shuttle bus). Just after turning off UT 9 and onto the Vistors Center/Watchman Campground Road, you'll cross the Virgin River. Immediately after this bridge, a small WATCHMAN TRAIL sign on the left side of the road marks the trailhead. No matter where you end up parking or leaving the bus, keep this location in mind. If you didn't happen to spot the sign on your way into the visitors center, simply locate the Virgin River on foot and look for the trail departing from the northwestern corner of the bridge.

48

Emerald Pools

Type: Desert; dirt and pavement; out-and-back; side trips possible

Season: Spring–Fall; possible in winter

Total Distance: 2.2 miles round-trip (can be looped with the Kayenta and Grotto Trails to add 1.5 miles)

Time: 40 minutes–1 hour

Rating: Moderate/Strenuous

Elevation Gain: 300 feet

Location: Zion Canyon, Zion National Park

Maps: USGS TEMPLE OF SINAWAVA US TOPO and USGS SPRINGDALE EAST US TOPO

Contact: Zion National Park, UT 9, Springdale, UT 54767; 435-772-3256; www.nps.gov/zion

Trailhead GPS Coordinates: Emerald Pools/Horse Corral: N37 15.053 W112 57.503

Comments: As of the publication of this book, the trail to the Middle Emerald Pools was closed without any scheduled reopening date.

OVERVIEW

Because of its moderate distance and unique environment, the Emerald Pools Trail is one of the most popular in Zion National Park. This trail accesses a moist, green notch in the mountains, rife with leafy trees and wildlife—all fed by a perennial stream. A rarity in the desert, this lush ecosystem is punctuated with three namesake pools. Especially in spring and early summer, waterfalls spill into these pools, sending a cooling mist into the air and slowly carving and deepening these broad, tranquil basins in the process. Though the Middle Emerald Pools Trail is closed indefinitely, the Lower and Upper Pools warrant the hike. If you have time, visit the Upper Pool, which is certainly the most spectacular of the two.

THE TRAIL

The Emerald Pools Trailhead shares its location with the horse corral. From the northern end of this midsized lot a paved path departs, and quickly crosses the North Fork of the Virgin River by way of a bridge. The trail immediately embarks on a rolling ascent through boxelder and cottonwood trees. On either side of the path, brush and trees grow densely in the sandy soil, thriving on the relative moisture of this shady canyon and its streams. Here you'll see herbaceous grasses and plants, numerous oak species, white fir and pinyon pine, willow, and sumac. Above all of this greenery, the Navajo sandstone cliffs of Zion Canyon soar nearly 1,000 feet.

After walking just 0.6 mile, you'll reach the Lower Emerald Pool. Offering viewpoints of

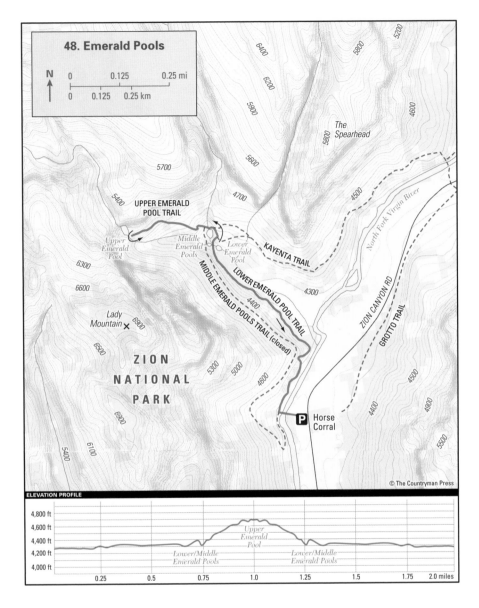

48. Emerald Pools

N

| 0 | 0.125 | 0.25 mi |
| 0 | 0.125 | 0.25 km |

The Spearhead

ZION NATIONAL PARK

Lady Mountain ✕

UPPER EMERALD POOL TRAIL

Upper Emerald Pool

Middle Emerald Pools

Lower Emerald Pool

KAYENTA TRAIL

LOWER EMERALD POOL TRAIL

MIDDLE EMERALD POOLS TRAIL (closed)

North Fork Virgin River

ZION CANYON RD

GROTTO TRAIL

P Horse Corral

© The Countryman Press

ELEVATION PROFILE

	4,800 ft					Upper				
	4,600 ft					Emerald				
	4,400 ft					Pool				
	4,200 ft			Lower/Middle				Lower/Middle		
	4,000 ft			Emerald Pools				Emerald Pools		

0.25   0.5   0.75   1.0   1.25   1.5   1.75   2.0 miles

the pool from afar, the trail then works its way up to and then behind the pool, squeezing between the water and the amphitheaterlike cliff behind it. Sandwiched between the cliff walls and the waterfall, hikers can look out through the ribbon of water, enjoying its misty spray. Above, the water spills over a hard capstone layer, then cascades 100 vertical feet into the pool below.

If you look at the walls above, you'll notice white and black streaks running down the curved cliff faces. Caused by mineral deposition, these streaks are lined with hanging gardens—riparian collections of flowering

Emerald Pools

Boulders en route to Emerald Pools

DAVID SJÖQUIST

plants, mosses, and ferns actually growing on the sheer Navajo sandstone walls. Say farewell to the pavement as you begin the final ascent to the Upper Pool. Though shorter than the first trail section, this portion grows steeper and more rugged. Able-bodied persons will find this trail casual; but those with knee problems or other physical limitations might find the incline and rocky steps challenging.

After passing behind the Lower Pool, the trail weaves between large boulders as it quickly climbs to a junction with the Kayenta Trail; follow signs pointing to the Upper Pool. An easy stream crossing and a minute later, you'll reach yet another junction for the Kayenta and Middle Pool Trails. Here you should again turn to head toward the Upper Pool. At the stream crossing you'll find yourself standing in a relatively open area on slickrock slabs. Though this clearing is fairly small, it affords views of classic Zion Canyon walls above. You don't have to look hard to see evidence of water seeping through the cliffs, rendering white streaks beneath horizontal seams.

You'll arrive at the upper pool more quickly than you'd expect. This pool sits at the base of a massive, U-shaped cliff. Here the stream that drains Heaps Canyon pours through a sharp notch at the top of the wall, passing an arch on its way down. Though many people visit this talus-lined pool—and you're almost guaranteed to share this space with many others—it nevertheless offers a hushed, tranquil atmosphere. As you prefer, you can either walk directly up to the water, or perch yourself farther back atop boulders.

Though the trail's popularity wards off skittish creatures, early and off-season visitors might have the luck of spotting mule deer, rock squirrel, bighorn sheep, kangaroo rats, or any other of the nearly 70 mammal species present in the park—all of which need water to survive. If near the pools at dusk, you're likely to see bats and hear canyon tree frogs, which become active in the evening.

From the Upper Pool, you'll have to backtrack at least to the Kayenta Trail. At this point, you can return to the horse corral via the same 0.6-mile route or you can take the 1.0-mile Kayenta Trail to The Grotto, and the 0.5-mile Grotto Trail to the horse corral.

FEES, RESTRICTIONS, AND PERMITS
Visitors to Zion National Park must pay $25 for a seven-day pass, and federal America the Beautiful passes are accepted; no dogs are allowed off-pavement in Zion National Park, so leave dogs at home

Upper Emerald Pool DAVID SJÖQUIST

49

Angels Landing

Type: Desert; dirt and pavement; out-and-back

Season: Spring–Fall; not to be hiked in bad weather

Total Distance: 5.5 miles round-trip

Time: 2–4 hours

Rating: Moderate/Strenuous

Elevation Gain: 1,600 feet

Location: Zion Canyon, Zion National Park

Maps: USGS TEMPLE OF SINAWAVA US TOPO

Contact: Zion National Park, UT 9, Springdale, UT 54767; 435-772-3256; www.nps.gov/zion

Trailhead GPS Coordinates: The Grotto: N37 15.562 W112 57.035

Comments: A spectacular hike with spacious overlooks of Zion Canyon and dizzying exposure, Angels Landing is not to be hiked if bad weather (wind, rain, snow, lightning) threatens.

OVERVIEW

Angels Landing is Zion National Park's most spectacular hike, with spacious overlooks of Zion Canyon and dizzying exposure. The first ⅔ of the trail, though steep, are well-developed and culminate at a lofty viewpoint overlooking Zion Canyon and the Virgin River. The final leg becomes technical and grows even steeper as it approaches Angels Landing proper. On this segment, hikers are presented with carved steps, hand chains, and knife-ridge scrambling with 1,000-foot-plus drop-offs on either side of the trail. This section is not to be hiked by the faint of heart, very young, or very old. If you're easily prone to vertigo, stick to the first section of the trail; you'll still be rewarded with amazing views and a great workout.

THE TRAIL

The trailhead for Angels Landing is at The Grotto. Ironically, this trailhead is easiest to access during peak season (April 1–October 31) due to Zion Canyon's mandatory shuttle bus policy being in effect during that time. Though the number of visitors is less during the shoulder seasons, the presence of passenger cars makes accessing this trailhead more tricky. The parking lot at The Grotto can fill quite quickly—so if doing this hike is important to you, consider arriving in the early morning. Alternatively, you can choose a backup parking area such as the Zion Lodge or Emerald Pools Parking. From Zion Lodge, you can hike 0.5 mile along the flat The Grotto Trail to reach The Grotto. If you park at

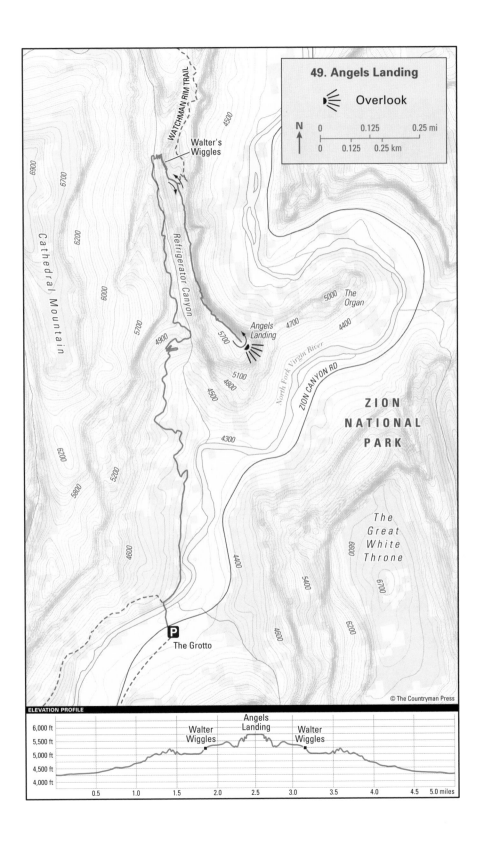

49. Angels Landing

Overlook

N

| 0 | 0.125 | 0.25 mi |
| 0 | 0.125 | 0.25 km |

WATCHMAN RIM TRAIL

Walter's Wiggles

Refrigerator Canyon

Cathedral Mountain

6900
6790
6200
5700
6000
4900
4500
5700
Angels Landing
5100
4900
4500
4300
4400
4600
5200
6200
5800

The Organ

5000
4700
4400

North Fork Virgin River

ZION CANYON RD

ZION NATIONAL PARK

The Great White Throne

6600
6700
6200
5400
4600

P The Grotto

© The Countryman Press

ELEVATION PROFILE

Angels Landing

Walter Wiggles

Walter Wiggles

6,000 ft
5,500 ft
5,000 ft
4,500 ft
4,000 ft

0.5   1.0   1.5   2.0   2.5   3.0   3.5   4.0   4.5   5.0 miles

Angels Landing itself, as seen from the trail

DAVID SJÖQUIST

the Emerald Pools Trailhead, you're just 1.6 trail miles south of the Angels Landing Trail.

Regardless of where you park or how you approach, the actual Angels Landing Trail starts at The Grotto Bridge, on the northwest side of the North Fork of the Virgin River. Broad, flat, and extremely well-developed, this trail's popularity is immediately evident. The trail heads roughly parallel to the river, climbing up and away from its sandy, cottonwood-lined banks. It turns to pavement after about 0.3 mile, and stays that way until the first major viewpoint—nearly 2 more miles. Though the first mile of the trail is among its least steep, you'll nevertheless roll quickly higher and higher toward the broken Navajo sandstone cliffs above.

The first major switchback section begins 1.0 mile into the hike. Here the trail steepens significantly, and leads up the steep, bowl-shaped mountainside. Paved in striated concrete, and fortified with stonewall foundation, this trail is quite steep in places as it zigzags among the broken cliffs you saw from below. Though challenging for the legs and lungs, this portion of the hike is utterly nontechnical and passable by anyone with a decent amount of fitness.

The first switchback section culminates by winding to a good viewpoint of itself and Zion Canyon before plunging into the narrow and shady Refrigerator Canyon. Here the trail flattens and gives hikers a reprieve from the steep hill-climbing. During the year's warmer months, this gorge between Cathedral Mountain and Angels Landing is a particularly welcome break from the switchback section below, featuring lower temperatures and a break from sun exposure.

Before you know it, the trail begins climbing again—slowly at first—up the sides of the canyon. Suddenly, you turn a corner to find yourself at the base of one of the trail's most famous sections: Walter's Wiggles. Looking up, you'll clearly see the steep set of 21 short switchbacks that carry the trail rapidly from the canyon bottom to its first major viewpoint—about 250 vertical feet in just a few minutes' walking.

The viewpoint at the top of Walter's Wiggles comes after about 2.25 miles of hiking, and is a popular regrouping area. Here the Angels Landing Trail meets up with the much longer, backcountry-style Watchman Rim Trail (which branches off to the north/left). If you've been properly hydrating, you'll enjoy the presence of a pit toilet. Regardless of whether you decide to continue to the actual Angels Landing summit and trail end, you should take a moment to enjoy views of the canyon and river below.

Angels Landing proper lies just 0.5 mile ahead, but the hike is hardly over. Looking at the cliffed-out finger ridge ahead, it's easy to understand that the trail dramatically changes character here. Those who are afraid of heights or unstable on their feet should turn around (or wait for other group members to return from the landing). This section of trail is not appropriate for young children. Regardless of age, ability, or immunity to vertigo, all hikers should absolutely avoid the next section of trail if any bad weather threatens, or if the trail has any ice or snowpack. Wind, rain, snow, and lightning greatly enhance the already high potential danger of this final and extremely exposed pitch. If in doubt, turn around!

If you're feeling up to the challenge, and the day's weather is perfect, put everything in your pack to free both hands. Tie your shoes securely, and start walking. Though much of the upcoming trail is lined by hand chains, you'll occasionally need to do a little route-finding to navigate from one post to another. Look for shoe-worn sandstone and carved steps. As the trail traverses this knife blade of sandstone, it rolls steeply, rising and falling as it makes its overall ascent to the top of Angels Landing.

Though not a huge area by any means, the summit is flat and a comfortable place to eat lunch in good weather. No handrails guard the edge, but if you're experiencing vertigo, simply sit down in the center of the landing to catch your bearings. If your stomach can handle it, peer over the edge. From the top of Angels Landing, you can see up and down the length of Zion Canyon. To the east, Echo Canyon forms a notch between Observation Point and Cable Mountain, to its south. To the north, you'll see a "mini Angels Landing," The Organ, and the North Fork of the Virgin River's Big Bend wrapping around it. Farther to the north, and beyond this bend, the famous Moonlight Buttress rock climbing route can be seen ascending the fairly obvious smooth column above a straight section of river.

When you're at the top of Angels Landing, you have no other practical choice than to return via the same 2.75-mile trail you just hiked. On the way down, be courteous to other hikers. Try to pass in places that are comfortable for both directions of travel. If you happened to notice any problems with the trail or foreboding weather patterns earlier, mention it to the people you meet.

FEES, RESTRICTIONS, AND PERMITS

Visitors to Zion National Park must pay $25 for a seven-day pass, and federal America the Beautiful passes are accepted; no dogs are allowed off-pavement in Zion National Park, so leave dogs at home

Check the Weather

The final pitch of the Angels Landing Trail features sheer drop-offs and extreme exposure to the elements. This trail is among Utah's most life-threatening if hiked in any kind of bad weather. Do yourself a favor, and check the weather before you hike to help yourself avoid lightning, wind, rain, and snowstorms. If you forgot to check before you came to Zion, ask a ranger or check the weather report at the Zion Canyon Visitors Center's backcountry desk.

View down Zion Canyon from the Angels Landing Trail   DAVID SJÖQUIST

50

Canyon Overlook Trail

Type: Desert; dirt, rock, and pavement; out-and-back

Season: Spring–Fall

Total Distance: 1.0 mile round-trip

Time: 20–40 minutes

Rating: Easy

Elevation Gain: 170 feet

Location: Eastern entrance, Zion National Park

Maps: USGS SPRINGDALE EAST US TOPO

Contact: Zion National Park, UT 9, Springdale, UT 54767; 435-772-3256; www.nps.gov/zion

Trailhead GPS Coordinates: Canyon Overlook Trailhead (east of Zion–Mount Carmel Hwy. [UT 9]): N37 12.809 W112 56.436

Comments: Because of its location at the top of the UT 9 tunnel, the Canyon Overlook Trail has a much higher starting elevation (5,180 feet) than the canyon floor hikes; watch for snow on this trail, present here long after it would be on the Watchman Trail (starting elevation 3,900 feet) or other lower-elevation routes.

OVERVIEW

Despite—or perhaps because of—its short length and its incredible views-for-effort bargain, the Canyon Overlook Trail is a Zion National Park classic. Given its brevity, minimal elevation gains, and the scenic landscape through which it passes, the Canyon Overlook Trail allows hikers the chance to access a spectacular viewpoint with very little time invested. With its trailhead just east of the UT 9 tunnel, this path begins more than 1,100 feet higher than the floor of lower Zion Canyon. Because of this elevation difference, the trail explores an environment completely different to that of Zion Canyon, trading in the canyon's red sheer cliffs for the high plateau's pale, striated, and round sandstone domes. The vantage point at the end of the trail affords generous vistas of Pine Creek Canyon and UT 9 switchbacking up its slopes. Even those weary of hiking in Zion National Park will enjoy this hike for the variety it adds to the palette.

THE TRAIL

No matter from which direction you arrive, you can't miss the Canyon Overlook Trail, whose trailhead sits immediately above the UT 9 tunnel on its north side. (If the parking lot directly above the tunnel is full, drive east just a few hundred yards to another pullout.) Before you even leave your car, you'll find yourself in a completely different landscape than Zion Canyon proper. Instead of sheer, dark red cliffs, you'll find yourself staring at a maze of cartoonlike sandstone domes—white

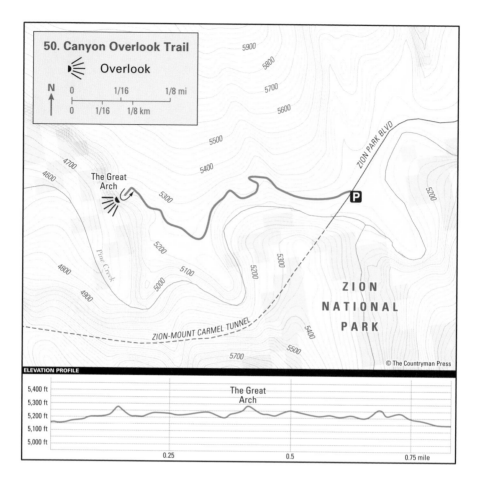

50. Canyon Overlook Trail

Overlook

N 0   1/16   1/8 mi

0   1/16   1/8 km

5900
5800
5700
5600
5500
5400
5300
5200
5100
5000
4900
4800
4700
4600
4500

ZION PARK BLVD

The Great
Arch

Pine Creek

P

ZION
NATIONAL
PARK

ZION-MOUNT CARMEL TUNNEL

5700   5500   5400

© The Countryman Press

ELEVATION PROFILE

5,400 ft			
5,300 ft		The Great	
5,200 ft		Arch	
5,100 ft			
5,000 ft			
	0.25	0.5	0.75 mile

and yellow, bulbous, and ringed with parallel stripes. This is because, at the parking lot, you're already more than 1,100 feet above the floor of Zion Canyon.

The trail begins by ascending quickly via steps and ramps carved directly into the stone. Making this short route even more accessible, the Civilian Conservation Corps added plentiful handrails along the way—so even those prone to vertigo feel at ease on this hike. On the earliest stretches of this trail, look down and directly to your left. The dark, deep, and narrow notch chasm below is the Pine Creek Narrows. The upper reaches of Pine Creek Canyon, pinching

down on itself, are a popular canyoneering route.

The trail soon bends to the right and into a moist notch in the mountainside. Here you are likely to spot grazing deer or other laid-back wildlife. After climbing more and swinging back to the left, you will catch more glimpses of the ominous-looking gash that is Pine Creek Narrows. Pause and listen for canyoneers.

Next, a sturdy, scaffoldinglike walkway leads past a cliffed-out portion of the route that would otherwise be inaccessible to foot traffic. The trail leads past an up-close view of hanging gardens and bids adieu to the

Pine Creek Narrows as it turns from dirt to slickrock slabs and enters a landscape of massive, gently sloped domes. The peculiar environment quite resembles Wile E. Coyote and Road Runner habitat, with comically shaped rocks leaning this way and that, perched atop smooth domes and among patchy juniper and pine trees.

Shortly after entering this zone, the trail reaches its end. Here, though you can't actually see it, you are actually standing atop a massive arch, appropriately named Great Arch. (If you drove up UT 9 from Zion Canyon, you'll have seen this to the left.) However, if you look far to the west, you'll be able to see the Towers of the Virgin,

Streaked Wall, East Temple and West Temple, Altar of Sacrifice, and the Beehives. In case you're not already familiar with these formations, a National Park Service placard at the trail's end labels these features clearly. Nearer to yourself, you'll see the switchbacks of UT 9 ascending Pine Creek Canyon, and where this canyon joins with Zion Canyon below.

FEES, RESTRICTIONS, AND PERMITS

Visitors to Zion National Park must pay $25 for a seven-day pass, and federal America the Beautiful passes are accepted; no dogs are allowed off-pavement in Zion National Park, so leave dogs at home

Looking down into Pine Creek Canyon from the Canyon Overlook   DAVID SJÖQUIST